Celebrating African-American Achievements

WHO'S WHO in BLACK Cleveland.

THE 2006 EDITION

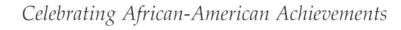

Photos taken at last year's Who's Who In Black Cleveland Unveiling Reception.

Celebrating African-American Achievements

WHO'S WHO
IN BLACK
Cleveland®
THE 2006 EDITION

Who's Who In Black Cleveland
is a registed trademark
Briscoe Media Group, LLC

Purchase additional copies online @
www.whoswhopublishing.com
Corporate Headquarters
Who's Who Publishing Co., LLC
1650 Lake Shore Drive, Ste. 250
Columbus, Ohio 43204

All Credit Cards Accepted
*Inquiries for **bulk purchases** for youth
groups, schools, churches, civic or
professional organizations, please call
our office for volume discounts.*

Corporate Headquarters
(614) 481-7300

Photo Credits
Rodney L. Brown Photography
Mychal Lilly

ISBN # 0-9763069-7-2
$24.95 each-USA

MEET THE TEAM AT

WHO'S *who*
PUBLISHING CO., LLC

1650 Lake Shore Drive, Ste. 250
Columbus, Ohio 43204

614-481-7300

C. Sunny Martin
Founder & CEO

Ernie Sullivan
Senior Partner

Carter Womack
Regional VP

Paula Gray
Asst. to the Publisher

Melanie Diggs
Senior Editor

Christy Smith
Production Manager

Ivory D. Payne
Sr. Graphic Designer

Rochelle Qualls
Executive Assistant

Nathan Wylder
Copy Editor

Philip Hickman
Copy Editor

Davina Jackson
Copy Editor

Good things have always come in different shapes, sizes, and colors.

At The Ohio Lottery, we're proud to celebrate diversity, and we congratulate everyone listed in Who's Who.

Your hard work has helped make the community a better place for all of us.

Odds Are, You'll Have Fun.

Supporting diversity

Invacare is proud to foster entrepreneurial and economic development within the African-American community through The President's Council and the Lorain County Urban League, by supporting their respective missions.

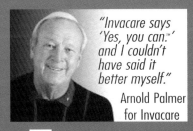

"Invacare says 'Yes, you can.™' and I couldn't have said it better myself."

Arnold Palmer for Invacare

Easter Seals National Corporate Sponsor.

INVACARE

Yes, you can.™

Who we are.

A COMMUNITY

University Hospitals Health System congratulates the 10 talented members of the UHHS medical team on their recognition in **Who's Who in Black Cleveland**. These individuals embrace the long-standing tradition: To Heal. To Teach. To Discover. We are proud of the standard of excellence our distinguished team demonstrates on a daily basis, and are inspired by the continuing dedication of our future medical leaders.

**UniversityHospitals
HealthSystem**

University Hospitals
of Cleveland

Photos by Donn R. Nottage

CONTENTS

STEPHANIE TUBBS JONES

**Representing Ohio's 11th Congressional District •
Committee on Ways and Means, Committee on Standards of Official Conduct**

Who's Who in Black Cleveland

Greetings:

It is with great pride that I salute *Who's Who in Black Cleveland* as you publish your 2nd edition of this high quality publication. Your 13 years of commitment of documenting African-Americans who are making outstanding contributions to the communities they serve is to be commended.

I so look forward to this publication which will feature a compilation of Cleveland's African-American most influential, business owners, community leaders, religious leaders, professionals, and many more. *Who's Who in Black Cleveland* will be an extremely important resource to the city Cleveland; it will create opportunities for individuals to market their services as well as a chance to be recognized for their many accomplishments. This publication will serve as a great resource and networking guide for our communities by highlighting positive role models, and providing motivation and inspiration to our youth - our leaders for the new millennium.

On behalf of the United States Congress and the residents of the 11th Congressional District, Ohio, I congratulate *Who's Who in Black Cleveland* on this your 2nd publication for the Cleveland area, and for the outstanding work you are doing by making this publication available in our great city of Cleveland, as well as in the Atlanta, Indianapolis, Cincinnati and Columbus areas. May you continue to be successful in all your future endeavors.

Stephanie Tubbs Jones
Member of Congress

BOB TAFT
GOVERNOR
STATE OF OHIO

FROM THE OFFICE OF
GOVERNOR BOB TAFT
NOVEMBER 1, 2005

It is my pleasure to extend my warmest greetings to the publishers, sponsors and readers of the 2005 issue of *Who's Who in Black Cleveland*. As Ohio continues its tradition of greatness, we must continue to recognize and embrace our diverse population.

Who's Who in Black Cleveland heralds the richness of our diversity by identifying and recording the achievements of Cleveland's most influential African-American business owners, community and religious leaders, professionals and many more who have contributed so greatly to the growth and development of our state. Many of the people listed in this publication will inspire our students -- Ohio's 21st Century leaders -- to strive to reach their full potential.

On behalf of all Ohioans, congratulations on this important work of reference.

Sincerely,

Bob Taft

Bob Taft
Governor

The City of Cleveland
Jane L. Campbell, Mayor

Greetings! As Mayor of the City of Cleveland, I am honored to extend best wishes to each of you for taking the time to learn more about the men and women represented in the Second Edition of Who's Who in Black Cleveland. As our community continues to grow more dynamic and diverse, it is important that we recognize those outstanding individuals who are moving Cleveland forward.

Who's Who in Black Cleveland is a valuable resource for citizens, businesses and visitors to our great City. Your publication is to be commended for highlighting outstanding African American achievers whose accomplishments and commitment contribute dynamically to the quality of life in Northeast Ohio.

I wish all the best to the team who has put this edition together, to the individuals who fill its pages and to everyone who uses this resource to move forward and build new networks within our community.

Sincerely,

Jane L. Campbell
Mayor

City of Cleveland

Office of the Council

Frank G. Jackson
President of City Council

Congratulations on the second edition of Who's Who in Black Cleveland.

Who's Who is an outstanding resource for the African-American community in Cleveland. It will serve as a networking tool for businesses and individuals; and it serves to recognize the contributions of those working in our community to make Cleveland a better place for African-Americans.

Those recognized in this edition of Who's Who in Black Cleveland have touched the lives of those in Greater Cleveland. They have reached out to their community to lend a helping hand, to generate support for one another and to create opportunities for each other. These are people who are the role models for today's youth; and they deserve nothing less than this prestigious recognition.

What better place is there to recognize these contributions than Cleveland? The City of Cleveland is home to the roots of African-American political power. When Carl B. Stokes was elected as the Mayor of the City of Cleveland, Cleveland voters signaled the dawn of a new era in American politics.

Today, the legacy strong African-American leaders, such as Stokes, carries on in Cleveland, which has given rise to scores of prominent Black politicians, business owners, religious leaders and community activists.

I am proud to join Who's Who in recognizing those who are making a difference in our community.

Sincerely,

Frank G. Jackson
President, Cleveland City Council

EXPERIENCE CASE.

Extending education beyond the classroom. Empowering students to change the world.

www.case.edu

Case Western Reserve University has been educating Cleveland's African American leaders for decades. Case salutes its distinguished alumni, faculty and staff for their contributions to the University and Cleveland community and congratulates those who have been honored for their accomplishments in this year's *Who's Who in Black Cleveland.*

CASE
CASE WESTERN RESERVE UNIVERSITY

Foreword

By The Honorable Louis Stokes

United States House of Representatives (Retired)

I want to thank Michael A. House, Connie Harper and John Lenear for inviting me to write the foreword to this first annual update of *Who's Who In Black Cleveland®*. It is also an honor for me to follow Carole F. Hoover, who authored the foreword for the first edition, 2004-2005.

As a native Clevelander, I was both excited and proud to see the inaugural edition of this book recognizing the men and women who made their mark in their specific occupations, professions, or in service to others in the Cleveland community. Cleveland has a long history of African Americans whose achievements in various fields of endeavor have earned them recognition both locally and nationally.

In the first edition of *Who's Who In Black Cleveland®*, founder and CEO C. Sunny Martin wrote a message in which he said, "The rich history and heritage of blacks in Cleveland has had a resounding effect on the rest of the nation..."

The reach of this statement is probably best demonstrated through the election in 1967 of my brother, Carl B. Stokes, as mayor of Cleveland. His election as mayor of Cleveland, which was then America's eighth largest city and only 37 percent black, not only established him as the first black mayor of a major American city, but also catapulted black political achievement to a new level throughout our nation.

Blacks all over America looked at his achievement as the pinnacle. It said to them that if a Carl B. Stokes could become mayor of Cleveland, they, too, could aspire for the highest elective offices in their cities.

Jevonne Stokes, Granddaughter of the late Mayor, Carl B. Stokes

His election brought politicians and political aspirants to Cleveland to find out how he did it.

Following Carl's election, we saw a spate of elections of black mayors in other major cities, such as Los Angeles, New York, Detroit, Philadelphia, Chicago, Atlanta, Dallas, Minneapolis and other cities around the nation.

According to "Black Elected Officials: A Statistical Summary, 2001," a report by the Joint Center for Political and Economic Studies, the total number of black mayors nationwide is now 454, which includes Mayors Michael Coleman (Columbus), Rhine McLin (Dayton) and Jack Ford (Toledo). Interestingly, many of today's black mayors followed the example set by Carl Stokes, of establishing coalitions of blacks, liberal whites and other ethnic or minority groups to get elected. Among black big city mayors, 57.1 percent have been elected in cities that do not have a black majority population.

We have made a lot of progress since that historic night in 1967 when the great-grandson of a slave, Carl B. Stokes, defeated Seth Taft, the great-grandson of an American president. According to the report of the Joint Center (which began its first year of keeping statistical data on black elected officials in 1970, just three years after Carl's election), in 1970 there were 1,469 black elected officials nationwide. As of 2001, the latest year for which the Joint Center has compiled data, the current total of 9,101 black elected officials represents an historic high.

While we have made significant gains in this and other areas of American life, I remain concerned about our need to redouble our efforts at minority business and entrepreneurship. I recall the night of Carl's election in 1967, when Dr. Martin Luther King, Jr. and I sat together in Carl's campaign headquarters. Carl had gone downstairs to a jubilant and tumultuous throng of people – at three o'clock in the morning.

Dr. King spoke of the significance of this night to all of America, and in particular, to Black America. He said, "Lou, we must now turn our attention to the development of economic power. No ethnic group in America has ever been able to achieve parity in this society without both political and economic power."

We must continue to pursue the challenge of Dr. King's prophetic words that night.

Keeping Kids Healthy.

Keeping Kids Happy.

Keeping Kids in School.

CLEVELAND
BROWNS
foundation

For more information visit clevelandbrowns.com.

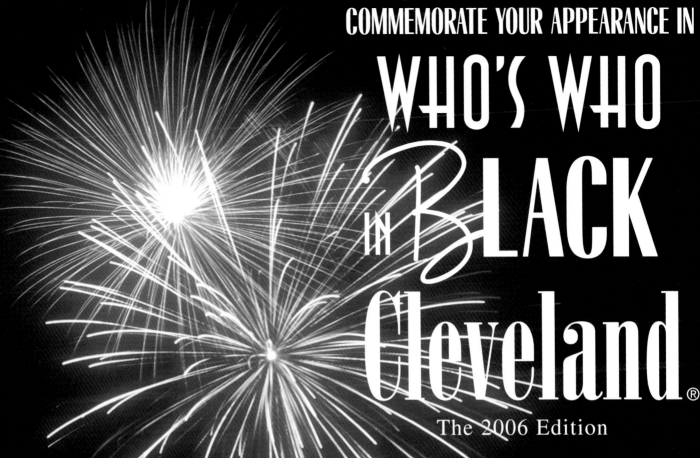

CiNTAS®
THE SERVICE PROFESSIONALS

Unique Perspectives.
Varied Cultures.
Innovative Ideas.

At Cintas, we're capitalizing on our greatest strength: **OUR PEOPLE**. As a leading provider of outsourced services, we embrace individuality in experience, age, appearance, physical ability, education, family status, and more. Our diversity has helped us to become one of the most successful companies in the country. It allows us to serve our customers better, which in turn, allows us to provide better opportunities for our employees.

For more information please visit our website at www.cintas.com.

A Message From The Founder & CEO

C. Sunny Martin

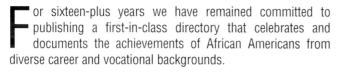

A Chance Encounter

For sixteen-plus years we have remained committed to publishing a first-in-class directory that celebrates and documents the achievements of African Americans from diverse career and vocational backgrounds.

Like most of you, we frequently talk about how important it is to show our young folks positive role models in their community. To that end, Who's Who Publishing Company continues to be committed in assisting our corporate partners in getting our publications into the hands of local school-age children.

It was on one such occasion that the Cleveland Cavaliers stepped up to donate a copy of the inaugural edition of *Who's Who In Black Cleveland*® to each library in the Cleveland Municipal School District. Likewise, Bruce Wimbish and M. Campy Russell of the Cleveland Cavaliers' front office saw fit to adopt a class at Martin Luther King, Jr. High School, and give each student a copy of our *Who's Who In Black Cleveland*® publication. I agreed to be in attendance that day and Michael House from the *Call & Post* newspaper came along to give some brief remarks.

The sixth grade students were all gathered in the school library and I asked if anyone could tell me who the first African-American mayor in Cleveland, Ohio was. Out of a class of approximately 17 students, one hand immediately went up. In the room was none other than the late mayor Carl B. Stokes' granddaughter, Jevonne Stokes.

I wish you could have seen the look on her face when she was handed the *Who's Who In Black Cleveland*® book that featured a special tribute to her grandfather prominently displayed on the front cover. Jevonne held that book so close to her and commenced to tell all of her classmates the story of how her grandfather became America's first African-American mayor of a major city. That school event was priceless, and it makes what we do at Who's Who Publishing worthwhile.

It is my hope that each of us can make a concerted effort to expose our young people to successful African-American role models in their own community who are and have been making a difference. The people you read about in this publication make the city of Cleveland a great place to live, work, raise a family, and even start a business. Clearly, what our young people see they can be! Like Jevonne, let us make them proud of the strong heritage passed down from a community of people who set the pace in a piece of American history.

Criteria for Inclusion

Who's Who In Black Cleveland® is an opportunity for us to afford a measure of recognition to the men and women who have made their mark in their specific occupations, professions, or in service to others in the Cleveland community.

A sincere effort was made to include those whose positions or accomplishments in their chosen fields are significant and those whose contributions to community affairs whether city-wide or on the neighborhood level have improved the quality of life for all of us.

The names of those brief biographies included in this edition were compiled from customary sources of information. Lists of a wide variety were consulted and every effort was made to reach all whose stature or civic activities merited their inclusion.

In today's mobile society, no such publication could ever claim to be complete; some who should be included could not be reached or chose not to respond, and for that we offer our apologies. Constraints of time, space and awareness are thus responsible for other omissions, and not a lack of good intentions on the part of the publisher. Our goal was to document the accomplishments of many people from various occupational disciplines.

An invitation to participate in the publication was extended at the discretion of the publisher. Biographies were invited to contribute personal and professional data, with only the information freely submitted to be included. The editors have made a sincere effort to present an accurate distillation of the data, and to catch errors whenever possible. However, the publisher cannot assume any responsibility for the accuracy of the information submitted.

There was no charge for inclusion in this publication and inclusion was not guaranteed; an annual update is planned. Comments and other concerns should be addressed to:

C. Sunny Martin, CEO
Who's Who Publishing Co., LLC
1650 Lake Shore Drive, Suite 250
Columbus, Ohio 43204
Phone: (614) 481-7300

E-Mail: sunny@whoswhopublishing.com
www.whoswhopublishing.com

A Message From The Cleveland Publisher

Connie Harper

"We recognize that it is important to demonstrate the accomplishments and the breath of possibilities of blacks, who serve as an inspiration for our youth."

The publishing team for **Who's Who in Black Cleveland®** is grateful for the warm reception our inaugural publication received.

The Cleveland edition is unique, as it is the only "Who's Who" city to have a publishing team. Michael House, John Lenear, Paula Morrison, Michael Nelson and yours truly worked together to produce this book. We were assisted by Kimberly Fleming.

We owe our thanks to Louis Stokes, the retired congressman, for writing the foreword for this second edition. Stokes, who retired from Congress after more than 30 years of leadership, will always be Congressman Stokes to us for his distinguished service to not only his district, but the entire nation.

It is certainly with pride that we showcase all the outstanding achievements and the rich history of blacks in the Greater Cleveland area. As a special feature of this edition we introduce to you some of the talented artists recognized locally and nationally for their amazing creativity. They are Ernestine and Malcolm Brown, Malcolm the artist and Ernestine the curator of the gallery that celebrates its 25th anniversary this year, as well as Neal Hamilton, Alice Seifullah, Ed Parker, Murphy Ajayi and Charles Pinkney. Further, we salute E.F. Boyd & Son Funeral Homes for a century of service to our community.

It is our desire that this publication will not only be informative, but also denote the variety of areas where blacks have and are making significant contributions to the development in a city that has historically set the pace for other cities.

We recognize that it is important to demonstrate the accomplishments and the breath of possibilities of blacks, who serve as an inspiration for our youth. It is impossible to tell the complete story, but it is with sincere gratitude that we thank those who shared their success in order to make this publication possible.

Our thanks are also given to C. Sunny Martin, founder and CEO of Who's Who Publishing Co., along with his wonderful staff for their dedication to producing an excellent publication.

Connie Harper

All for one. One for all.

800.820.CAVS   cavs.com

The right health insurance. Right where you need it.

Ohio's Get-Well Card.™

MEDICAL MUTUAL™

SuperMed®

Luke Smith

Since 1934, Medical Mutual™ has been Ohio's health insurance company. Our card is your passport to good health. It gives you access to the largest network of doctors and hospitals across the state. Backed by the most responsive customer service anywhere. That's our commitment to Ohioans. So you can focus on what's most important. Getting well.

Visit MedMutual.com.

Turner
Building the Future

Turner 1422 Euclid Ave., Suite 1400 Cleveland, OH 44115 T: 216.522.1180 F: 216.522.0240

WILLIAM F. BOYD

A Lifetime Devoted to Service

William F. Boyd

This year the Boyd Funeral Homes are celebrating 100 years in the business.

In a professional career that spans more than six decades, William F. Boyd, Sr. has touched the lives of many generations of Cleveland families. Boyd is the patriarch of one of the city's premier African-American funeral homes. Although semi-retired, Boyd still serves as chairman of the board of E.F. Boyd & Son Funeral Homes, Inc. a firm founded by his father, Elmer F. Boyd in 1906.

William F. Boyd has been a good friend to the community and he has earned its loyalty. When Boyd took the helm of the family business 58 years ago, times were tough, and the average African American was struggling to make ends meet. During those lean years, death care fees had to be kept low, because many African Americans were poor people without burial insurance.

Boyd was actively involved in community life and often the people who came to him for funeral arrangements were neighbors and friends. It was not uncommon for Boyd to conduct funerals that were paid for in small weekly installments.

"Sometimes we really had to work with the family," Boyd said. "We'd hold some remains for five or six weeks to allow people to scrape together even part of the expenses."

Boyd and his wife, Mary Webster Boyd, who is also a funeral director, put in long hours, working side by side for more than 25 years to grow the business. With the help of their children and grandchildren, they have turned the funeral home into one of the city's most stable family-owned businesses. Under his leadership, E.F. Boyd & Son has grown from one small funeral parlor to three large funeral homes in Cleveland, East Cleveland and Warrensville Heights.

William F. and Mary Boyd

Top: Euclid Avenue in East Cleveland. Bottom Left: East 89th Street in Cleveland. Bottom Right: Emery Road in Warrensville Heights.

All three of Boyd's children have joined the business. William "Pepper" F. Boyd II is the chief executive officer, and daughters Marina Grant and Marcella Cox are vice presidents. "Serving the community is not just what my father does, it's who he is," said Pepper Boyd.

The firm also includes a son-in-law and some fourth-generation family members. "I am so pleased that so many members of my family have decided to join the business," Boyd said. "It's something I never expected to happen. It touches me to know that my father, then me, and now my children and grandchildren have all been involved with different generations of the same families."

Boyd's civic, philanthropic and professional contributions to the Greater Cleveland community are many and outstanding. He served as president of the Buckeye Funeral Directors Association, and he founded one of the most profitable minority-owned credit unions in the state of Ohio.

He was one of the first African Americans elected to the Cleveland Municipal School Board, where he served for two terms.

Boyd has served as both a trustee and officer of the Cleveland Urban League and the NAACP. He was president of the board of the Fairfax Renaissance Development Corp. and vice president of the Eliza Bryant Center. He has been awarded the Silver Beaver Award from the Boy Scouts of America. Likewise, he received the Humanist Award from the United Black Fund and the President's Award from the Buckeye State Funeral Directors and Morticians Association. He has also been inducted into the Glenville Hall of Fame.

Boyd was named Man of the Year by Antioch Baptist Church, where he served as a trustee for many years, and he was a recipient of the Black Professional Association Charitable Foundation's Life Achievement Awards. He is an avid golfer and a member of Gaylord's Social Club.

**Moving Businesses Forward.
Moving Communities Forward.
Moving Lives Forward.**

We're your Greater Cleveland Regional Transit Authority. And while it's our business to take over 50 million passengers from place to place every year, it's our mission to make Greater Cleveland a better place to live and work. Which is why we've launched initiatives such as the Euclid Corridor Transportation Project, which will spur regional economic development, and the Commuter Advantage program, offering area employees discounts on public transportation fares. And with our new clean-air fleet of buses that are 100% wheelchair-accessible, we've shown improvement in reliability, on-time performance, and customer satisfaction. At RTA, we're proud of the progress we've made today. And we're looking forward to moving Cleveland towards a brighter tomorrow.

rideRTA.com

Global Presence. Local Expertise.

We are SIRVA, the world's largest global relocation services business. With offices in over 40 countries and Global Certified Providers in more than 175 countries, we're setting new industry standards for worldwide point-to-point control.

We're also setting new standards for customer satisfaction by providing your transferees with one-call assistance, single-source reporting and on-site expertise for any situation. At SIRVA, we're continually redefining relocation to make the process faster and easier than ever before.

6070 Parkland Boulevard
Mayfield Heights, OH 44124

1.800.341.5648
www.sirvarelocation.com

relocation redefined®

LIVE ON FIVE →

→ **ON YOUR SIDE WITH BREAKING NEWS**

→ **HEALTH AND CONSUMER STORIES**

→ **ACCURATE, DOPPLER 5000 WEATHER FORECASTS**

← **AT 6:00 AND 11:00**

→ **NEW STORIES**

→ **LATE-BREAKING COVERAGE**

→ **5 ON YOUR SIDE INVESTIGATIONS**

NEWS CHANNEL 5
ON YOUR SIDE

WHO'S NEXT?

The achievements and dedication of the 2005 Who's Who In Black Cleveland honorees makes life better for all of us and leaves a lasting legacy for tomorrow. We salute you not only for being named Who's Who, but for inspiring Who's Next.

That's a mission worth investing in.

A bank invested in people.

 **Huntington**

huntington.com

MWH

Proudly Celebrates African American Achievement and Congratulates Who's Who in Black Cleveland

MWH has been a pioneering force in technology and infrastructure delivery for over 150 years. With 6,100 specialists in 36 countries, MWH's global team includes many of the brightest scientists, technology experts, engineers and constructors in the world.

A Recognized Industry Leader Around the Globe

Norman Gadzinski, V.P.
1300 East 9th Street, Suite 1100
Cleveland, OH 44114
tel: 216-621-2407
fax: 216-621-4972

www.mwhglobal.com

Energy is just one of the things we generate. Dominion dollars and volunteers help power scholarships, mentoring programs, education grants, minority-owned businesses, and other community initiatives. See how you can get involved at www.dom.com.

Our employees all have something in common. Imagination.

GE employees are as diverse as our products and services. That's because we bring together the best imaginations from diverse people. We're 315,000 minds operating in 100 countries, making over 25,000 products. Without diversity, we just wouldn't be GE.

To learn more, visit ge.com.

 imagination at work

Cleveland's
INTERESTING PERSONALITIES

Financial Education Center

A Passion to Serve and Build

Bruce D. Murphy

By Rhonda Crowder

In his younger days Bruce Murphy wanted to be a sports broadcaster, but did not want to relocate to small town America to get his start. So, he pursued another passion – helping people make better lives for themselves. This was a passion he inherited from his father, who spent his life in public service working for the State of Ohio and local politicians.

Banking, on the other hand, was an occupation he stumbled into, since he's always managed his career by simply knowing the direction he was going as opposed to the destination. "What I do want to be is engaged with providing tangible, meaningful services to people," says Murphy, president of community development banking at KeyBank.

Murphy is proud of the work that Key allows him to do in the area of urban initiatives. Murphy and his team have built a business strategy to provide products and services for low- to moderate-income people. The most notable programs include a check cashing service, Key Bank Plus, and the free financial education center located at Key's Buckeye branch.

Murphy says he's thankful the company has allowed him and his team to create the groundbreaking products and services that tangibly affect people's lives, and considers himself fortunate to work for an institution that cares about diversity.

"I have a deep passion for taking and leveraging what an institution like Key offers and I want to take those tools and make them available to the broader community, not just the African-American community," shared Murphy. "I think our company has very strong values and a genuine interest in ensuring that who we are as an institution is ethical and is relevant to the markets that we are in. For me it's about working for an institution that cares."

Murphy has been with KeyBank for 15 years, starting out on the human resources side of the business, then serving as district president before stepping into his current position. Prior to coming to Key, he worked at Mellon Bank in Pittsburgh for 13 years. On a football scholarship, he attended the University of Pittsburgh, where he obtained an undergraduate degree in communications and a master's degree in public management.

Despite being born in Youngstown, he's always had a special affinity for Cleveland since he often traveled here to visit his grandmother, who lived in the Kinsman area.

Murphy's active memberships include the Community Reinvestment Committee of the Consumer Bankers Association, Leadership Cleveland, and Alpha Phi Alpha Fraternity, Inc. He is also board president of the United Black Fund, board chair for Recovery Resources, and a board member of A.M. McGregor Home.

A recipient of many awards, it's the Louis Stokes Community Partner award from the Cleveland Housing Network, which he recently received, that means the most to him. Carl Stokes' election as mayor of Cleveland is his earliest recollection of being a proud African American. He is also a recipient of the Call & Post Foundation's 2005 W.O. Walker Community Excellence Award.

In his spare time, Murphy loves to cook, entertain and attempt, he says, to play golf. He also enjoys spending time with his wife, Michele, and their three children.

Murphy is honored to be listed among the *Who's Who in Black Cleveland*® for the second time and believes the directory is an important tool, because it shows the breath and the scope of capability in the community.

"I feel we should focus on the least of God's people."

Rev. William F. Crockett

By Rhonda Crowder

The Reverend William F. Crockett is a hardworking yet humble man who has worked tirelessly towards influencing the political process and assisting troubled youth.

Born in Birmingham, AL, Crockett moved to Cleveland in 1948. He became involved with the political process in Cleveland during the late '60s, helping both Louis and Carl Stokes raise funds and run campaigns for political offices. During that time, Crockett also became the first black man to serve as clerk of the United States Postal Union.

"At that time being involved in politics was important for advancing in the workforce," he said. To that end, Crockett associated himself with various projects and organizations designed to empower African Americans. At the NAACP, he served as chair of the labor and industry committee and spearheaded successful efforts to get minorities appointed to directorships and managerial positions with the Cleveland Public Library. He also served as an Urban League of Greater Cleveland board member, and as executive vice president of the Carnegie Roundtable.

Crockett also understood the importance of an education. He graduated from Baldwin-Wallace College, earning an MBA in systems management in 1976. He also attended Case Western Reserve, and John Carroll and Cleveland State universities, but pursued a master's of divinity degree at Ashland Theological Seminary. "I believe we were put here for a purpose," Crockett said.

In doing God's work, he served as youth minister and interim pastor at Shiloh Baptist Church; director of the Baptist Ministers Conference Health and Welfare Fund; president and chair of the East Side Cleveland Clergy for United Way; and as an instructor at Olivet Institutional Baptist Church Christian Education Institute.

His most challenging and rewarding community improvement efforts include service as Protestant chaplain and board member of Young Men's Chance for Change, where he helped troubled youth turn their lives over to Christ.

In 1989, he founded Bill Crockett Ministries with the goal to bring the Bible into the lives of those who lack it, and as another effort to help youth. Crockett also serves as a meeting planner at the National Baptist Convention, a position he's held since 1992.

In 2002, Crockett was elected the 36th imperial potentate of Prince Hall Shriners, an organization dedicated to dispensing charity and assisting in benevolent purposes, as well supporting individuals with common interests. As potentate, he focused on education and youth development, with an emphasis on at-risk and high-risk youth programs. He also initiated voter registration and education programs because he believes educating voters is a critical part of the process. Crockett is a past grand master in Ohio and Louisiana, as well.

Former Masonic involvement includes service as worshipful master (No. 11), most wise master (Hiram Rose Croix Chapter), commander in chief (Bezaleel Consistory No. 15), associate editor of *LAMP* (Prince Hall Grand Lodge publication) and illustrious potentate (El Hasa Temple No. 28).

Crockett has over 30 years of experience working with troubled youth and has been a consultant to inner-city, faith-based, and community outreach youth programs. He is a member of Zeta Chapter, Delta Mu Delta National Honor Society for Business Graduates, and Kappa Alpha Psi Fraternity, Inc. Crockett has also been inducted into the African-American Hall of Fame in Alliance, Ohio.

Married to his wife Laura since 1952, they have one daughter, Rysia.

THE CITY OF WARRENSVILLE HEIGHTS, OHIO

MARCIA L. FUDGE
MAYOR

Photo by Mychal Lilly

On a Fast Track Paved with Success and Service

The Honorable
Marcia L. Fudge

By Jacqueline Kelly

With the coming of the new millennium, history was made twice in Warrensville Heights, Ohio. For the first time since the city's founding 193 years ago, an African American was elected mayor. The event was twice as significant because the mayor, Marcia L. Fudge, was also the first female to lead the city.

Marcia Fudge has been on the leadership fast track all of her life. After graduating from Shaker Heights High School, Marcia received a bachelor of science degree in business administration from The Ohio State University. Always seeking opportunities for enrichment, she continued her education by earning a juris doctorate from Cleveland Marshall College of Law, Cleveland State University in June of 1983.

Professionally, Mayor Fudge has had a diverse employment career. She has held top level managerial positions in private industry and nearly every level of government. She has been employed by the cities of Cleveland and Bedford, Ohio, Cuyahoga County, the State of Ohio, and the Congress of the United States of America. Each professional position has taken her a step higher on her career ladder, helping to prepare her for her latest role as mayor.

As a law clerk, Mayor Fudge honed the writing and legal research skills that contributed to her success as a visiting judge. She also put her business skills to work in Cuyahoga County, serving as the director of personal property taxation, deputy county auditor of the estate tax department, director of the budget commission, and as a budget and finance officer for the county prosecutor's office. Most recently, she was chief of staff for U.S. Congresswoman Stephanie Tubbs Jones.

Mayor Fudge has been well schooled. As a solo law practitioner, visiting referee, and acting judge she observed, thought, and acted with her best judgment. These characteristics helped her to be successful in her civic endeavors, including serving on the boards of the Cleveland Public Library and Alcoa Aluminum, and on the Judge Lloyd O. Brown Scholarship Committee.

As mayor of Warrensville Heights, she has put together a team which has spearheaded an economic revival in the city. Since her election, there has been a flurry of new construction, including the recently completed Marriott Hotel, a senior citizen's housing complex, and an upscale housing subdivision. Mayor Fudge has further increased the city's tax base and created new jobs by attracting businesses such as Sherwin Williams Aerosol Research Division, Marcus Thomas Advertising, and Heinen's Supermarkets, which relocated its corporate headquarters to the city.

Mayor Fudge has devoted her life to community service and is deeply committed to social justice issues. She was the 21st National President of Delta Sigma Theta Sorority, Inc., and currently chairs the social action commission for the national public service organization. Mayor Fudge credits her faith in God and a strong family for her temperament and drive to succeed.

Success Runs in Our Race

SUCCESSGUIDE 2005
SUCCESSGUIDE 2005
SUCCESSGUIDE 2005
SUCCESSGUIDE 2005
SUCCESSGUIDE 2005
SUCCESSGUIDE 2005
SUCCESSGUIDE 2005
SUCCESSGUIDE 2005
SUCCESSGUIDE 2005
SUCCESSGUIDE 2005
SUCCESSGUIDE 2005
SUCCESSGUIDE 2005
SUCCESSGUIDE 2005
SUCCESSGUIDE 2005
SUCCESSGUIDE 2005
SUCCESSGUIDE 2005
SUCCESSGUIDE 2005
SUCCESSGUIDE 2005
SUCCESSGUIDE 2005
SUCCESSGUIDE 2000 - 2001
SUCCESSGUIDE 2002-2003

"You cannot do anything of any significance by yourself."

George C. Fraser

By Rhonda Crowder

Some would argue it's what you know while others proclaim it's who you know, but networking guru George C. Fraser believes both aspects are extremely important when entering the ballpark of life. He sees life as a three-legged stool with education, marketable skills and the ability to develop and maintain relationships being the three legs, and he believes the key to success is directly related to one's willingness to ask for help.

According to Fraser, relationships are critical and building relationships stems from one's ability to work with and through other people; the ability to cultivate, nurture and develop various relationships; to build a team and become a part of the team; to love and be loved; and the ability to lead and follow. "Without relationships you have no business, and without relationships you have no business being in business," he says.

Fraser believes profound ideas are simple ideas and that someone must deliver the spark to ignite the idea. Therefore, he created and is committed to delivering the idea of success, wealth creation, and networking to the African-American community as a whole.

One of 11 children, he grew up poor and in foster care in Brooklyn, NY. However, he's thankful that his father, a taxi driver, did not pass his poverty onto his children.

Fraser received his executive training at Tuck School of Business at Dartmouth College. He went on to work in management with Procter & Gamble, the United Way and Ford Motor Company for 17 years – work he believes prepared him for his calling.

He wrote two critically acclaimed books, *Success Runs in Our Race: The Complete Guide to Effective Networking in the African American Community* and *Race for Success: The Ten Best Business Opportunities for Blacks in America.*

Success Runs in Our Race, a book he wrote ten years ago, has become a modern-day classic and required reading at 60 Historically Black Colleges and Universities.

Additionally, Fraser has appeared on more than 250 television and radio talk shows, and has almost 120 worldwide speaking engagements per year, where he discusses success principles, effective networking, wealth creation, ethics, and the importance of diversity. The prestigious publication *Vital Speeches of the Day* selected five of Fraser's speeches for worldwide reprint and distribution, making him the first professional speaker in America to accomplish such a feat. He was also named one of *Upscale Magazine's* top 50 power brokers in black America.

Considered one of the foremost authorities on networking and building effective relationships, Fraser is the chairman and CEO of FraserNet Inc., which publishes the award-winning *SuccessGuide Worldwide: The Networking Guide to Black Resources*. FraserNet also annually hosts black America's largest networking event, the PowerNetworking Conference – designed to promote economic development by teaching participants how to leverage resources and connect the dots in their business and personal lives.

The work Fraser does is geared toward stopping the transference of generational poverty, building self-esteem, addressing the issues plaguing the African-American community, and spiritual empowerment. By promoting "can do/must do" thinking, he hopes his message is passed on, improved upon, and continuously implemented, thus closing the income and wealth gap in America.

A recipient of an honorary doctorate degree of humane letters from Jarvis Christian College, George Fraser has been married to his wife, Nora Jean for 33 years. They have two sons, Kyle and Scott.

Photo by Mychal Lilly

Knocking Down Doors to Build Buildings

Robert P. Madison

By Rhonda Crowder

During the 1940s, it was unheard of for a black man to even think about being an architect, let alone become one, but Robert P. Madison was up to the challenge. He knew what he was going to be since the age of seven, when his mother took one look at a drawing he brought home from school and told him he was going to be an architect.

On some level, Madison has been involved with the design or construction of every major project in Cleveland's downtown renaissance. His most notable local projects include the RTA Waterfront Line, Rock n' Roll Hall of Fame and Museum, Great Lakes Science Center, Cleveland State University's Science and Research Center, Langston Hughes Branch Library, Quicken Loans Arena, Cleveland Browns Stadium, and the list goes on.

Madison is licensed to practice architecture in 22 states and has designed structures throughout the United States and in Africa. Of all the structures he's designed, the U.S. Embassy in Dakar, Senegal, West Africa is his most significant. "When I went there to design the embassy I was going back to the place were my ancestors come from," he says. "That, symbolically, was the most significant, meaningful structure."

Madison admits his success didn't come easy because the world wasn't ready for a black architect. In fact, he saw how his father, a civil engineer, was turned down for jobs because of his ethnicity; like so many others before him, Madison had to knock down doors so he could build buildings. He graduated from East Technical High School with honors in math and science and attended Howard University's School of Architecture until leaving to fight in World War II. He served his country until he was wounded in action.

It has been said that the greatest misfortunes often bring about unforeseen rewards; this was the case for Madison. He returned home with a Purple Heart and three Battle Ribbons, then attended the Western Reserve University School of Architecture, a school he applied to twice. His first application was denied because it didn't accept "Coloreds" at the time.

After receiving his bachelor's degree in architecture, Madison attended Harvard University, where he obtained his master's degree in architecture. He also received a Fulbright fellowship at L'Ecole des Beaux Arts, in Paris, where he studied architecture and urban design.

Despite having the credentials, some didn't believe he could do the work that requires accuracy, attention to detail, and a strong sense of math and physics. However, Madison was determined to prove them wrong. He worked as an assistant professor of architecture at Howard University before opening his firm in Cleveland in 1954, the first in Ohio founded by an African American and ninth in the nation.

If you're wondering how many firsts one black man can rack up in a lifetime, ask Madison, chairman and CEO of Robert P. Madison International Inc. Architects, Engineers and Planners. He was the first African American to graduate from Western Reserve University School of Architecture, and to register to practice architecture in Ohio. He was also the first African American to design a world renowned building, to design a building for the State of Ohio, to design a branch office for a major corporation in Ohio, to design a major building in Cleveland, and to serve on the board of trustees at Case Western Reserve University. Madison has also received numerous awards and honorary degrees.

Believing it to be his obligation to mentor and support minorities pursuing careers in architecture, his firm has trained over 200 African-American architects and engineers, and he established the Robert P. Madison Scholarship in Architecture Fund, administered by The Cleveland Foundation. He also visits schools to speak to children and offers one piece of advice to aspiring architects: "I think you have to like it, and if you like and love it, you'll do well, but it's not to be taken easy."

Madison is still practicing, and he refers to architectural work as doodling with a purpose in mind. So every time Madison sits down to doodle, leading to a design for a school, church, stadium or museum, he proves the possibilities are endless.

A Results-Oriented Approach Nets Strategic Alliances

Brian E. Hall

By Rhonda Crowder

Industrial Inventory Solutions, LLC is the parent company of Industrial Transport Inc. (a Cleveland-based freight transportation company) and iSource Performance Materials, LLC (a warehousing and distribution company). As chairman and chief executive officer of Industrial Inventory Solutions, it is Brian E. Hall's responsibility to oversee daily operations concerning freight transportation and the distribution of the safety and specialty industrial chemical products throughout the United States.

Hall's high motivation level and results-oriented approach to business helps him to successfully interact with representatives from Ford Motor Company, DaimlerChrysler, General Motors, Sears, Goodyear, and the many other industry leaders that are included among Industrial Inventory Solutions' customer list.

Currently, Industrial spots 40,000 trailers a week at 12 plants spread throughout Ohio, Michigan, Illinois, Missouri, Wisconsin and California. Each day, iSource ships 2,000 adhesives, sealants, epoxies, paints, lubricants and safety products as it represents leading industrial companies such as Dow Chemical, Sherwin Williams, LPS, and others.

When Hall is not working, he is involved in several civic and community projects. He is founder and past president of the President's Council, an organization made up of CEOs from some of Cleveland's largest African-American businesses. The President's Council was established in 1996 to provide entrepreneurial and economic development in the African-American community. It was also formed to advance the growth of African-American companies by fostering strategic alliances with majority CEOs of other corporations in Northeast Ohio.

In 1987, Hall established the Tremont Advisory Group at Tremont Elementary School, a mentoring program that guides 12 young African-American males. The group continues to maintain contact with 50 percent of the young men, assisting them with employment leads and opportunities.

In the past, he has sat on numerous boards of directors, including the AAU Junior Olympics Board, the American Red Cross, Greater Cleveland Growth Association, Cleveland Convention & Visitors Bureau, and the Visiting Nurses Association. He also served as an adviser to ShoreBank. Hall currently serves on 11 boards and is co-chair of the Initiatives on Economic Inclusion.

He has been named the Leadership Cleveland Herbert E. Strawbridge Volunteer of the Year two years in a row (2001 and 2002), received the 2003 Nortech Innovative Business Award, and was recognized as a *Black Enterprise* 2003 Top 100 MBE.

Hall received a bachelor's degree in business management and an executive MBA from Baldwin-Wallace College. He also attended the prestigious Minority Business Executive Program and subsequent advanced programs at Dartmouth College's Amos Tuck School of Business.

Brian and his wife, Susan, have two children and live in Shaker Heights.

Many African
Americans have
had their dreams
come true...

...You can, too.

Financial Planning for a well-balanced future.

No matter where you are in life and no matter where life takes you,
Fifth Third is there with a variety of products and services to fit your
needs. From checking and savings accounts to loan and investing
options, Fifth Third is there to offer assistance as you grow
into financial maturity and independence. Fifth Third
is more than simply a bank...we are a life-long financial partner.

1-877-579-5353

Working Hard To Be The Only Bank You'll Ever Need.®

Memories can be as precious as jewels.
Protecting them can be as easy as sharing them.

We realize all of the names of history makers didn't make it into history books.
That's why we'd like to acknowledge all of those who withstood and endured, who dried tears
and cried tears, who stepped in and courageously kept on. Who defied injustice to any as proudly as
they praised justice for all. Who believed in right enough to suffer wrong. Who hurt and too often bled
but never gave up the fight. Who mourned and yet still marched, who clasped hands and walked on,
who sat in but most of all stood up for civil rights.

Although the world may not know your individual names,
together you made a world of difference and changed the course of American History.
We Salute You All!

**American Family Insurance is proud to help protect
all the things that matter most.... Even precious memories.**

Cuyahoga Community College

Opened in Cleveland in 1963, Cuyahoga Community College is Ohio's first and largest community college, serving approximately 60,000 students each year. More than 700,000 students have come through Tri-C's doors during the past four decades.

Our curriculum includes nearly 1,000 credit courses in 70 career and technical programs and the liberal arts.

Our student to teacher ratio is 19 to 1 and tuition is the lowest in Northeast Ohio.

85% of our students find jobs in Northeast Ohio.

87% of our students would recommend Tri-C to someone seeking the same kind of program they studied.

The mission of Cuyahoga Community College is to provide high quality, accessible and affordable educational opportunities and services – including university transfer, technical and lifelong learning programs – that promote individual development and improve the overall quality of life in a multicultural community.

TRI-C CONNECTS YOU
to your future

www.tri-c.edu   **WHERE FUTURES BEGIN™**   1.800.954.tri-c

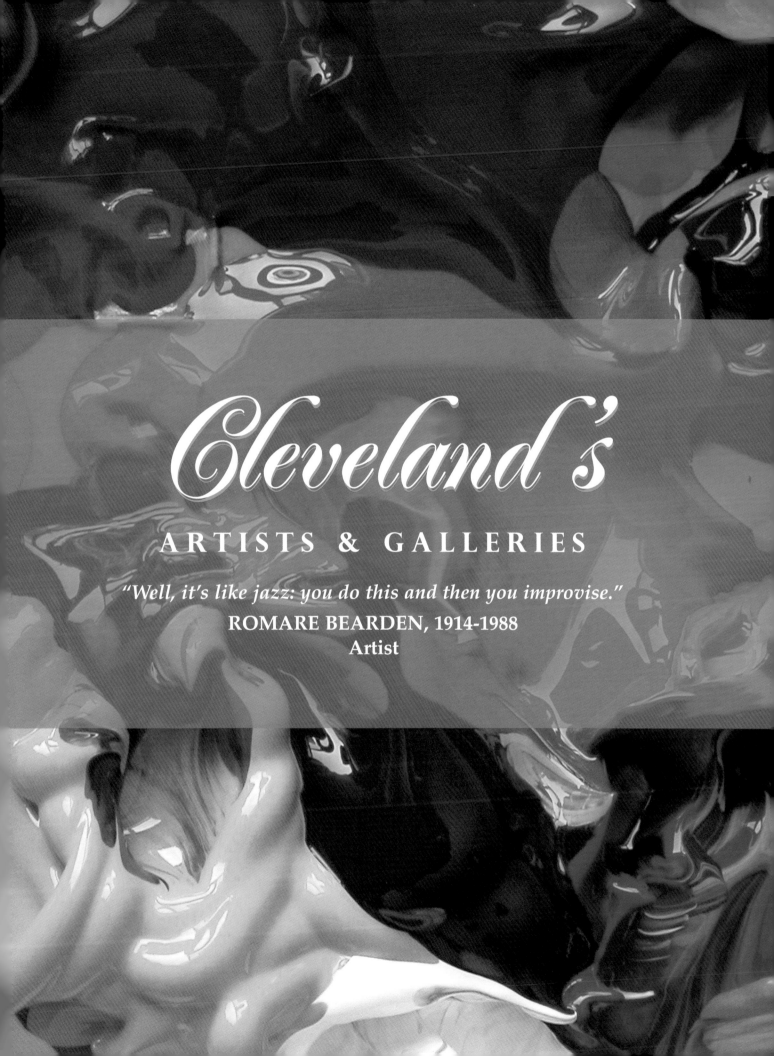

Cleveland's

ARTISTS & GALLERIES

"Well, it's like jazz: you do this and then you improvise."
ROMARE BEARDEN, 1914-1988
Artist

Murphy Ajayi, Ph.D.

By Jacqueline Knox Kelly

Dr. Murphy Ajayi is a renowned sculptor in Nigeria. He has produced several monumental outdoor sculptures, mosaic murals, and wall art that is erected in a dozen major Nigerian cities. His visually striking sculptures range in size from tabletop statues to gigantic monuments more than 85 feet high. "I have a reputation in Nigeria because so many of my sculptures are in public places," he said.

Here in the United States, Dr. Ajayi's reputation is growing, not only as an artist but also as an award-winning teacher and lecturer. Ajayi received his bachelor's and master's of art degrees in fine arts in Nigeria. He recently earned a doctor of philosophy degree at Union Institute and University in Cincinnati, Ohio. He is professor of pan-African studies at Kent State University, Geauga, and Twinsburg Center, where he introduces students to African arts, theater, drama, and culture. He also participates in the broad spectrum of theater activities both in front of and behind the curtain.

Dr. Ajayi blurs the line between the artist and the teacher. For him, both roles are integrated. The fusion is natural for Ajayi because all art forms are interwoven into the fabric of African life and culture. Ajayi says that everything he imparts as a teacher, he learns from his art. "He who educates through art must be a practitioner of art," said Ajayi.

One of Dr. Ajayi's notable public sculptures created in Cleveland include "The Louis Stokes Community Visionary Award," a 42-inch high bronze sculpture awarded annually by Fairfax Renaissance Development Corporation to an individual or group. Replicas were acquired by Congressman Charles B. Rangel and former Cleveland Mayor Michael R. White. Ajayi was also commissioned to create a life-size sculpture of Langston Hughes for Cleveland's Karamu House.

Malcolm & Ernestine Brown

By Jacqueline Knox Kelly

He's a brilliant visual artist and educator. She's an arts advocate, civic leader and gallery director. Together, the husband and wife team of Malcolm McCleod Brown and Ernestine Turner Brown has devoted the past quarter century to enhancing the cultural landscape of northeast Ohio and beyond.

Malcolm Brown's distinguished arts career expands nearly four decades. A Virginia native, Malcolm earned a bachelor of arts degree at Virginia State College and master of arts degree at Case Western Reserve University. He is a member of the prestigious American Watercolor Society, and is internationally exhibited and collected. He has received worldwide exposure through the films *Waiting to Exhale* and *The Antwone Fisher Story*. His artwork is represented in more than two dozen major institutions, including the Cleveland Museum of Art, and is currently traveling with The Grant Hill Collection of African American Art: Something All Our Own.

A Youngstown State University graduate, Ernestine Brown worked as a teacher in the Cleveland Public Schools, and then as a part-time instructor at Cuyahoga Community College, before opening the Malcolm Brown Gallery in Shaker Heights, Ohio. Under her directorship, the gallery has gained national and international acclaim for increasing awareness and appreciation of the visual arts. "My mission is to expose new and seasoned audiences and museums to a broader spectrum of art and artists," said Ernestine.

Among the renowned African-American artists whose works have been showcased in the Malcolm Brown Gallery are Elizabeth Catlett, Romare Bearden, and Selma Burke.

This year the gallery is celebrating its 25th anniversary with an exhibition by the gallery's namesake, entitled Malcolm Brown: Caribbean Journey. Inspired by travels to isles of the Caribbean over the past two years, Brown's vivid palette weds abstract and figurative imagery to create 25 watercolor and acrylic paintings of lush landscapes, seascapes, and street scenes.

Neal Hamilton

By Jacqueline Knox Kelly

Since 1979, visual artist Neal Hamilton has had phenomenal success as an illustrator, graphic designer, photographer and painter. Although he has been painting all of his life, Hamilton took a ten-year break to pursue other artistic opportunities. Hamilton is a Clevelander with what many would consider the dream job. For the past nine years, he has combined his passion for music with visual art to become the official photographer of the Rock and Roll Hall of Fame and Museum.

Hamilton was an art prodigy. As a six-year-old art student at the Cleveland Museum of Art, he outperformed children twice his age. He later studied at Cuyahoga Community College and Cooper School of Art. A chance meeting with former Cleveland Browns football player Ben Davis led to his introduction to fellow artist Gary Thomas, who became his mentor.

Hamilton began his professional art career in the 70s with Artist Studios, where he sharpened his skills as a graphic designer and illustrator. He later operated his own enterprise, Livewire Studios, which quickly became known in Cleveland for cutting edge graphic arts and design. His major clients included American Greetings and Goodyear Tire Company.

During his tenure with the Rock Hall, Hamilton created many memorable projects including a series with Aretha Franklin, whom he photographed with golf icon Tiger Woods. He documented the opening of the John Lennon exhibition and chronicled the historic visit of President Bill Clinton to the Rock Hall.

Periodically, during his self-imposed hiatus from painting, Neal has felt the urge to get back to his art, but when a tragic house fire destroyed his home and studio, he turned to his painting for solace and experienced an artistic rebirth. With his passions for design and painting rekindled and fueled by the music he loves, Neal began to paint feverishly. With all of his supplies destroyed, he began creating with an arsenal of unorthodox tools and leftover cans of house paint.

For the first time in his life, Hamilton feels that all his experiences and creative passions have finally found a home in his portraits of rock icons. The result is mesmerizing pop art: paints layered, mediums melded, canvases pushed and prodded into life, saturated with vibrant colors and the soul of rock and roll. The images are intense and revealing, rock stars with eyes that stare into your soul, colors that accentuate their mood — sensuality, mystery, or in-your-face flamboyancy. In these portraits of rocks icons, Neal Hamilton feels that, at long last, his experiences and creative passions have found a home.

Photo by Mychal Lilly

Edward Everett Parker

By Jacqueline Knox Kelly

Retired college professor Edward Everett Parker is a master artist, educator, and entrepreneur. Parker is the founder and director of the Snickerfritz Cultural Workshop for the Arts, Inc., located in the Edward E. Parker Creative Arts Complex in East Cleveland, Ohio. The complex, which also includes gallery and classroom space, meeting rooms, a number of small businesses, and one of the area's more quaint bed and breakfast facilities, is housed in a converted nursing home that sat vacant and dilapidated for seventeen years before Parker purchased and rehabilitated the facility.

The complex has been a dedicated influence in the development of cultural and artistic expression and appreciation for more than nineteen years. It serves as a venue for the exhibition and display of works of area artists. Parker describes himself as a "Theme Artist," whose vision has long been inspired by African-American history and culture. His better known works include a life-sized sculpture of the Chicken George character from Alex Haley's Roots, and a celebrated series of African-American clown sculptures and prints. He is currently working on a mixed media series entitled *Be Bop Meets Hip Hop*.

Parker earned a bachelor's degree in art from Central State University in Wilberforce, Ohio, and a master's degree in art education from Kent State University. He taught in the Cleveland Public Schools, and served as the head of the art department at Audubon Junior High. Later, he was a professor and arts coordinator at Cuyahoga Community College, where he taught for nearly twenty years.

Parker resides in East Cleveland, Ohio and has served on the board of trustees for the East Cleveland Library.

Photo by Mychal Lilly

Charles Pinkney

By Jacqueline Knox Kelly

Don't try to pigeonhole Charles Pinkney. He abhors stereotypes. Pinkney has made a concerted effort to develop all of his many talents—photographer, writer, and painter—to the fullest. Like all renaissance men, he aspires to excellence in multiple fields. Pinkney discovered painting the first time his mother, at a teacher's suggestion, took him to the Cleveland Museum of Art.

"I was seven years old and I knew then I wanted to be a painter," he said.

When Charles was ten years old, his mother became ill and Charles became reclusive and withdrawn, spending much of his time drawing as a way to gain attention and praise. Two years later, when his mother died, drawing and painting helped him get past his loss.

Pinkney continued to paint, but his career took a temporary detour when he discovered he could paint with his camera. During a tour of duty in Europe with the Army, Charles became fascinated with the work of a German artist named Gruenwald who painted black people during the 16th century. Using a Leica camera won in a card game, he developed his first photojournalism essay, featuring pictures of Gruenwald's hometown and family.

After his discharge from the Army, Charles attended Kent State University where he studied art and history. Although he wanted to paint, by that time he was married with a family to

support. Focusing on more practical endeavors, he accepted a job with *The Pittsburgh Press* newspaper and became one of the first black photojournalists in the country to work for a major publication. Never one to rest on his laurels, Pinkney was always looking for new intellectual challenges. In the 80s, Pinkney published *The Chesnutt Record*, a literary magazine that served as an intellectual forum for writers and artists in northeast Ohio.

Pinkney says seascapes, landscapes and still life paintings are his passion. A world traveler, Pinkney was on a trip to San Diego, California when he fell in love with the scenery of the area and embarked upon his most prolific period as a painter. Influenced by the prospect of becoming a part of the vibrant local art community, he relocated to Southern California where, for the next several years, the ocean near La Jolla was his favorite subject.

Devoid of human images, the land and seascapes and still life paintings afford Pinkney racial anonymity. Then, just when you think you know who Pinkney is not, he reveals himself in portraits of black people. He says he paints them because he wants to erase negative stereotypes and show the true beauty of his race.

Alice Hill Seifullah

By Jacqueline Knox Kelly

Alice Seifullah has been a professional artist for more than 30 years. She is an accomplished portrait artist whose commissioned works hang in homes, businesses and galleries throughout the United States. A native Clevelander, Seifullah's natural talents as an artist became apparent during childhood when she was awarded a scholarship for Saturday classes at the Cleveland Institute of Art. She majored in fine arts at The Ohio State University and the Cooper School of Art, where she obtained an associate degree in fashion illustration.

For most of the last decade, Alice Seifullah combined her love of 1940s fashion with her interest in painting and music to create unusual boutiques in downtown Cleveland and University Circle. Seifullah's ateliers were more than just unique shopping experiences, they were destinations. In addition to being places to shop for exquisite vintage clothing, fashion accessories, and household collectibles, the shops were a gathering place for musicians, writers, students, and other artists. Seifullah's work, in addition to the work of other artists, was always on display in the space. Seifullah's drawings and paintings include portraits of people both real and imaginary. Her faces are so universal that viewers often mistake her fantasy faces for real people they know.

Shiefullah is a deeply religious person. Although her religious roots are planted firmly in the Baptist tradition, Alice's spiritual evolution includes a deep exploration of Islam. Her father, the late Rev. Luther Hill, a Baptist preacher, was a pastor at Mt. Sinai Baptist Church which her grandfather founded. She says her work is intended to be spiritually uplifting. As a result, Madonna and Child subjects and other religious references are dominant themes throughout her work.

Seifullah is a lover of all of the arts. On any given day a shopper could observe the artist at work, or enjoying an impromptu jam session, poetry reading, or book signing. These days, Seifullah devotes herself to painting, drawing and practicing the violin, an instrument she studied as a child and recently rediscovered. She is a member of Delta Sigma Theta Sorority, Inc. and plays with The Melting Pot Orchestra, a multi-cultural ensemble which plays inspirational music. Seifullah's and her husband Alan, chief communications officer of the Cleveland Municipal School District, reside in Cleveland. They have five children.

The Sherwin-Williams Company
celebrates diversity
in our people, our suppliers
and our valued customers.

SHERWIN WILLIAMS.
sherwin-williams.com

For information on
Ulmer & Berne LLP,
contact
Inajo D. Chappell,
ichappell@ulmer.com
216.931.6140

Leonard D. Young
lyoung@ulmer.com
216.931.6220

At Ulmer & Berne LLP, we consider diversity to be fundamental to our success. It promotes a broader, richer work environment. It replaces tired, conventional solutions with creative ideas. It enriches individual assets and strengthens our collective value.

ulmer | berne | llp
ATTORNEYS

www.ulmer.com

Cleveland   Columbus   Cincinnati   Chicago

*Virginia is 72, lives on her own
and still has a pre-schooler.*
You can help.

Enough love to raise the grandchildren but not enough income to feed them.

For more than 50,000 deserving residents in our community who struggle to make ends meet, the Hunger Network of Greater Cleveland is the answer. We're the area's largest network of food pantries and soup kitchens. Your donations allow hundreds of volunteers to purchase food, assemble balanced meals, and distribute them to qualified caring families like Virginia's.

Make a donation that makes a difference.

HUNGERNETWORK
OF GREATER CLEVELAND

You can see it working.℠

To donate, please call 216-619-8155, or mail your donation to Hunger Network of Greater Cleveland, 614 W. Superior Ave., Suite 744, Cleveland, OH 44113. THANK YOU.

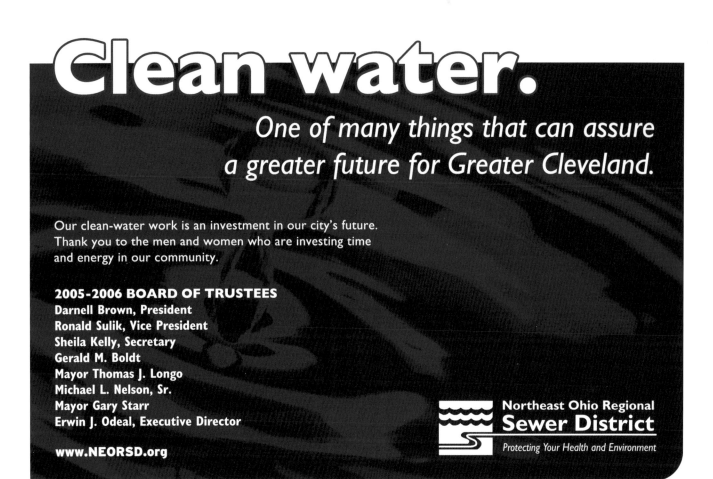

Clean water.

One of many things that can assure a greater future for Greater Cleveland.

Our clean-water work is an investment in our city's future.
Thank you to the men and women who are investing time
and energy in our community.

2005-2006 BOARD OF TRUSTEES
Darnell Brown, President
Ronald Sulik, Vice President
Sheila Kelly, Secretary
Gerald M. Boldt
Mayor Thomas J. Longo
Michael L. Nelson, Sr.
Mayor Gary Starr
Erwin J. Odeal, Executive Director

www.NEORSD.org

Northeast Ohio Regional
Sewer District
Protecting Your Health and Environment

Investing in our future. Drawing commerce to Cleveland. Improving our quality of life.

Boyd & Son inc.
Funeral Home & Crematory

*Four Generations Serving You
for 100 Years in a
Tradition of Quality, Compassionate Care*

- *Pre-Need
  Arrangements*

- *Organ and
  Air-Conditioning*

- *On-Site Crematory*

- *Ample Parking*

- *Handicapped
  Facilities*

- *Complete Services
  Within All Means*

*2165 East 89th Street
Cleveland, OH 44106
(216) 791-0770 Fax (216) 421-2776*

*15357 Euclid Avenue
East Cleveland, OH 44112
(216) 541-2856
Fax (216) 541-4197*

*25900 Emery Road
Warrensville Hts., OH 44128
(216) 831-7906
Fax (216) 831-7916*

Celebrating African-American Achievements

WHO'S WHO
in BLACK
Cleveland
THE 2006 EDITION

Order Additional Copies Online
www.whoswhopublishing.com
614.481.7300

PARTNERS FOR POTENTIAL

Partnering with Urban Youth of Promise for a Stronger Greater Cleveland Community

By virtually every statistical and anecdotal measurement we are losing our most talented youth, this is true across almost every demographic group in Northeastern Ohio. As employers we have been impacted by the "brain drain". Finding and recruiting the best talent within Northeastern Ohio is increasingly more difficult.

Partners for Potential's intent is to create the next generation of business and community leaders within the inner city by giving the most gifted minority youth, scholarships, mentoring, jobs, the opportunity to work together on community service projects and, ultimately, college tuition reimbursement. Joined by our corporate and non-profit partners we will mentor and train inner city youth to become successful businesspeople and professionals who will stay and participate in Northeastern Ohio communities. To stop the "brain drain" and build leaders who will, as so many have before, bring opportunity and prosperity to our inner cities, we are looking for corporations to give early support to these kids. As any single effort, we are bound to failure, unless linked to all of the other corporate and philanthropic efforts to retain and build on Northeastern Ohio's pool of talent.

Edward J. Davidson
CEO Partners for Potential

Reggie Rucker
Executive Diretor

6065 Parkland Blvd. Cleveland, OH 44124

www.partnersforpotential.org
800-399-2626

INTERCONTINENTAL HOTEL CLEVELAND
EXCEPTIONAL EVENTS, LUXURIOUS ACCOMMODATIONS AND SERVICE LIKE NO OTHER

Whether it's the site of a corporate conference, the setting for an intimate dinner for two, or the location for a plush overnight stay, the InterContinental Hotel Cleveland offers unparalleled service in an atmosphere suited for any occasion.

Located just minutes from the heart of downtown, InterContinental Hotels Cleveland boasts three unique properties on the world-famous Cleveland Clinic Campus. As a member of the InterContinental Hotels Group, the AAA Four Diamond InterContinental Hotel Cleveland is part of one of the most sophisticated hospitality companies in the world, with a reputation for luxurious accommodations, exceptional facilities, and meticulous personal attention.

HIGH-TECH SPECIAL EVENTS

At the InterContinental Hotel Cleveland, special events are state of the art. From the 35,000-square-foot conference center to its 300 guestrooms and 23 suites, the hotel offers some the most advanced technology available.

The 500-seat amphitheater is equipped with cutting-edge technology.

An ideal setting for a variety of events, the hotel's amphitheater hosts a data port for a high-speed Internet connection, a conventional modem, and an audience response system keypad, which can be used to poll the audience. The amphitheater also can be divided into two smaller theaters, and activities can be broadcast to The Cleveland Clinic, hotel guestrooms, eight breakout rooms, or any teleconferencing facility in the world. The state of the art conference center was recently awarded the grand prize for "Best Presentation Rooms" in *Presentations* magazine's guide to the best facilities.

The elegant ballroom can accommodate up to 1,100 guests and can be separated into three sections.

The InterContinental Hotel also houses an 8,000-square-foot, double-height ballroom (18 feet) featuring viewing screens that drop from the ceiling for audiovisual presentations. Plus, the hotel features spacious reception areas and function rooms for smaller events.

But technology doesn't stop here. Hotel guestrooms also feature impressive technology, including a PC hook-up, a dual-line phone with data port for a computer, and high-speed Internet access.

For Shelli Weisz, director of implementation services for Beachwood-based TMW Systems, holding her company's annual User Group conference at a technologically-advanced location was imperative. "As the leading worldwide supplier of dispatch operations software, our clients look to our company to be an innovator in technology," said Weisz. "Being a technology-centered hotel, InterContinental is a great fit for our company, and it gives us all the high-tech equipment we need for successful meetings."

Since 2003, when the hotel first opened, Weisz has hosted approximately 600 attendees at InterContinental for each of the company's three-and-a-half-day conferences.

CATERING TO YOUR NEEDS

When it comes to outstanding cuisine to meet your unique taste, InterContinental Hotel Cleveland offers a variety of choices.

For events ranging from intimate birthday parties, business conferences, and exquisite weddings, the InterContinental catering team works closely with clients to develop the menu, food presentation, and personalized service desired.

Recently host to Indian, Lebanese, and Greek traditional weddings, the catering staff at InterContinental has significant experience with different ethnic cuisine and decor.

Classics, the only AAA Five Diamond restaurant in Ohio, serves traditional French cuisine with a modern twist. Featuring a new lunch menu designed to be served within one hour and a revamped dinner menu offering several new classic dishes, Classics also controls one of the largest and most extensive wine collections in Ohio. For fine food in a more casual setting, the InterContinental Hotel offers the Grill Room at Classics and the North Coast Café. The Grill Room at Classics features a simple, yet sophisticated menu, with traditional American favorites and unique creations. The North Coast Café offers an international buffet and a continental à la carte selection.

GLOBAL INFLUENCES

Reflective of its diverse staff and global influences, a large mosaic of a seventeenth century old-world map greets guests as they enter the hotel lobby.

InterContinental Hotels Group is the world's most global hotel company and the largest by number of rooms. With more than 35,000 hotels and 535,000 guestrooms across nearly 100 countries and territories, the InterContinental Hotels Group understands the value of diversity in the workplace and in the community where it operates.

Blending consistent global standards with the culture of the city, the InterContinental Hotel Cleveland is home to employees from 21 countries versed in 17 languages, including Arabic, French, Romanian, Russian, and Spanish, among others.

INTERCONTINENTAL.
HOTEL
CLEVELAND
9801 Carnegie Avenue Cleveland, OH 44106
216.707.4185 www.cleveland.interconti.com

Olivia C. Brown, CPA
Hotel Manager
The InterContinental Hotel Cleveland

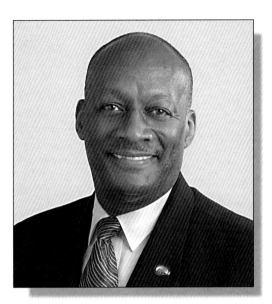

George F. Burress
Lieutenant
Cleveland Clinic Foundation Police Department
The InterContinental Hotel Cleveland

Olivia C. Brown is the hotel manager for the InterContinental Suite Hotel Cleveland and Cleveland Clinic Guesthouse. In this role, Olivia oversees daily operations of the 395-room hotel and Guesthouse and is responsible for hotel profitability, employee development and guest satisfaction.

Prior to her time with the Suite Hotel, Olivia served as executive assistant manager for the Crowne Plaza Royal Palm Miami where she oversaw the daily operations of the 417-room hotel. With 15 years of experience in the hospitality industry, Olivia has held various corporate positions with InterContinental, including managing the audit department for the worldwide hotel group and serving as a general manager trainee at the InterContinental Chicago.

Olivia received a degree in hospitality and tourism administration from the Centennial College of Applied Arts and Technology in Toronto, Ontario. She also completed the managerial accounting/finance program at Toronto's Ryerson Polytechnic University. She is a certified public accountant and an active member of the National Association of Black Accountants.

Born in Jamaica, Olivia was raised in Canada and currently resides in Twinsburg with her husband, Otto, and twins, Sidney and Sebastian.

George F. Burress is a lieutenant with the Cleveland Clinic Foundation Police Department. As lieutenant, George is responsible for ensuring the safety of all guests and staff of the three InterContinental Hotel properties on the Cleveland Clinic Campus. He is in charge of the hotel security team, lead investigator for all hotel incidents, and director of security for more than 600 rooms. As part of the hotel's protective service team, George is responsible for ensuring the safety of VIPs and dignitaries visiting the three InterContinental Hotel properties.

Collectively, George has more than 35 years of law enforcement experience and was temporarily assigned to the Department of Justice Gang Task Force as the only representative from the Cleveland Clinic Foundation Police Department. George has also worked for the Cuyahoga County Sheriff's Department and the East Cleveland Police Department, where he served on the auxiliary unit. A Vietnam War veteran, he has received numerous honors from the police department.

George has an associate degree in law enforcement from Cuyahoga Community College. He is a native of Cleveland and currently resides Euclid. He and his wife, Dorothy, have eight children.

Corporate Spotlight —————————————————

I
INTERCONTINENTAL.
HOTEL
CLEVELAND

Leola Daniels
Catering Coordinator
The InterContinental Hotel Cleveland

Ronnie Eason
Executive Sous Chef
The InterContinental Hotel Cleveland

Leola Daniels is the catering coordinator for the three InterContinental Hotel properties on the Cleveland Clinic Campus. As catering coordinator, Leola plans ten to fifteen events per month, accommodating as many as 500 guests. She oversees all details for these events, managing everything from personnel and budget to food selection.

Prior to joining InterContinental in January of 2005, Leola served as a human resource and financial manager for Sabathani Community Center, a Minneapolis-based center for underprivileged families. She began her career in television production and has produced programs for Discovery, Discovery Kids, The Learning Channel, HGTV, and PBS. Leola has earned numerous honors for her work in this area, including a number of local Emmy Awards and a national Emmy Award for *Newton's Apple*, a children's program on PBS.

Leola earned her associate degree in accounting from St. Paul Technical College, and is currently attending classes at Cleveland State University. A resident of Cleveland Heights, Leola was born in Tokyo, Japan, and has two adult daughters, Nicole Marie and Noelle.

Ronnie Eason is the executive sous chef for the InterContinental Suite Hotel Cleveland where he prepares daily breakfast, lunch and dinner menus for Citrus, the hotel restaurant. Located on the grounds of the Cleveland Clinic Campus, the restaurant specializes in the preparation of comfort food. In addition to his roles at Citrus, Ronnie helps coordinate catering requests and prepares food for special events held on the hotel property. He is also responsible for supervising food preparation, initiating food and supply orders, and training and evaluating the food service staff.

Prior to his time with InterContinental, Ronnie served as sous chef for AVI Food Service, the cafeteria for approximately 800 employees at the Cleveland Clinic. He also served as swing chef at Cleveland's former Omni International Hotel, as head chef at the Aramark cafeteria at Case Western Reserve, and as a line cook at the Cleveland Marriott.

Ronnie attended Central Texas College after retiring from the United States Navy, and received a culinary arts degree from the Pennsylvania Institute of Culinary Arts.

An avid pool player, Ronnie currently resides in Cleveland. He has one daughter, Veronica.

INTERCONTINENTAL.
HOTEL
CLEVELAND

Corporate Spotlight

Sharon Ensley
Front Office Manager
Cleveland Clinic Guesthouse
The InterContinental Hotel Cleveland

Henry D. Sams
Service Center Manager
The InterContinental Hotel Cleveland

Sharon Ensley has served as front office manager for InterContinental's Cleveland Clinic Guesthouse for seven years. In this role, Sharon is responsible for fulfilling guest requests, handling concerns, overseeing front office personnel, and assisting in the development of formal training programs. She also prepares daily reports and logs for the hotel manager and assists all departments in obtaining appropriate information regarding special groups, inventory, and guest information.

She has previously served as a front desk agent for the Cleveland Clinic Guesthouse under the management of Bolton Square Company and as a mortgage lien typist for Cuyahoga County Clerk Gerald E. Fuerst. A devoted employee, Sharon has been recognized as Manager of the Month during her time with InterContinental, and was named Employee of the Month during her time with the Bolton Square's Cleveland Clinic Guesthouse.

Sharon earned her associate degree in paralegal courses and clerical training from the Academy of Court Reporting in Cleveland. She enjoys reading novels by Stephen King and Norma Roberts and spending time with her three children, Alexis, Briana, and Donovan. Sharon resides in Cleveland Heights.

Henry Sams is the service center manager for the InterContinental Hotel Cleveland. His department is responsible for the "One Stop Shop" point of contact to guest satisfaction. The team coordinates with other operating departments throughout the hotel to ensure guest needs are met. This process is done through a computer program call Espresso, which directs the requests to a cell phone by text message. In addition, Henry monitors wake-up and emergency calls, and manages maintenance on more than 690 guestroom phones.

Henry has been with InterContinental Hotel Cleveland for six years, beginning as a front desk agent at the Cleveland Clinic Guesthouse. He later became front desk supervisor and was promoted to front desk manager and assistant front office manager before being named to his current role.

Henry holds a bachelor's degree in nutrition and hospitality management from Alabama A&M University. He resides in Euclid and enjoys spending time with his wife, Aisha, and his four-year-old daughter, Tierra.

INTERCONTINENTAL.
HOTEL
CLEVELAND

Michele Steele-Thompson
Hotel Training Manager
The InterContinental Hotel Cleveland

Trudy Thompson
Front Office Manager
The InterContinental Hotel Cleveland

Michele Steele-Thompson is the hotel training manager for the three properties of InterContinental Hotel Cleveland. Michele started her tenure with InterContinental Hotels Group at the Crowne Plaza Kingston in Jamaica as the training manager and was later promoted to the director of human resources and training.

In her current role, Michele is responsible for conducting training-needs analysis and developing an annual training plan. Michele conducts training for all employees, instructs trainers, and develops and manages training programs for the hotel. She developed the hotel's signature customer service program "Corner Stones of Service" and conducts its leadership development programs.

Michele has worked for some of Jamaica's most reputable organizations, including Runaway Bay Heart Hotel and Training Institute; Mothers Enterprises Ltd, Jamaica's largest local fast-food chain; and the Planning Institute of Jamaica.

Holding a degree in institutional management and catering from the University of Technology Jamaica, Michelle also was awarded a certificate for advanced small quantity food preparation/baking from the George Brown College in Toronto.

A native of Kingston, Jamaica, Michele lives in Oakwood, Ohio, with her children Brittney-Lee and Orlando.

Trudy Thompson is the front office manager for the InterContinental Suite Hotel. In this position, he manages all front office activities including guest relations, agents, doormen, and bellmen. Trudy has worked at the InterContinental Suite Hotel for more than four years, managing his staff to ensure a quality experience for every guest.

Prior to his time with InterContinental, Trudy served as the owner of Jon Brittain Florist, Inc. He has also worked at Acme Spirally Wound Paper Products, Heights Auto/Jim's Towing, Cleveland Catholic Diocese, St. Timothy Church, and the Ohio Bureau of Employment Services.

Trudy attended Ohio University, majoring in management. A native of West Virginia, he resides in Cleveland.

INTERCONTINENTAL.
HOTEL
CLEVELAND

Antoine Torbert
Chief Engineer
The InterContinental Hotel Cleveland

Antoine Torbert is the chief engineer for the InterContinental Hotel Cleveland, where he supervises a staff of 21 employees. In this position, Antoine oversees maintenance for 700 rooms and manages scheduling, payroll, vendor contract negotiations, and equipment on the hotel's three properties. He has 18 years of progressive managerial and technical experience, and is responsible for the hotel's three restaurants, a ballroom, and meeting space operations. He also coordinates functions with the VIP staff at the Cleveland Clinic. Antoine began his career as a groundskeeper and worked his way up the ranks to his current position.

Antoine previously worked at the Radisson Hotel and Conference Center and the Omni International Hotel. He has received certification in interaction management, technical training, field service, refrigerant transition and recovery, heating refrigeration, and building construction.

A member of Calvary Hill Missionary Baptist Church, Antoine serves on the usher board. He is an avid fisherman and a Cleveland Cavaliers fan.

Antoine and his wife, Charlene, live in Cleveland Heights and have one daughter, Jordyn.

Antoinette Wimberly
Assistant Executive Housekeeping Manager
The InterContinental Hotel Cleveland

Antoinette Wimberly is the assistant executive housekeeping manager for the Intercontinental Guesthouse Hotel, supervising a staff of 45 people. Antoinette oversees all room attendants and housekeeping personnel, identifies training needs, and prepares a weekly schedule for her staff.

She is additionally responsible for maintaining a steady flow of communication with the front office and engineering staff, monitoring and ordering inventory, and personally inspecting guest rooms to ensure they meet the highest standards.

Employed with the hotel since 1997, Antoinette has worked her way from room attendant to manager, also serving as an administrative office assistant. She has previously worked as a home care provider in the private sector.

Antoinette enjoys cooking, shopping, and spending time with her 15-year-old son, Carlos. She resides in Cleveland.

National City®

CORPORATE SPOTLIGHT

National City®

Corporate Spotlight

Ervin G. Brabham
Senior Vice President,
Business Information Officer
National City Corporation

Ervin Brabham is the business information officer for the corporate administration portfolio. In this position he is responsible for management of all information systems related activities that support human resources, finance, corporate risk, legal, and information protection.

Ervin has been employed in the financial services industry for 18 years. One of his major accomplishments was contributing to the creation of an electronic standard allowing transfer of property appraisal and title data to the top 20 financial services companies.

Ervin received a bachelor of arts degree from the University of South Carolina. He completed an executive education program at the Duke University's Fuqua School of Business. He is currently enrolled at Case Western University in the executive master of business administration program in Cleveland.

He is native of Columbia, South Carolina. Currently, Ervin, his wife Loretta, and their daughter live in Aurora. Their son Daniel resides in Columbia, South Carolina.

Felicia Plummer Davis
Assistant Vice President,
Human Resources
National City Corporation

Felicia Davis is the program manager for corporate operations and information services and the consumer and commercial loans leadership program at National City. She currently oversees the recruiting, development, and strategic planning for the program. In this role, she also manages the internship and mentoring programs. Prior to managing the Associate program at National City, Felicia was responsible for launching the preferred vendor program in training and development, and was part of the team to lead the design and implementation of a corporate university.

Before joining the financial services industry, Davis was a commodity management buyer for First Energy Corporation. This role also included managing all aspects of the development and implementation of the retail operation for the Cleveland Electric Formula Classic to promote the use of electric vehicles.

A native of the Cleveland area, Davis recently completed the master's degree program for diversity management at Cleveland State University. She is a member of the Society for Human Resource Professionals and the Black Data Processing Association, and she serves on the board of the Legacy Village Lyndhurst Community Fund of the Cleveland Foundation.

National City.

B orn in Cleveland and a product of Cleveland Public Schools, John Hairston III is an assistant vice president with National City Bank. As a cash management officer, he works with small businesses to structure accounts and information services to meet their specific needs.

John has served as a board member for Glenville Development Corporation, and the Academy of Finance. This past year, he was inducted into *Kaleidoscope Magazine*'s Forty under 40 Club, which recognizes 40 African Americans, ages 40 and under, who are making significant contributions in the Greater Cleveland area and within their organizations.

John received a bachelor of science degree from the University of Akron. In 2004, he completed his master of business administration degree from the Weatherhead School of Management at Case Western Reserve University.

John feels his greatest accomplishment is his relationship with his family. He feels blessed to have Allison as his wife of 16 years, and two children, his daughter Taylor (13) and son Mark (7).

John Hairston III
Assistant Vice President,
Cash Management
National City Bank

K enya Bennett Jackson is a project manager with National City Bank (NCB)'s small business credit services division. In this position, she managed the implementation and execution of the small business replacement underwriting system ($1 million project) by coordinating testing, defect resolution, business requirement fulfillment and post-production system stabilization. Previously, Kenya served as the credit analyst manager for small business underwriting, and led a team of 15 associates responsible for underwriting 16,000 commercial loan requests.

Kenya was a 2004 Team Excel Award nominee for Competitive Spirit (NCB's highest honor), 2003 NCB Sales Champion for Indirect Leasing, and a 2003 *Kaleidoscope Magazine* Forty Under 40 Club member.

A native of Louisville, Kentucky, Kenya received a bachelor of science degree in biology and a master of business administration degree from the University of Kentucky. Since making a home in Cleveland, she has served as an OHIO Reads tutor, a United Way loaned executive, and vice chair for the associate board of Recovery Resources. Kenya is also an active participant in NCB's MBA Leadership Program recruitment efforts.

Kenya is married to Shawn Jackson, the Lowe's sales operations manager with GE Consumer & Industrial.

Kenya Bennett Jackson
Vice President & Project Manager
National City Bank

National City® ————————————— Corporate Spotlight

Carolyn Lee
Vice President &
Supplier Diversity Manager
Corporate Strategic Sourcing
National City Corporation

Carolyn Lee is the supplier diversity manager for National City Corporation. She joined National City Bank (Cleveland) in 1981 as a management development trainee and has maintained a wide array of positions. Her efforts include process improvements and infrastructure development; W/MBE recruitment and advocacy; hosting and participation in small business networking and educational forums; and the monitoring and reporting of program achievements. The corporate supplier diversity objective is to create an inclusive organizational culture exemplified by diversity within the procurement practices and vendor pool, which will ultimately promote the economic growth of the local business communities.

Lee is a board member of the Northern Ohio Minority Business Council, a member of the Urban Financial Services Coalition and the Society for Human Resource Management, and most importantly, an active member within Zion Chapel Missionary Baptist Church.

A committed wife, mother, daughter, and granddaughter, and a Cleveland native, Lee resides in the southeastern Cleveland area with her husband, three daughters, mother, and grandmother. She believes that diversity is a pivotal factor in the future performance success of individuals, organizations, and society as a whole.

Buffie Patterson
Assistant Vice President,
Cash Management Operations
National City Bank

Buffie Patterson is assistant vice president and department manager for remittance services, and is responsible for one of National City's largest operating departments. In this position, she manages lockbox and image services, account reconcilement, controlled disbursement, and draft processing for corporate clients.

Buffie has actively served on several nonprofit boards and committees, including the United Way of Central Ohio's Education Vision Council and the Prevention Council of Central Ohio. She currently serves as secretary for the Cleveland Northeast Ohio Chapter of the National Black MBA Association.

Buffie received a bachelor of science degree from The Ohio State University and a master's degree in business administration from Franklin University. Her work experience includes operations management, industrial engineering, corporate training, retail sales, and retail banking. She is also a licensed real estate sales agent in the State of Ohio.

Buffie is a native of Columbus, Ohio, and currently resides in Strongsville.

NationalCity®

Antionette Rollins is a vice president with National City in the small business banking department. In this position, she assists small businesses to manage cash flow, finance growth and acquisition, increase wealth and/or security, reduce operating costs, reduce risk, and manage the personal finances of the owners and employees.

Antionette has received a number of recognitions during her ten years at National City. She was recognized for her top annuity sales in 2001 with a trip to Las Vegas. Her overall sales performance has also been ranked in the top ten percent of the corporation. These performances have earned her recognition as a Sales Champion in 2002 and 2004, sending her to both Florida and Puerto Rico.

In addition to graduating as valedictorian of her high school class, Antionette earned her bachelor of arts degree from Case Western Reserve University. In 1999, she completed the Retail Management Development Program at National City and was promoted to branch manager.

A native of Cleveland, Antionette is the wife of Raymond (Torry) Rollins II and the proud mother of two children, Devon and Dominique.

Antionette J. Rollins
Vice President,
Small Business Banking
National City Bank

Sam Scruggs is senior vice president and field employment manager in the corporate human resources division for National City Bank. In this position, he develops talent acquisition strategies to support both corporate and field based lines of businesses for National City.

A 1976 graduate of John F. Kennedy High School and member of the George E. Mills Gallery of Excellence, Sam left Cleveland to attend the University of Cincinnati to pursue a degree in business. While at UC, he co-founded the Association of Black Business Students and earned a bachelor of business administration degree in marketing and economics. Sam recently returned to Cleveland to join National City after a successful career in marketing, operations, logistics and human resources with several Fortune 500 companies across the U.S.

Most recently, Sam worked for Regions Financial Corporation in Birmingham, Alabama, where he was senior vice president of corporate human resources. While in Birmingham he served on several civic boards. Sam is also a member of Kappa Alpha Psi Fraternity, Inc.

Sam is the husband of Deborah Key Scruggs and the proud father of two sons, Samuel III and Tyler.

Samuel E. Scruggs, Jr.
Senior Vice President,
Field Employment Manager
National City Corporation

National City.

Michael J. Taylor
President
National City
Community Development Corporation

Michael J. Taylor is president of the National City Community Development Corporation (CDC), the first community development corporation founded by a financial services company. The CDC has invested more than $886 million in revitalizing neighborhoods throughout Ohio, Indiana, Illinois, Kentucky, Michigan, Missouri, and Pennsylvania.

Taylor has more than 20 years of banking experience, serving as the CDC's community development specialist and as commercial and community development manager for National City Bank in Southeast Michigan. He expanded the CDC investment and loan portfolio in Illinois and Indiana, and coordinated the corporation's commercial community development lending activities for the Southeast Michigan Region. He directed bank commercial loan activities in the Detroit Empowerment Zone and functioned as product manager for the Initiative Small Business Loan Product. Previously, he served as executive director for the Saginaw Economic Development Corporation in Saginaw, Michigan.

Taylor has a bachelor's degree in business administration and a master's degree in administration from Central Michigan University. He received a 2000 National City Bank of Michigan/Illinois Excel Award, the highest recognition award an employee can receive, for outstanding contributions and service to the community.

Mark J. Williams
Senior Vice President
National City Corporation

Mark Williams is a senior vice president in National City Corporation's wholesale bank, where he leads the wholesale banking decision support group. He is responsible for developing and driving business unit growth strategies and providing sales management infrastructure. Prior to joining National City, Mark held various executive positions at Capital One Financial Corp. (director-operations strategy, U.S. Card Operations); McKinsey and Company (associate principal); and GE Aircraft Engines.

Mark was nominated to *Kaleidoscope*'s Forty Under 40 (Class of 1997). He is an advisory board member for Metaloy, Inc. and is an assistant scoutmaster for Boy Scouts of America.

Mark holds a master of business administration degree from the Harvard Graduate School of Business (Baker Scholar). He also holds a master of science degree in aerospace engineering from the University of Cincinnati and a bachelor of science degree in aerospace engineering from Polytechnic University.

Mark, an avid pilot and scuba diver, resides in Solon, Ohio with his wife Tonie, their son Jordan, and daughter Mikaelle.

Cleveland's

MOST INFLUENTIAL

*"Life has two rules: number one, never quit!
Number two, always remember rule number one."*

DUKE ELLINGTON, 1899-1974
Composer and Band Leader

Rashidah Abdulhaqq
Member, Board of Education
Cleveland Municipal School District

A s a member of the Cleveland Municipal School District's Board of Education, Rashidah Abdulhaqq sees the system continuously improving. As the client information specialist for the Hunger Network of Greater Cleveland, she identifies policies that impact low income families who utilize the hunger centers.

Rashidah assists families and seniors in the city by participating in a variety of volunteer efforts, services, and activities. She serves as a board member of the Girl Scouts of Lake Erie Council and the Greater Cleveland Health Education Service Council, and as an advisor to the Cleveland Communities Organized Against Lead. In April of 2005, she was elected to the steering committee for the Council of Urban Boards of Education of the National School Boards Association.

On May 22, 2005 Rashidah was honored by the Taskforce for Community Mobilization and Peace in the Hood when she received the Al Hajj Malik Shabazz Integrity Award for Education.

She attended Cuyahoga Community College and has completed numerous trainings and in-services.

Born in Arkansas and reared in Cleveland, Rashidah is the mother of grown children, and many have adopted her. Her grandchildren attend Cleveland Schools.

The Honorable
Ronald B. Adrine
Judge
Cleveland Municipal Court

A life-long resident of Greater Cleveland, Judge Ronald Adrine graduated from Fisk University and the Cleveland-Marshall College of Law. After passing the bar in 1973, he entered the private practice of law with his father, the late Russell T. Adrine. He also worked as an assistant Cuyahoga County prosecutor and served as senior staff counsel to the U.S. House of Representatives Select Committee on Assassinations. Then in 1981, he decided to run for a seat on the municipal bench. He won, and has been reelected three times, without opposition, to full six-year terms, the most recent being in November of 1999.

Over the years, Adrine has belonged to more than 50 organizations, served on the boards of more than 30 of those organizations, and held a leadership position on more than 12 of those boards.

Adrine, co-author of "Ohio Domestic Violence Law," has lectured extensively on domestic violence issues here and around the country, as well as in the Virgin Islands and Puerto Rico.

Dr. Daisy Alford-Smith is chief operating officer for the International Commission on Healthcare Professionals, a nonprofit healthcare organization.

Previously, Alford-Smith was the first African-American woman to serve as director of the Cleveland Department of Public Health. She also served as deputy director of the Ohio Department of Human Services, and as director of Case Western Reserve University's Center for Urban and Minority Health.

Alford-Smith's affiliations include The Links, Inc., Alpha Kappa Alpha, Inc., and the Cleveland Council of Black Nurses. She has been recognized by *Crain's Cleveland Business* as one of Northeast Ohio's Leaders of Today, and one of Cleveland's Most Influential Women. She is also one of the founding members of the Cleveland chapter of 100 Black Women.

Alford-Smith earned a bachelor of science degree in nursing from the University at Albany, State University of New York; a master of science degree in technical education from the University of Akron; and a doctorate in urban education from Cleveland State University.

Alford-Smith is married to Kenneth D. Smith, and she is the proud mother of Kym Sellers, Kelli Wilson, and William Alford.

Dr. Daisy Alford-Smith
Chief Operating Officer
International Commission on
Healthcare Professionals

Carolyn W. Allen is an attorney advisor for NASA Glenn Research Center. She came to that position in 2001 after serving as a magistrate for the Cleveland Municipal Court.

Carolyn grew up in the Glenville Community of Cleveland, where she received her diploma from John Hay High School. She graduated from Central State University in Wilberforce, Ohio, and completed her law degree in 1972 at Case Western Reserve University.

Carolyn practiced law in Columbus, Ohio, where she was active in civil rights litigation for minority employment in the Columbus police and fire departments. In 1975, she became the first African-American female executive director of a Legal Aid Society.

Carolyn returned to Cleveland in 1978 and served as an assistant United States attorney. She later became the first African-American safety director for the City of Cleveland. She served in that capacity in the administration of Mayor Michael R. White, who then appointed her to the position of chief city prosecutor.

Carolyn is active in her community in the areas of community development and mental health. She is married to Robert L. Allen, and has two beautiful daughters, Cicely and Tiffany.

Carolyn Watts Allen
Attorney Advisor
NASA Glenn Research Center

Paul W. Allison
Vice President, External Affairs
The Illuminating Company,
a FirstEnergy Company

P aul W. Allison is the vice president of external affairs for the Illuminating Company, a FirstEnergy Company. He is responsible for all external affairs of the company including addressing customer service matters, managing the company's corporate giving program, and working with community organizations. He also manages the company's area managers in conducting governmental relations with local officials in Illuminating Company's service territory.

In his current position, Mr. Allison is a strong supporter of community programs and organizations in the Greater Cleveland area such as Habitat for Humanity, United Way Services, Holiday Lighting, and other community activities. Mr. Allison also serves as the vice president of the Akron City School Board.

A member of Leadership Cleveland's class of 2005, Allison graduated cum laude from John Carroll University with a bachelor's degree in 1975. In 1978, he received his law degree from The Ohio State University School of Law. Before joining FirstEnergy, he was a partner and attorney at law with Buckingham, Doolittle & Burroughs, LLP.

A native of Cleveland, Allison resides in Akron with his wife, Anna, and their two children, Mackenzie and Paul, Jr.

Warren E. Anderson
President & General Manager
The Anderson-Dubose Company

W arren Anderson is the president and general manager of The Anderson-Dubose Company. The Anderson-Dubose Company is a distributor of McDonald's products to over 270 restaurants in northeastern Ohio, western Pennsylvania, and West Virginia. Anderson-Dubose is one of 40 McDonald's distributors in North America. Anderson-Dubose is currently the 17th largest African-American industrial-service company in the United States, and the number one largest African-American company in Ohio.

In 1998, Ernst & Young named Warren a Northeast Ohio Entrepreneur of the Year. He received the NAACP Distinguished Service Award in 1995, and was the African American Businessman of the Year in 1994 by *Kaleidoscope Magazine.*

Warren graduated from the University of Michigan's School of Literature, Science, and Arts. He majored in radio and television production with a bachelor of general science degree in 1974. He then entered the University's School of Communication, and graduated with a master's degree in 1976 in broadcast journalism.

Warren is from Detroit, Michigan. As a child, he spent several years in Nigeria, Tanzania, and Zambia. He has two children, son Khari, and daughter, Alayna.

Cleveland's
MOST INFLUENTIAL

Judge Randolph Baxter is the chief judge of the U.S. Bankruptcy Court for the Northern District of Ohio. Initially appointed to a 14-year term in 1985, Baxter is currently serving a second 14-year term. In 1999, he became one of five charter judges to serve on the Sixth Circuit Court of Appeals' Bankruptcy Appellate Panel.

A native of Columbia, Tennessee, Baxter is a graduate of Tuskegee University and the University of Akron Law School. He was former secretary of the National Conference of Bankruptcy judges. In 1995, Chief Justice William Rehnquist appointed him to a four-year term on the Federal Judicial Center's Bankruptcy Education Advisory Committee.

The author of numerous judicial opinions and articles, Baxter holds memberships in the American, National, and Federal Bar Associations.

A former U.S. Army officer, Baxter was awarded the Bronze Star for Valor, while serving as a tank platoon leader in the Republic of Vietnam with the 11th Armored Calvary Regiment. He later achieved the rank of captain, and commanded a tank company before resigning his commission and returning to civilian life in 1971.

Baxter and his wife, Yvonne, have two sons and two daughters.

**The Honorable
Randolph Baxter**
Chief Judge
U.S. Bankruptcy Court for the
Northern District of Ohio

LySandra Baynard is a senior vice president for MBNA America, a financial services firm headquartered in Wilmington, Delaware. As the personnel director, she manages recruiting and people relations. In addition to her personnel role, she is also the regional site director.

LySandra received her bachelor's degree in human resources from the University of Delaware. She earned her professional certification from the American Association of Affirmative Action and is a member of *Kaleidoscope Magazine*'s 40/40.

LySandra relocated to Cleveland in March of 2004. She lives with her spouse and has three daughters, LyShantia, Kycia, and Vaniesha. She is the proud grandmother of two grandsons.

LySandra Baynard
Senior Vice President
Regional Site Director
MBNA

Teresa M. Beasley
Director of Law
City of Cleveland

Teresa M. Beasley, director of law for the City of Cleveland, leads the litigation, prosecutorial, and transactional work of 81 lawyers in both criminal and civil divisions. She advises Mayor Jane Campbell and Cleveland City Council on critical legal issues facing the city and its citizens.

Before being appointed director, Beasley was chief counsel and chief assistant director of law of real estate and development. She was responsible for leading Cleveland's renaissance through major development projects that involve negotiating, drafting, and reviewing complex real property and development-related contracts.

Prior to joining the city in October of 2002, Beasley was a senior associate of Walter & Haverfield. She began her law career as in-house counsel for The Lincoln Electric Company.

Beasley earned her bachelor's degree from the University of Alabama and her juris doctorate degree from the Cleveland-Marshall College of Law. She has been a speaker at many professional organizations and is active with The Cleveland Foundation. She is a member of the 2004 class of Cleveland Bridge Builders, *Kaleidoscope Magazine*'s Class of 2005 Forty Under 40, and Delta Sigma Theta Sorority, Inc.

Sheryl King Benford
General Counsel
Greater Cleveland Regional
Transit Authority

Since April of 2000, Sheryl King Benford has served as the Greater Cleveland Regional Transit Authority's general counsel and deputy general manager of legal affairs. She supervises a staff of 40 employees who handle litigation, labor issues, workers' compensation, risk management, safety, and the office of equal opportunity. She has more than 25 years of public service in Cleveland-area legal and education circles.

Benford previously worked as the law director for the City of Shaker Heights, assistant law director for the City of Cleveland, in private practice, and as a public school teacher and administrator. An assistant dean at the Cleveland-Marshall College of Law at Cleveland State University, she later taught there and served as president of the Alumni Association board of trustees.

Benford is affiliated with many professional organizations including Delta Sigma Theta Sorority, Inc. She has also held numerous leadership roles with the International Municipal Lawyers Association. She has received the Distinguished Alumna Award from the Cleveland-Marshall Law Alumni Association, among many other awards and distinctions.

The widow of Ronald Benford, Sheryl is the proud mother of daughter, Dory, and son, Kevin.

The Honorable Fletcher D. Berger is currently councilman at large for the City of Bedford Heights, Ohio. He previously served a term as Ward Three councilman and ran for Mayor in 2003. He is also an elected precinct committee executive person in Bedford Heights.

Fletcher retired from Ameritech/SBC after 23 years in management. He is a veteran of the United States Army and served in Vietnam.

Fletcher holds a bachelor of science degree in business administration and accounting from Franklin University.

Fletcher is married to Melva and they have an adult daughter.

**The Honorable
Fletcher D. Berger**
Councilman At Large
City of Bedford Heights

The Honorable Judge Patricia Ann Blackmon sits as a three-term incumbent on the Eighth District Court of Appeals in Cuyahoga County, Ohio. Presently the administrative judge of the court, her term will expire in December of 2005.

Judge Blackmon received her juris doctorate degree from Cleveland Marshall College of Law at Cleveland State University. She served as a chief prosecutor for the City of Cleveland and was the city's first night prosecutor. Blackmon also served as an assistant director of the Victims/Witness Program and as a professor at Dyke College.

Blackmon's honors include induction into the Ohio Women's Hall of Fame, and she received the 1996 Alumna of the Year Award from Cleveland-Marshall College of Law. Further, she and Judge Sara J. Harper were the first African-American women elected to the Court of Appeals for the State of Ohio, Eighth Judicial District.

Judge Blackmon is a member of Olivet Institutional Baptist Church, Delta Sigma Theta Sorority, Inc., and Black Women's PAC. She is a trustee on the board of Lake Erie College and a commissioner on the Ohio Supreme Court's Client Security Fund.

**The Honorable
Patricia Ann Blackmon**
Judge
Eighth District Court of Appeals

Alexandria Johnson Boone
President & CEO
GAP Communications Group

Alexandria Johnson Boone has served as president and CEO of GAP Communications Group since its inception in May of 1994. GAP Communications is a full-service public relations, advertising, marketing, fundraising, and special events firm based in Cleveland. Under her leadership, GAP has gained local, regional, and national recognition for its quality public relations, publicity and marketing services, and its creative communications programs.

Ms. Boone, a Cleveland native, is a proud graduate of Cleveland Public Schools. She holds a master's degree from the Weatherhead School of Management at Case Western Reserve University, a certificate from the Amos Tuck School of Business at Dartmouth College, and she was a 1997 National Fellow in the Boston University School of Public Health's Join Together Program. She was also a member of Leadership Cleveland in 1987-1988.

Prior to founding GAP Communications Group, Ms. Boone served as a senior vice president at a Cleveland public relations firm and as a public information officer for the federal government for five years.

Throughout her career, Ms. Boone has received several awards for her business and professional achievements, and has been recognized for numerous communications industry accomplishments.

The Honorable Patricia J. Britt
Councilmember
City of Cleveland

Patricia J. Britt was born and raised in Cleveland's Ward 6, which she has represented on Cleveland City Council since 1995. Councilwoman Britt works hard to establish and maintain partnerships between industry, education, banking, and health care in an effort to make the community a clean, beautiful, and safe place for people to live, work, and raise their families.

During her tenure, Ward 6 has seen a new housing development, which Councilwoman Britt has worked to match with economic development opportunities. Britt believes that economic development opportunities are vital in revitalizing the ward and allowing residents to become self-sufficient.

She has focused much of her time and energy on bringing two major county projects to Ward 6 that will create up to 400 jobs, $50 million in development, and the possibility of several new ancillary businesses on Quincy Avenue.

Councilwoman Britt is currently a member of the National Black Caucus of Local Elected Officials, and a member of St. Adalbert Catholic Church. In addition, she is on the faculty at Case Western Reserve University's Mandel School of Applied Social Sciences.

As chief operating officer for the City of Cleveland, Darnell Brown oversees the departments of public service, public utilities, parks, recreation and properties, and port control. He works to ensure that the highest quality of basic city service is delivered to Cleveland residents.

This 29-year veteran began his career with the City of Cleveland Division of Water Pollution Control. As commissioner, he later administered and controlled a division of more than 160 employees with a $24 million budget. Additionally, during the first 11 months of the Campbell administration, Brown served as acting director of the Department of Public Utilities, which has a budget of $423 million and 1,700 employees.

Brown is a mayoral appointee for the Cleveland Foodbank, the Northeast Ohio Regional Sewer District, and the Doan Brook Watershed Partnership, where he served as board president for the last three years. He also serves as board president for the Cuyahoga County Board of Mental Retardation and Developmental Disabilities.

Brown attended Ohio University in Athens, Ohio. He is married to Terri Hamilton-Brown, president of University Circle Inc., and they have two children, Danielle and Kenneth.

Darnell Brown
Chief Operating Officer
City of Cleveland

Harvey L. Brown has been a resident of Bedford Heights for 30 years, and actively serves as the Ward 2 councilman in the city. Currently, Harvey serves as the chairperson for the council cable and infrastructure and capital improvement committees.

A graduate of Jackson State University in Jackson, Mississippi, Harvey retired from the Cleveland Public School System, where he worked for 32 years as an art teacher. For 30 years he served as the chairman of the department of fine arts at Central Intermediate School.

Harvey is a devoted member of the Bedford Heights Democratic Club, Lions Club, American Federation of Teachers, the Cleveland Teachers Union, and the Affinity Baptist Church Morning Praise Voices.

Harvey is the recipient of several awards and honors including the Central Intermediate School Teacher of the Year (1973, 1978, 1984, 1996, 2002); M.A. Hanna Teacher of the Year (1993-1994); and Cleveland CAVS Teacher of the Month (March 1996).

Harvey is married to Delores Wright Brown, is the father of Marcie Knuckles and Stefanie Brown, father-in-law to Kevin Knuckles, and grandfather to Kevin Jr. and Malia Knuckles.

Harvey L. Brown
Ward 2 Councilman
City of Bedford Heights

Terri Hamilton Brown
President
University Circle Incorporated

Terri Hamilton Brown is president of University Circle Incorporated (UCI). The first African American and first female to lead the organization, Brown has been dedicated to promoting cooperative efforts in shaping a better Cleveland. Since joining UCI, she has worked to expand outreach efforts to communities both near and far, including surrounding African American and Italian neighborhoods, Westside communities, and cities outside of the region.

Previously, Brown was executive director of Cuyahoga Metropolitan Housing Authority (CMHA) for four years. Prior to CMHA, she served eight years with the City of Cleveland, Department of Community Development, where she became its director and also established the Housing Construction Office.

Brown is a distinguished product of the Cleveland community and holds a bachelor's degree in economics from the University of Chicago and a master's degree in city planning from Massachusetts Institute of Technology.

She serves on the boards of The Cleveland Foundation, Greater Cleveland Partnership, ShoreBank Cleveland, and Neighborhood Progress Incorporated.

Brown is married to Darnell Brown, chief operating officer for the City of Cleveland.

Terry Butler
District Vice President of Access
and College Pathway Programs
Cuyahoga Community College

Terry Butler is the vice president of Access and College Pathway Programs at Cuyahoga Community College, and serves as the interim president of Cuyahoga Community College's Metropolitan Campus.

In his positions, Butler provides executive level vision, academic leadership, and direction to the college. Planning, direction, management, and evaluation of instructional, student development, and support service programs are among his responsibilities.

As interim president of the Metropolitan Campus, Butler is also responsible for the productivity and performance of the faculty, administrators, and staff of that campus as well as the budget and resource development supporting their existing and planned programs.

As vice president of Access and College Pathway Programs for the college district-wide, he is responsible for strategic planning, tactical implementation and supervision of the Bridges/PASS (Partnership for Achieving Student Success) Program. He is likewise responsible for the Educational Opportunity Programs (EOP), Youth Technology Academy (YTA), and local operations of the Science Engineering and Mathematics and Aerospace Academy (SEMAA).

Butler holds a bachelor of science degree from Kent State University and a master's degree in education administration from Cleveland State University.

B arbara Byrd-Bennett is an experienced teacher, supervisor, manager, administrator, and researcher of urban education. She is widely regarded as one of the nation's top urban educators.

Byrd-Bennett grew up in Harlem, attending public school. She graduated high school at age 16 and received a bachelor of arts degree in English from Long Island University at 19. She holds a master of arts degree from New York University and a master of science degree from Pace University. Additionally, she was a Penn fellow at Teachers College of Columbia University during her doctoral studies.

In New York City, Byrd-Bennett taught at the elementary and high school levels, served as a school principal and district administrator, held two urban superintendencies, and held two adjunct professorships. She came to Cleveland in November of 1998, chosen by Mayor Michael R. White to be the district's first CEO.

Byrd-Bennett is a daughter, a wife, a mother, and a proud grandmother of twin boys. Someone who has an insatiable appetite for all types of music—especially jazz, she is a gardener, a painter, and a lifelong reader.

Barbara Byrd-Bennett
Chief Executive Officer
Cleveland Municipal School District

R enee Cash is president of Ray's Sausage Company, Inc., which was established by her father, Raymond Cash, Sr. Ray's Sausage Company is family-owned and now operates under the second and third generation of the family. Ray's manufactures fresh pork and beef sausage, souse meat, headcheese, beef souse, Italian turkey and beef links, and pork and beef links. Ray's strives to provide the best products for their customers. Their motto is, "Shop where it pays and bring home the Ray's."

Renee is a member of the Kentucky State Alumni Association, Eta Phi Beta Sorority, Inc., the National Register of Who's Who, the National Association for Female Executives, the National Rifle Association, and St. Timothy Baptist Church.

In 1968, Renee received a bachelor of science degree from Kentucky State University and in 1969, she received a degree in corrective therapy. She was formerly a health and physical education teacher in the Cleveland Public School system.

Renee's hobbies are bowling, golf, and fishing. She also enjoys listening to music and traveling.

A native Clevelander, Renee is the proud mother of two daughters, Leslie Renee and Lisa Rae'.

Renee Cash
President
Ray's Sausage Co., Inc.

**The Honorable
Roosevelt Coats**
Councilmember
City of Cleveland

C leveland City Councilman Roosevelt Coats champions race relations and is an advocate for low-income persons, the elderly, and the homeless. Representing Ward 10, Coats has worked to secure funding for neighborhood recreation services and retail rehabilitation; has sponsored legislation to assist victims of ethnic intimidation; and supports funding for meals programs and improved housing.

His commitment to these issues was formed when he was a teenager in Alabama during the civil rights movements. Councilman Coats participated in the famous Selma to Montgomery March, and was in Birmingham during the height of the violence.

Councilman Coats is on the board of directors of the National League of Cities, and is past president of the National Black Caucus of Local Elected Officials.

A graduate of the Leadership Cleveland Class of 1991, Coats earned an associate degree from Dyke College and served in the United States Air Force. Coats serves as a steward of Lee Memorial A.M.E. Church where he has been a member for more than 20 years.

Tillie Taylor Colter
Alpha Omega Chapter President
Alpha Kappa Alpha Sorority, Inc.

T illie Taylor Colter is the president of the Alpha Omega chapter of Alpha Kappa Alpha Sorority, Inc. Alpha Omega is the oldest graduate chapter of Alpha Kappa Alpha. In her position as president, Tillie leads 435 active members and 40 committees. Along with chapter operations, she oversees the Alpha Omega Foundation, which specifically deals with educational programs for community outreach.

Former chair of the Collinwood High School music department, Colter is a 2001 Hall of Fame inductee for the Gradsnet Foundation of Cleveland. The Ohio Music Education Association honored her in 1994 for 25 years of service as an outstanding educator; in 1988, she served as the director of the Greater Cleveland Pan-Hellenic Choir.

In addition, Tillie has served on the community boards of The Cleveland Opera, The Cleveland Rock and Roll Hall of Fame, and The Cleveland Orchestra. She holds both her bachelor's and master's degrees in music education from the University of Arkansas-Pine Bluff, and Cleveland State University.

A native of Big Spring, Texas, Tillie is married to Reverend Dempsey D. Colter. She has two daughters, Tillie Lynnette and Nina Raquel, and three grandchildren, Brittney, Randy, and Amber.

After vigorously campaigning on a platform of economic development and family issues, Kevin Conwell was elected to represent Ward 9 on Cleveland City Council in November of 2001.

For the past six years, Kevin was operations manager for the Fathers and Families Together Program of the Center for Families and Children. As operations manager, he coordinated the delivery of parenting classes and job placement services to fathers in locations throughout the city of Cleveland.

Kevin graduated from Glenville High School. In 1986, he earned a bachelor's degree from Kent State University.

Kevin has received numerous accolades from his community including the 2001 National Father of the Year Award from the National Fatherhood Initiative and numerous accolades for helping homeless people and people with disabilities.

Kevin has shared 16 years of marriage with his wife Yvonne Spauling-Conwell. They have a son, Kevin, Jr., and two daughters, Krystle and Krystina.

**The Honorable
Kevin Conwell**
Councilman, Ward 9
Cleveland City Council

Fred M. Crosby has been the chairman of the Crosby Furniture Company for the past 11 years. Before that, he was the president of the company for approximately 30 years. Crosby Furniture Company handles retail sales and serves as a finance company.

Fred's board affiliations include chairmanships of Intercity Bank, the Ohio Council of Retail Merchants, and First National Bank. He is the vice-chairman of Forest City Hospital and the NAACP, and the treasurer for the Urban League. A trustee of the Cleveland Growth Association Chamber of Commerce and the American Automobile Association, he is also a founding partner of COSE (Council of Smaller Enterprises).

Fred has served many commissions, including his appointment by Governor Rhodes to the Task Force on Small Business; an appointment by Governor Celeste to the Ohio Boxing Commission; and his appointment by Governor Gilligan to the Workers' Compensation Board. Mayor Voinovich appointed him to the Cleveland Port Authority. Later, as governor, Voinovich appointed him to Ohio's Small Business Development Corporation.

A native of Cleveland, Fred and his wife, Phendalyne, have three adult children, Fred, James, and Llionicia.

Fred M. Crosby
Chairman
Crosby Furniture Company, Inc.

Barbara J. Danforth, Esq.
Executive Director
YWCA of Greater Cleveland

As executive director of the YWCA of Greater Cleveland, Barbara J. Danforth draws upon her educational and professional experience to implement the YWCA's mission of empowering women and eliminating racism. Under her leadership, the YWCA has completed a major renovation project at the North Central YWCA, and has unveiled a new membership model that helps professional women succeed in the workplace.

Prior to joining the YWCA in 1996, Danforth worked for the Cuyahoga County department of children and family services as legal administrator. Additionally, she worked for Mayor Michael White, and the law firm Sindell, Sindell and Rubenstein.

Selected as a *Crain's Cleveland Business* Woman of Note in 2001, Danforth was the featured guest speaker for the Smart Business Network's 2004 Women in Business conference.

Danforth has a bachelor's degree in sociology from Eastern Michigan University, and a juris doctorate from the University of Pittsburgh.

An active member of New Freedom Ministries, she is the current president of the United Way's Council of Agency Executives. She is past president of the board of directors of Youth Visions, and has been a trustee to the Harambee Services to Families.

Bob Dean
Diversity Manager
Cleveland-Cuyahoga County
Port Authority

Bob Dean personifies continual motion with measurable results. Whether he is performing his full-time duties as the Cleveland-Cuyahoga County Port Authority diversity manager, serving as a councilman-at-large in the City of Warren, or personally procuring 700 winter coats for inner city kids, Bob is everywhere.

Bob's past and current achievements include the President's Volunteer Action Award, the Institute for Public Service Jefferson Award, and the Greater Cleveland YMCA Volunteer of the Year "Best of the Best" Award. He has also been inducted into both the Trumbull County Afro-American Hall of Fame and Warren High School's Distinguished Alumni Hall of Fame.

Bob's professional endeavors reflect a long list of "firsts." These include the first full-time equal opportunity specialist in Air Force history, the first diversity manager at the Cleveland Port Authority, and the first African-American director in the Mayor's Citizens' Assistance Office in Houston, Texas.

Bob distinguished himself during a 20-year career in the U.S. Air Force, retiring as the most decorated senior master sergeant in his field.

Bob is married to Nedra Dean and has three children, Brian, Ayanna, and Taigi.

Michael DeBose was appointed to the Ohio House of Representatives on February 13, 2002. He is currently serving his first elected term as the representative for the 12th House District.

DeBose worked as a planning manager for the Cuyahoga Metropolitan Housing Authority from 1992 to 2000, and as a building and grounds superintendent for Cuyahoga Development and Sanitary Engineering from June of 2000 to February of 2002.

A lifelong Cleveland resident, DeBose has been very active in his community. He is the founder and former president of the Cleveland School of the Arts' PTA and is a regular volunteer for the Cleveland Municipal School District. He has also served as a member of the Cleveland School Board and is a member of the Lee Harvard Community Association, the NAACP, and the Ohio Legislative Black Caucus.

DeBose attended Cleveland State University where he earned a bachelor of arts degree in mass media communication. He has also received a certificate in public administration from David N. Myers College, a Bible certificate from Moody Bible Institute, and he is a licensed and ordained minister at Zion Chapel Baptist Church in Cleveland.

Michael has been married to Cheryl for 24 years and is a loving and proud parent of three children.

**The Honorable
Michael DeBose**
**State Representative
Ohio House of Representatives**

George F. Dixon, III is the first African-American male to serve as president of the American Public Transportation Association (APTA). As the leading industry group in North America, APTA serves more than 90 percent of passengers using transit in the U.S. and Canada.

Dixon has been active with APTA for many years on their governing boards and executive committees, and has been a presenter at many national conferences. He chairs a policy committee for the Transportation Research Board, and is active in the Conference of Minority Transportation Officials. In addition, Dixon has served on the GCRTA board of trustees since 1992, and has been its president since 1994. He also serves on the board of the Northeastern Ohio Areawide Coordinating Agency, a five-county transportation planning organization.

President Clinton appointed Dixon to represent public transportation interests on the Federal Advisory Committee to reduce greenhouse gases. In 2001, Ohio Governor Bob Taft appointed him to an eight-year term on the Ohio Turnpike Commission.

Dixon served on the Board of Education of the Cleveland Municipal Schools from 1998 to 2003. He owns Cleveland's popular Lancer's Steakhouse, and is active in many community groups.

George F. Dixon, III
**President, Board of Trustees
Greater Cleveland
Regional Transit Authority**

Ed E. Duncan
Partner
Tucker Ellis & West LLP

Ed Duncan is a partner in the Cleveland office of the law firm of Tucker Ellis & West LLP, and is in his 30th year of practice, primarily in the area of insurance litigation.

Ed has written numerous coverage opinions, has appeared in trial and appellate courts throughout Ohio, and has successfully argued two cases in the Ohio Supreme Court. He has lectured on insurance coverage issues and has authored several publications, including the chapter on insurance coverage for contractors in *Ohio Public Contract Law: Second Edition.*

Ed received his undergraduate degree, with honors, from Oberlin College, and was awarded his law degree from Northwestern University Law School.

Ed is very active in the Cleveland community. He is a past board member of the Glenville YMCA and the Ohio Board of Building Standards, and he is a regular volunteer at St. Martin de Porres School.

The Honorable
Alison L. Floyd
Judge
Cuyahoga County
Court of Common Pleas

The Honorable Alison Lisa Floyd, judge in the Cuyahoga County Court of Common Pleas juvenile division, began her first six-year term as judge on January 2, 2001. Previously, she was a judicial magistrate in the court's domestic relations division. She has also served as a judicial law clerk with the court judges Stephanie Tubbs Jones, Carl J. Character, and Daniel Gaul.

Floyd is the past president of the Norman S. Minor Bar Association, and a life member of the Eighth District Judicial Conference. She served as a judicial panelist for the Ohio Center of Law-Related Education, a statewide mock trial competition for Ohio high school students. Floyd serves on the board of trustees for the Phillis Wheatley Association and Emeritus House, Inc. In 1995, she was the recipient of the Phillis Wheatley Association's board of trustees, Jane Edna Hunter Award.

Recently, Floyd completed the leadership-training curriculum provided by The Cleveland Growth Association as part of the Leadership Cleveland class of 2003.

Judge Floyd and her husband, attorney Lawrence R. Floyd, reside in Solon, Ohio with her stepchildren. They attend Mt. Sinai Baptist Church in Cleveland, Ohio.

Cleveland's
MOST INFLUENTIAL

Mark S. Floyd is a partner in Thompson Hine's labor and employment practice group. He has a focus on employment litigation, principally in defense of management in alleged discrimination, wrongful discharge, covenant not to compete, and trade secret litigation.

Mark also has extensive experience in traditional management labor representation, including contract negotiations and matters involving grievance, arbitration, and administrative hearings on behalf of both private and public sector clients. He has represented clients in matters before the Occupational Safety and Health Administration (OSHA).

Prior to joining Thompson Hine, Mark was a partner for seven years at a Cleveland-based law firm. He brings more than two decades of experience with him to Thompson Hine, with an extensive background in the areas of labor, employment, employment litigation, OSHA, and immigration law.

Mark received a juris doctorate degree in 1983 from Columbia Law School, where he served as the articles editor for the Columbia Journal of Art and The Law. In 1980, he graduated from Stanford University with an artium baccalaureus (bachelor of arts) degree in music (with honors) and political science.

Mark S. Floyd
Partner & Vice Chair,
Labor & Employment Practice Group
Thompson Hine LLP

In November of 2003, Karen L. Gilliam was elected to council, Ward 4 in the city of Bedford Heights, Ohio. She currently chairs the legislative/education committee and is a member of the community life, cable television, and economic development committees. Karen is director of employee relations and development for Kent State University in Kent, Ohio. In this position, she leads a team responsible for providing personal and professional growth opportunities, performance management, policy and procedure interpretation, and informal mediation services for the university community.

Karen is a member of Homeowners of Metro Estates (HOME) and Organization Development (OD) Connection. Likewise, she is a lifetime member of the National Black MBA Association, a trustee board member of Sunny Acres Foundation, and a volunteer facilitator for Voices & Choices.

She has a bachelor's degree in business from Notre Dame College, a master's degree in business from Baldwin-Wallace, and she is a doctoral candidate in Antioch University's doctor of philosophy in leadership and change program.

A native Clevelander, Karen is the wife of John Gilliam, a mother of four, John, Carlo, Bianca, and Danielle, and grandmother of eight.

The Honorable
Karen L. Gilliam
Councilwoman
City of Bedford Heights

Louise J. Gissendaner
Senior Vice President,
Director of Community Development
Fifth Third Bank

L ouise J. Gissendaner is a senior vice president and director of community development for the Fifth Third Bank (Northeastern Ohio). Gissendaner's primary responsibility is working with housing, economic, and community development organizations to assist with the development of affordable housing, community revitalization, and programs that assist minority business enterprises. She joined Fifth Third Bank in October of 1995 with more than 24 years of experience in banking.

Currently, Gissendaner serves as the board chair for the Akron Urban League and is the founder and president of Sankofa Fine Art Plus. Some of Gissendaner's other board commitments include Blossom Board of Overseers, Marcus Garvey Academy, and the Urquhart Memorial Foundation. In addition, she serves on the five-member city of Akron Planning Commission and is a member of the city of Cleveland's Bureau of Cultural Arts advisory board and the East Cleveland Mayor's advisory committee.

Gissendaner is currently a member of the Black Professional Association, the Urban Financial Services Coalition, and Delta Sigma Theta Sorority, Inc. She received her undergraduate degree in communications from Kent State University and resides in Akron, Ohio.

Donald Graham
Executive Vice President,
Consumer Lending Division
Fifth Third Bank

D onald Graham is the executive vice president of Fifth Third Bank's consumer lending division for Northeastern Ohio, Western Pennsylvania, and Western New York. He also is the market president for the Akron region. In addition, he directs the community development line of business for the Northeastern Ohio market.

Prior to his career with Fifth Third, Graham was a zone manager with Ford Motor Company. He is also a veteran of the U.S. Army, having served a tour of duty in Vietnam, where he was awarded the Army Commendation Medal for meritorious service.

Graham earned a bachelor's degree in business administration from Youngstown State University, where he was a member of the varsity basketball team. He then went on to earn a master of business administration degree from Xavier University in Cincinnati, and a certification in accounting from the College of Mt. Saint Joseph.

A life member of Omega Psi Phi Fraternity, Inc., Graham is also a member of Faith Fellowship Church.

Active in the community, Graham serves on numerous nonprofit and civic boards. Also, he serves on the Fifth Third Bank Northeast Ohio board of directors.

The Honorable Wendolyn Grant is currently council at large for the City of Bedford Heights. As a councilmember, she has served on all standing committees as a member or chair. She is presently the chair of the safety and economic development committee, and she serves on the public works, finance, and planning commission. Wendolyn is also the SBC associate director of marketing.

An executive committee member of the Democratic Party since 1998, Wendolyn has been appointed by Ohio Governor Bob Taft to the State Fire Commission and by the county commissioners to the Cuyahoga County Housing Consortium. She is a current trustee for the Bedford City Schools Foundation and UHHS Bedford Medical.

Because of her community involvement at a professional and social level, she was selected to the Women of Professional Excellence by the YWCA/CAVS Organization and was featured in *Kaleidoscope Magazine*, both in 1999.

Wendolyn resides in Bedford Heights with her husband of 35 years, Larry Grant. She takes pride in her son Allen Grant, his wife Angel, and their precious son Alec.

**The Honorable
Wendolyn J. Grant**
Councilmember at Large
City of Bedford Heights

The Honorable Emanuella Groves was elected to the Cleveland Municipal Court on November 6, 2001, and with no opposition, she was reelected to a six-year term in 2003.

Groves grew up in a family of eight children and graduated from Canton McKinley High School in 1975. An honors student, she obtained a bachelor's degree in business management from Kent State University in just three years time. While attending law school at Case Western Reserve University, she met attorney Greg Groves and the two married in 1981.

Groves started her legal career balancing the rights of victims and defendants as an assistant Cleveland police prosecutor. In 1983, she became the first black attorney hired at the Cuyahoga Metropolitan Housing Authority and negotiated the first tenant management contract in the State of Ohio.

In addition to raising two children, Angela and Greg, Groves finds time to volunteer in the community as well as her church, Liberty Hill Baptist, where her husband serves as a deacon.

**The Honorable
Emanuella Groves**
Judge
Cleveland Municipal Court

**The Honorable
Deborah A. Hill**
Councilmember, Ward Two
City of Warrensville Heights

The Honorable Deborah Hill proudly serves the constituents of Ward Two in Warrensville Heights. Striving to empower residents to participate in government on the local and national levels, Hill is a member of the Tri-City Democratic Club, former chairperson of the public safety committee, and chairperson of the tax review committee. She is currently serving a four-year term as a Cuyahoga County Executive Board member of the Democratic Party, and is a member of the Northeast Ohio City Council Association.

Hill is a charter member of the Greater Cleveland chapter of the Coalition of 100 Black Women, and a member of the National Black Caucus of Elected Officials, the National League of Cities (Leadership Training Council), and Alpha Kappa Alpha Sorority, Inc. She is also an active member of the Southeast Seventh Day Adventist Church and serves on the Allegheny West Conference Executive Board of Seventh Day Adventist.

Hill earned her bachelor of arts degree in sociology from Knoxville College and her master's degree in social science administration from Case Western Reserve University. She is also a licensed independent social worker by the State of Ohio.

Dr. Bessie House
President & Chief Executive Officer
B. House Communications, Inc.

Dr. Bessie House is an award-winning author and poet, public speaker, professor, and administrator at Kent State University, and an entrepreneur. She is also an expert on entrepreneurship and economic development in the United States. She is the executive director and founder of the Center for the Study and Development of Minority Businesses at Kent State University, and the director of the Entrepreneurial Academy in the Cleveland Empowerment Zone.

Dr. House is also the president and chief executive officer of B. House Communications, Inc., through which she provides educational training on economic development issues through workshops, keynote speeches, and other consulting activities. She serves on the board of directors of Health Legacy of Cleveland, and the Northeast Ohio chapter of the National Black MBA Association.

Dr. House has published three books and numerous scholarly articles, including the critically acclaimed, "Confronting the Odds: African American Entrepreneurship in Cleveland, Ohio." She has received numerous honors and awards, including the Henry Howe Book Award and the 2004 Phenomenal Woman of the Year Award.

She is married to Dr. Maurice A.E. Soremekun, and they have three children, Yomi, Jadesola, and Adrianna.

Michael A. House is president and chief operating officer of the *Call & Post* Newspapers, a King Media Corporation in Cleveland, Ohio. He oversees operations of the company's weekly editions in Cleveland, Columbus, Cincinnati, and the state.

Michael is president of the Call & Post Foundation, which annually hosts the W.O. Walker Salute to Community Excellence Awards. Prior to joining King Media, Michael served as president of Amalgamated Publishers, Inc.

The National Newspaper Association named Michael Publisher of The Year for 2003-2004 for establishing the *Call & Post* as one of the top black newspapers in America. Additionally, he is a member emeritus of the Cleveland Chapter of the National Alliance of Market Developers (NAMD). Michael is past national president of NAMD and a current a board member. He also sits on the boards of The Urban League, The Hunger Network, and MOTTEP.

Michael received his bachelor of arts degree from Howard University, and earned his master of business administration degree from Baruch College, City University of New York.

A native of Louisville, Kentucky, he is married to Doris House, and is the proud father of Robert, Margoit, William, and Crystal.

Michael A. House
President & Chief Operating Officer
Call & Post Newspapers

Dr. Edgar B. Jackson, Jr. is a practicing physician, special advisor to the president of University Hospitals of Cleveland, and a man who has dedicated his career to encouraging minority students to pursue medical careers.

Raised in Rison, Arkansas and Cleveland, Jackson graduated from Case Western Reserve University (CWRU) with a bachelor's degree, and later with a medical doctorate. He later became the first African-American professor of clinical medicine at CWRU.

Jackson became University Hospitals chief of staff and senior vice president of clinical affairs. He created the Douglas-Satcher Clerkship for minorities, and helped found the Otis Moss, Jr.-University Hospitals Medical Center.

Currently the health director for Shaker Heights, Jackson serves on numerous civic boards and is a deacon at Olivet Institutional Baptist Church. One of only 500 physicians in the National Academy of Sciences, he is the second African American elected to the American Board of Internal Medicine board of governors.

In Jackson's honor, University Hospitals of Cleveland created the first endowed chair for an African-American physician in Cleveland.

Jackson and his wife of 47 years, Thelma, are parents to three children and have five grandchildren.

Edgar B. Jackson, Jr., M.D.
Health Director
City of Shaker Heights

**The Honorable
Frank G. Jackson**
President
Cleveland City Council

Born and raised in the neighborhoods of Kinsman and Central, the Honorable Frank Jackson served his country in the Army in Vietnam. Upon returning home, Jackson worked minimum wage jobs, and at the age of 27, he used his G.I. Bill to take courses at Cuyahoga Community College. He continued his education at Cleveland State University, where he earned a bachelor's degree in urban studies and history and a master's degree in urban affairs.

After completing his master's degree, Jackson was a night clerk for the Cleveland Municipal Clerk of Court's Office while putting himself through law school at the Cleveland-Marshall College of Law. With the support of his wife, Edwina, Jackson became an attorney and started his legal career as an assistant city prosecutor.

In 1989, Jackson ran for and won a seat on Cleveland City Council, representing Ward Five. Since becoming a councilman, he has delivered approximately $500,000,000 of economic and community investment to Ward Five. In 2001, he was elected president of the council. As president, Jackson has focused on reinvigorating Cleveland and cultivating the belief that Cleveland can thrive. He was a mayoral candidate in the 2005 election.

Leonard B. Jackson
Commissioner of Athletics
Cleveland Municipal School District

Leonard B. Jackson is the commissioner of athletics for the Cleveland Municipal School District and a 12-year member of the Ohio High School Athletic Association (OHSAA) district athletic board. Former Northeast Ohio Athletic Administrator of the Year, Jackson received the Ohio Interscholastic Athletics Administrator Association's Sportsmanship, Ethics, and Integrity Award in 1996. In 2001-2002, he was elected as OHSAA's first African-American board of control president.

In 2003, the Cleveland Board of Education honored Jackson for his outstanding commitment to Cleveland's children when the state-of-the-art East High School gymnasium was dedicated and named the Leonard B. Jackson Gymnasium.

Jackson has served in numerous organizations that include the Council for Economic Opportunities in Greater Cleveland, the Cleveland Sports Commission, the Governor's Commission on Ohioan Outdoors, and Olivet Institutional Baptist Church.

Jackson graduated from New Stanton High School in Jacksonville, Florida. He holds a bachelor's degree in health and physical education from Central State University, and a master's degree in school administration from Cleveland State University.

Jackson and his wife, Micheline, have two daughters, Lynnette Michelle and Cheryl Yvette. In 1987, Jackson was awarded the Father of the Year Leadership Award.

Stanley Jackson, Jr. is an attorney and international sports agent. In this position, he practices in a variety of areas such as sports, entertainment, real estate, and intellectual property. Stanley is a NFL, NBA, and MLB sports agent, representing numerous athletes internationally. He has functioned as legal advisor to Don King Productions, and is likewise the advisor and legal counsel to Monarch and Xcel Sports Management, companies of boxing promoter and manager Carl King. In addition, he is advisor and legal counsel to William D. Hall of Holly Development.

Stanley earned his juris doctor degree from the University of Dayton School of Law. He earned a bachelor of arts degree and a master's degree in public administration and international affairs from Bowling Green State University, where he also received a private pilot's license.

Stanley is a young, aggressively innovative attorney. He is an executive board member of the Norman S. Minor Bar Association and a member of Alpha Phi Alpha Fraternity, Inc.

A native of Cleveland, Ohio, Stanley is a proud alumnus of St. Ignatius High School. He is a member of the Airplane Owners and Pilots Association.

Stanley Jackson, Jr.
Attorney & International Sports Agent
The Law Office of Stanley Jackson, Jr.

An Alabama native, the Honorable Mabel Jasper grew up on Cleveland's east side and graduated from Glenville High School at the age of 16. Then it was on to Kent State University, where in just three years time she earned a bachelor's degree with a teaching certificate.

After teaching for 20 years, Jasper enrolled in the Cleveland-Marshall College of Law, and after passing the bar, she worked in private practice serving as general counsel for a local savings and loan association. From there, Jasper became an assistant attorney general and trial attorney for the Bureau of Workers' Compensation. Then it was on to Cuyahoga County Domestic Relations Court, where she served as a magistrate. After four years in that role, Jasper decided it was time to run for office, and in 1987, she was elected to serve on the Cleveland Municipal Court. She was reelected in 1993 and 1999.

Jasper is a member of many civic and professional organizations. She is an active member of the Delta Sigma Theta Sorority, Inc., a past president at Rotary East, and she has served as a deacon at Mt. Zion Congregational Church.

The Honorable
Mabel M. Jasper
Judge
Cleveland Municipal Court

Gary Johnson, Sr.
President
Amalgamated Transit Union-Local 268

Gary Johnson, Sr. has been the president and business agent of the Amalgamated Transit Union-Local 268 for two years. The branch has 2,000 active union members and 500 retirees. The Amalgamated Transit Union (ATU) is one of the largest labor unions in Cuyahoga County.

ATU Local 268 represents the majority of the employees including all bus and rail operators at the Greater Cleveland Regional Transit Authority (GCRTA).

Johnson has been an ATU Local 268 member for the past 20 years, and formerly served as an assistant trustee to the Local. He is the vice president of Cleveland AFL-CIO, and chairs the Buckeye Transit Career Ladder Partnership, a cooperative effort of several large transit systems in Ohio that train people for transit jobs. He lobbies hard for key transportation funding issues.

Johnson is the president of the RTA Hayden Federal Credit Union and has been honored for his outstanding service there. He has also received various awards and honors from the ATU Black Caucus, the ATU International Women's Caucus, and the George Meany Center for Labor Studies.

A native of Cleveland, Johnson and his wife, Tangee, have five children.

The Honorable
Kenneth L. Johnson
Councilmember
City of Cleveland

Ward 4 Councilman Kenneth L. Johnson, a life-long resident of the Buckeye-Shaker neighborhood, was first elected to Cleveland City Council in 1980. Since then, Johnson has worked to bring new development, new investment, and new jobs to his community. He also instituted citywide computer training programs, and initiated a volunteer program in Ward 4 to assist senior citizens and disabled residents.

Johnson chairs the public parks, recreation and properties committee. He believes quality recreational programming is a priority for Cleveland's residents because it helps young people develop socially, learn leadership skills, and stay healthy. Since being elected, he has instituted free camping, started a holiday basketball tournament that attracts 450 participants annually, and created basketball leagues at all Cleveland recreation centers. Johnson is responsible for a $500,000 donation from the NFL to the muni football league. His success in improving recreation in Cleveland caused the city to name a recreation center in his honor.

Councilman Johnson is proud of his seven boys, ages ten to 34, including a medical student, a lawyer, a firefighter, and two recreation directors.

Cleveland's
MOST INFLUENTIAL

A graduate of Glenville High School, the Honorable Larry Jones received his bachelor of arts degree from Wooster College and his juris doctorate from the Case Western Reserve University Law School. He worked as assistant Cuyahoga County prosecutor from 1978 until 1981, when he won a seat on the Cleveland City Council. After serving five years as Ward 10 councilman, he was elected judge of the Cleveland Municipal Court in 1987, and he was reelected in 1993 and 1999.

In 1995, Jones was selected by his colleagues and remains today the presiding and administrative judge of the Cleveland Municipal Court. In 1998, he began overseeing the Greater Cleveland Drug Court, a program designed to hold drug offenders accountable and provide treatment resources to break the cycle of drug abuse and drug-related crimes.

Jones is a member of four bar associations and many community and civic-oriented groups, including the NAACP, 100 Black Men of Greater Cleveland, Inc., and several Masonic organizations.

The Honorable
Larry A. Jones
Presiding & Administrative Judge
Cleveland Municipal Court

Since February 9, 2002, Peter Lawson Jones has been a member of the Board of Cuyahoga County Commissioners. The only African-American county commissioner in the state of Ohio, Jones previously served more than five years in the Ohio House of Representatives, where he was the ranking member of the House Finance and Appropriations Committee.

Jones, a graduate of Harvard College, magna cum laude in government, and Harvard Law School, is a partner with the national firm of Roetzel & Andress. He formerly served as the vice mayor and as a councilman in the City of Shaker Heights.

Among his many honors, Jones is a graduate of the Leadership Cleveland program and is listed in *Who's Who Among Black Americans.* He has also received an honorary doctorate of letters from David N. Myers University; was named an Ohio Super Lawyer for three consecutive years; and was inducted into the Shaker Heights Alumni Association Hall of Fame. His play, *The Family Line,* has been produced in several venues.

Jones and his wife, Lisa, are the proud parents of three children, Ryan, Leah, and Evan.

Peter Lawson Jones
Commissioner
Cuyahoga County

The Honorable
Stephanie Tubbs Jones
Representative,
11th District of Ohio
U.S. House of Representatives

A lifelong resident of the 11th District, the Honorable Stephanie Tubbs Jones was the first African-American woman elected to the United States House of Representatives from Ohio. She has championed economic development, health care, and quality education for all children. She serves on several House committees, is an active member of the Congressional Black Caucus, and chairs its housing task force. Tubbs Jones is also active in the Democratic Caucus and works for candidates throughout the country.

In addition to several civic and professional memberships, Tubbs Jones is a trustee for Bethany Baptist Church, the Community Re-Entry Program, and a Leadership Cleveland alumna. She served as a board of regents member for the National College of District Attorneys and Case Western Reserve University's Franklin T. Backus School of Law.

A graduate of Cleveland Public Schools, Tubbs Jones earned a degree in social work from Case Western Reserve University, Flora Mather College. She received her juris doctorate degree from Case Western Reserve School of Law.

Tubbs Jones was married to Mervyn L. Jones, Sr., (deceased) for 27 years and is the proud mother of Mervyn Leroy Jones, II.

Dr. Eugene J. Jordan
President & Founder
Jordan Dental Centers

Dr. Eugene Jordan is a certified doctor of dental surgery who has devoted much of his time to serving the Cleveland community in dental medicine and human rights. He is a pioneer in private dental group practice with two locations in the Cleveland area. He also pioneered the Mobile Dental Health Units that currently serve Cleveland Head Start Centers.

Dr. Jordan is currently a trustee for the National Dental Association. He has been a member of the Cleveland executive board of the NAACP for 20 years, and he is the founder and president of the Underground Railroad Society.

He has received the Black Social Worker's Martin Luther King Humanitarian Award; NAACP's Freedom Award; Omega Psi Phi Fraternity's Chapter Man of the Year Award; and Citizen of the Year Award.

Dr. Jordan earned his bachelor's degree in biology from Capital University, and his dental degree from Howard University. He later earned a bachelor's degree in business administration from Myers University.

Eugene is married to Bernice Cockrell Jordan, and he has three children, Dr. Joy A. Jordan, Dr. Martin E. Jordan, and Dr. Michael W. Jordan.

D r. Joy," as she is affectionately called by many of her patients, devotes most of her career to ensuring that children have healthy minds as well as bodies to meet the challenges of today's world.

Dr. Joy serves as president of the National Dental Association, and president of the East Cleveland Board of Education simultaneously. She recently received the YWCA Woman of Achievement Award, the Howard University Outstanding Leadership Award, and the NAACP Martin Luther King Award.

In addition, Dr. Joy was recently named one of the 100 Most Influential Black Americans by *Ebony* magazine. She was appointed by Ohio Governor Bob Taft to the Dentist Loan Repayment Advisory Board, and was named adjunct professor of clinical dentistry at Case Western Reserve University.

Dr. Jordan received her bachelor of science degree in microbiology, and her doctor of dental surgery degree from Howard University.

Presently, Dr. Jordon is a practicing dentist at Jordon Dental Center, dental director at the maximum security male prison facility in Ohio, and a leader in her community. Additionally, she serves as the center dentist for the Cleveland Job Corps Program.

Dr. Joy A. Jordon
President, National Dental Association
President, East Cleveland
Board of Education

S tate Representative Annie L. Key has been a member of the Ohio House of Representatives since January of 2001. A native of Camden, Alabama, she represents the 11th District, which includes Cleveland's Fifth, Sixth, Seventh, Twelfth, and Sixteenth Wards, Newburg Heights, Cuyahoga Heights, and Brooklyn Heights. Key is the ranking Democratic member on the House Ethics and Elections Committee. She is also a member of the Criminal Justice and Transportation and Public Safety Committees.

Key's professional affiliations include membership in the Rainey Institute, Black Women's Political Action Committee, the National Council of Negro Women, Inc., the NAACP, and the Cuyahoga Women's Political Caucus. She attended Cleveland State University and Cuyahoga Community College.

Prior to joining the state legislature, Key was employed with Ohio Bell and later with AT&T. She has one daughter, Stephanie, and attends the Church of Christ on the Boulevard.

The Honorable
Annie L. Key
Representative, 11th District
Ohio House of Representatives

Loretta Kirk
National Chair
Conference of Minority
Transportation Officials

L oretta Kirk is national chair of the Conference of Minority Transportation Officials (COMTO), which has more than 2,200 members at every level of transportation. Kirk has been active in COMTO for more than 20 years. A past president of the Cleveland chapter, she won the 1999 Gerald A. Anderson Sibling Award.

A certified public accountant, Kirk has worked for the Greater Cleveland Regional Transit Authority for more than 24 years. As a member of the executive management team, she plays a key role in managing RTA's annual operating budget of $230 million.

Kirk received the Professional Award from the National Association of the Negro Business Professional Woman's Club, and the Phenomenal Woman Award for contributions to her profession and her community.

A graduate of Cleveland State University, she has studied at the International Transit Student Program, the University of Southern California, and Northern University. A member of the American Public Transportation Association's financial management committee, Kirk is a past local president of the Institute of Internal Auditors. Further, she is past president and national second vice president of the Eta Phi Beta Sorority Inc.'s Gamma chapter.

Gerald Levert
Entertainer & Producer
Trevel Productions

O ne of the most recognizable musical voices of his era, Gerald Levert's career has spanned more than 20 years and produced 17 gold and platinum records.

Gerald received his musical education very early by studying his father, Eddie Levert, Sr., of the legendary O'Jays. At Shaker Heights High School, he regularly appeared in plays, musicals, and talent shows, while touring with his dad in the summers.

His first success as an artist and songwriter came when he, Marc Gordon, and his brother, Sean Levert, recorded and released "I'm Still." Atlantic Records signed the young trio, and their first release entitled *Pop Pop* climbed to number one on the charts.

In 1991, Gerald embarked on a solo career. His platinum selling debut, *Private Line*, started an eight-album run of gold and platinum records.

A songwriter and record producer, Gerald has spurned hits for several other artists including Anita Baker, Barry White, Keith Sweat, New Edition, and the O'Jays. He also gives back to his community by offering musical opportunities to others.

His production company, Trevel Productions, opened in 1988 and has achieved a level of longevity rare in the music business.

Michael R. Lisman works as a senior vice president and director of community development banking for Charter One Bank (a part of the eighth-largest bank holding company in the U.S., owned by the Royal Bank of Scotland, the world's sixth-largest bank). A graduate of Kent State University in Kent, Ohio, he is a licensed social worker and a trained community mediator.

Lisman is a 2003 recipient of the W.O. Walker Award for Community Excellence from the Call and Post Foundation. A member of the Special Contributions Fund board of trustees of the National NAACP, his personal credo is, "Wisdom is better than strength."

Lisman serves as vice chairman of the employment cluster of the UWS Investment Committee. He serves on the Akron NAACP executive committee, the Cleveland NAACP executive committee, and NCA board, as well as the executive advisory boards of National Black MBA of Cleveland and NPRC Business Advisory Council.

Lisman is a member of the Association for Conflict Resolution, BPA, and Ohio Fair Housing Congress. He holds life membership with Golden Heritage and is a member of the NAACP.

Elder Michael R. Lisman
Senior Vice President & Director,
Community Development Banking
Charter One Bank

Elected to Village of Highland Hills Council in 2000, the Honorable Danita Jo Love currently serves as council president. She is chair of the finance committee, oversees the council's agendas, and gives direction to the clerk of council. She previously served as chair of the rules and public works committees.

The vice president of the Northeast Ohio City Council Association, Danita is an active member of the National League of Cities, where she serves on numerous constituency groups and committees.

Danita works full-time at a prominent law firm in downtown Cleveland as a graphic production artist, which enhances her knowledge and provides necessary tools to govern and lead her community.

Danita's administrative and management experience, along with computer and design expertise, gives her flexibility to assess and analyze effectively. A creative, quick, and efficient pathfinder, she is always ready to learn and pitch in as a team player.

Danita graduated from John Hay High School, attended Cuyahoga Community College and Cleveland State University. A faithful member of Affinity Missionary Baptist Church, she is the proud mother of two sons, Jovon and Delbert.

The Honorable
Danita Jo Love
Council President
Village of Highland Hills

Pamela Marshall-Holmes
Regional Vice President
Community Service & Development
Cleveland Clinic Health System-East

Pamela Marshall-Holmes began her professional career at Cleveland Clinic Health System (formerly Meridia Health System) as director of social services at Euclid Hospital in 1980. In 1994, Pamela accepted the position of vice president of community service and development.

Pamela holds a master's degree in social work from the University of Pittsburgh. An active member of the Cleveland chapters of Jack & Jill, The Links, Inc., and The Northeasterners, she currently serves on the boards of Kid's Health 20/20 and the Center for Families and Children.

Her other honors include being named among the 2002 Top Ladies of Distinction by the March of Dimes and the Greater Cleveland chapter of Top Ladies of Distinction, Inc. She was also featured in *Kaleidoscope Magazine's* "Saluting Women Who Give Back." She is a member of the 2005 Leadership Cleveland class.

Pamela resides in Beachwood, Ohio where the mayor honored her with "Pamela Holmes Day" in 2000. She is married to Stefan, vice president of public funds for First Merit Bank. Her daughter, Heather, is a graduate of Bowling Green State University, and her son, Chase, is a senior at Beachwood High School.

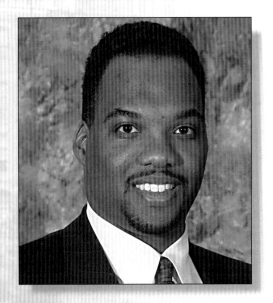

**The Honorable
Lance T. Mason**
Representative, 8th District
Ohio House of Representatives

Representative Lance T. Mason is the assistant minority whip of the House Democratic Caucus. Mason was appointed state representative to the Ohio House of Representatives in February of 2002, filling the vacancy created by Commissioner Peter Lawson Jones.

Previously, Mason was the district director for Congresswoman Stephanie Tubbs Jones. As district director, he supervised a staff of seven and operated the district office for the congresswoman. His primary responsibility was to serve the needs of the more than 575,000 constituents in the 11th Congressional District. Prior to his service in the congressional office, Mason served as an assistant county prosecutor and handled several high profile felony cases, including a capital murder, kidnapping, felonious assaults, rapes, and robberies.

Representative Mason has been a trial lawyer in the private practice of law for more than ten years. He currently works in the litigation group at Baker & Hostetler LLP. He holds a bachelor of arts degree with honors from the College of Wooster and a juris doctorate from the University of Michigan Law School.

Melodie Mayberry-Stewart is the first-ever chief technology officer (CTO) for the City of Cleveland. In this role, she oversees the development and implementation of information technology and telecommunications strategies.

Prior to becoming the City's CTO, Melodie was the founder and chief executive officer of the Black Diamond IT Consulting Group, LLC. She was the first black female general manager and vice president of corporate and shared services for worldwide delivery of IT systems for the BP Amoco Corporation.

Melodie holds a doctorate with an emphasis in information technology management from the Peter F. Drucker Executive Management Center of Claremont Graduate University. She graduated, cum laude, with a double-major bachelor's degree from Union College, a master's degree from the University of Nebraska, and a master of business administration degree in finance from Pepperdine University.

An active member in the community, Melodie has held high-ranking positions in several organizations. She is currently the president and board trustee of the Pine Valley Forge Foundation. Additionally, she has been featured as one of *Ebony* magazine's "100 Most Promising Corporate Women."

Melodie has one son, George Mayberry.

Melodie I. Mayberry-Stewart, Ph.D.
Chief Technology Officer
City of Cleveland

The Honorable Anita Laster Mays was elected to the Cleveland Municipal Court in November of 2003. In a given week, Judge Laster Mays presides over 200 criminal cases and oversees a civil docket where cases do not exceed a $15,000 award.

Laster Mays was named a 1986 Pace Setter, became an honored member of Who's Who Worldwide, and in 1996 was awarded as an Outstanding Alumnus of the Cleveland Public Schools. She is a member of Sigma Gamma Rho Sorority, Inc., The Black Women's Political Action Committee, and Providence Missionary Baptist Church. Laster Mays volunteers to assist the youth with tutoring or career days, recognizing that they are the future. She often says that "Killing time murders opportunity."

In 1986, Judge Laster Mays received a bachelor of science degree in business administration from The Ohio State University. In 1992, she received her juris doctorate degree from Cleveland-Marshall College of Law.

The Honorable
Anita Laster Mays
Judge
Cleveland Municipal Court

Valarie J. McCall
City Clerk, Clerk of Council
Cleveland City Council

The youngest city clerk, clerk of council in Cleveland's history, Valarie J. McCall brings energy and structure to the offices of Cleveland City Council. She oversees Cleveland City Council's staff of 41 and interacts with the 21 council members and their assistants.

Prior to becoming the clerk of council, McCall served as the director of the empowerment zone, where she was responsible for a $200 million budget.

McCall shares her energy by serving on numerous boards and organizations. Her achievements earned her several awards, including the prestigious Cleveland State University-awarded Alumni Emerging Leadership Award.

Her leadership allowed McCall to travel to Japan with the American Council of Young Political Leaders. In 2003, she became an American Marshall fellow of the German Marshall Fund, which fosters transatlantic partnerships to build international relations.

A native Clevelander, McCall graduated from Martin Luther King Law & Public Services Magnet High School. She has a bachelor's degree in social work from Cleveland State University and a master's degree in public administration from Cleveland State University's Levin College of Urban Affairs. McCall is a member of The Word Church.

Dr. Charles S. Modlin, Jr.,
M.D., FACS
Kidney Transplant Surgeon
Cleveland Clinic Foundation

Dr. Charles S. Modlin is a kidney transplant surgeon and urologist at the Cleveland Clinic Foundation, Lerner College of Medicine of Case Western Reserve University.

In 1983, Modlin graduated from Northwestern University, and in 1987, he received his medical degree from Northwestern University Medical School. He completed a six-year surgery/urology residency at New York University in 1993 and then a three-year kidney transplant fellowship at the Cleveland Clinic Foundation. He joined the staff in 1996.

Modlin has served as director of renal transplantation at St. Elizabeth's Hospital and Akron City Hospital. He has authored scientific publications and presented research. He is leading Cleveland toward elimination of health disparities as founder and director of the Cleveland Clinic's Minority Men's Health Center.

Modlin is one of only 15 African-American transplant surgeons in the United States and the only black urologist trained in transplantation surgery. He was voted as one of "Cleveland's Most Interesting People" in the first edition of *Who's Who In Black Cleveland*®. He is also the health committee chair of the 100 Black Men and NAACP.

Dr. Modlin has four children, and his wife Sheryl is an anesthesiologist.

E ducation was always emphasized in growing up," recalls the Honorable Judge Lauren C. Moore, who graduated with honors from Shaker Heights High School and then attended Spelman College, where she received a degree in English. The lure of a family and law school scholarship brought her back home to Cleveland, where she attended Case Western Reserve University to earn her juris doctorate.

After passing the bar in 1987, Judge Moore went to work for the Legal Aid Society as both a civil attorney and public defender. Nine years later, she decided to run for judge on the Cleveland Municipal Court. Unsuccessful in her first two attempts, she was asked to serve as chief prosecutor for Cleveland and then assistant Cuyahoga County prosecutor, until she was elected to the bench in 2003 after garnering 77 percent of the popular vote.

Judge Moore is very involved in the community and has participated in several mentoring and tutoring programs for young people.

**The Honorable
Lauren C. Moore**
Judge
Cleveland Municipal Court

T he Reverend Dr. Otis Moss, Jr. is pastor of Olivet Institutional Baptist Church in Cleveland.

Called to the ministry at age 17 while a student at Morehouse College, Moss completed his education with mentors like Dr. Benjamin E. Mays and friends like Dr. Martin Luther King, Jr. He earned a master of divinity degree from the Morehouse School of Religion, Interdenominational Theological Center, and a doctor of ministry degree from the United Theological Seminary.

Moss was the third co-pastor to serve Dr. Martin Luther King, Sr. at the historic Ebenezer Baptist Church in Atlanta, where he also established the Ebenezer Baptist Church Credit Union. From 1971 to 1996, Moss served on the national board of the Martin Luther King, Jr. Center for Non-Violent Social Change.

Moss is a Prince Hall, 33rd-degree Freemason, a life member of the NAACP, and a life member of the Alpha Phi Alpha Fraternity, Inc. He is also chair of the Morehouse College board of trustees.

Moss is married to the former Edwina Hudson Smith, and they have three children, Kevin, Daphne (deceased), and Otis, III.

Rev. Dr. Otis Moss, Jr.
Pastor
Olivet Institutional Baptist Church

Frederick R. Nance
Managing Partner
Squire, Sanders & Dempsey L.L.P.

Frederick R. Nance is managing partner of the Cleveland office of Squire, Sanders & Dempsey L.L.P. His legal practice focuses on commercial litigation, sports law, construction law, white collar crime, public-private partnerships and project counseling.

Nance was primary outside counsel to the City of Cleveland and former Cleveland Mayor Michael White for more than ten years. He is currently counsel to NBA-star LeBron James and to the Cleveland Browns on various commercial matters.

Nance is recognized in *The Best Lawyers in America* (2003-2005), and has been a Leading Lawyer in Northeast Ohio by *Inside Business* (2001-2004). In 2004, he was named one of America's Best Corporate Lawyers by *Corporate Board Member*, and in 2005, he was selected for the cover and featured in *Ohio Super Lawyers.*

In addition to various professional bar associations, Nance is a member of the boards of Baldwin-Wallace College, the Urban League of Greater Cleveland, United Way of Greater Cleveland, and the Catholic Charities Foundation.

In 2005, Nance received the American ORT Jurisprudence Award, The Leukemia & Lymphoma Society's Service to Mankind Award, and the Norman S. Minor Bar Association's Trailblazer Award in 2004.

Michael L. Nelson, Sr.
Principal Owner
The Law Offices of
Michael L. Nelson, Esq.

Michael L. Nelson, Sr. is principal owner of The Law Offices of Michael L. Nelson, Esq., where he specializes in public finance, civil and criminal litigation, and small business development. He has provided legal counsel on some of this region's most dynamic projects.

In addition to his law practice, Michael serves on the board of trustees of the Northeast Ohio Regional Sewer District, to which he was appointed by former Mayor Michael R. White, and reappointed by Mayor Jane Campbell. He also serves on the Central State University board of trustees, to which he was appointed by Governor George Voinovich and reappointed by Governor Bob Taft.

Michael graduated from Central State University and Case Western Reserve University School of Law. A member of Kappa Alpha Psi Fraternity, Inc., he is the founding president of the 100 Black Men of Greater Cleveland, and parliamentarian for the 100 Black Men of America.

A native of Cleveland, Michael is a proud father of son Michael Jr., daughters Nichole, Ebony, and Rayne, and a grandfather of Cornell, Cameron, and Christopher.

The Honorable Ruby Nelson serves as councilmember for the City of Warrensville Heights to a diverse constituency in Ward 4 that consists of homeowners, multi-level dwellings, and small businesses. In this position, she chairs the personnel, compensation and benefits, and senior citizens committees. She also serves as vice chair of the tax review board, and as a member of the finance committee.

From 2001 to 2003, Ruby served as chair of the Civil Service Commission for the City of Warrensville Heights. From 2002 to the present, she has served as chair of the Cuyahoga County Auditors Citizens Advisory Board. Ruby is serving her second four-year term as a Cuyahoga County executive committee member.

In 2003-2004, Ruby was a private contractor for the Cuyahoga County Department of Senior and Adult Services and the Community Office on Aging.

A native of Cleveland, Ruby is a member of Mt. Zion Fellowship Church in Highland Hills, Ohio. She is a widow and the proud mother of four adult children, Charniese, Carlton, Dwan, and Kyle.

**The Honorable
Ruby Nelson**
Councilmember
City of Warrensville Heights

Njeri Nuru-Holm is vice president for student affairs and minority affairs at Cleveland State University. Some of her previous roles include serving as dean of the School of Communication at Gallaudet University and clinical director at St. Elizabeth's Hospital.

Nuru-Holm holds bachelor's and master's degrees from Howard University, a doctor of philosophy degree from the University of Maryland, and certificates from Harvard University. A fellow of the American Speech-Language-Hearing Association, she is co-founder of the National Black Association for Speech-Language and Hearing.

Nuru-Holm is an alumna of Leadership Cleveland and has been featured on radio and in *The Plain Dealer* and *Kaleidoscope Magazine*. One of *Cleveland* magazine's 50 Most Interesting People in Cleveland, her leadership has been recognized by YWCA Women of Achievement, CSU Women Who Make a Difference, and as CSU Mentor of the Year.

She is a member of The Links, Inc., Alpha Kappa Alpha Sorority, Inc., and an honorary member of Alpha Lambda Delta and Phi Alpha National Social Work Honor Society.

Nuru-Holm and her husband, Dr. John Holm, live in Cleveland Heights. Her two daughters live in Maryland and California.

Njeri Nuru-Holm
Vice President,
Student & Minority Affairs
Cleveland State University

John C. Pace, Jr.
President & Chief Executive Officer
World-Class Event Management, Inc.

John C. Pace, Jr. is president and CEO of World-Class Event Management, Inc. He previously served as president of the River Front Classic & Jamboree, where he was responsible for the day-to-day operations and administration of the football "Classic" game held in Cincinnati.

Currently, John is president and CEO of The P&G Ohio Classic & Jamboree and The College Basketball All-Star Game events. During his tenure with the River Front Classic, he developed programs that generated more than $13 million annually for Cincinnati's economy and more than $1 million in financial support for Historically Black Colleges and Universities.

Additionally, John served as development and marketing director for the Martin Luther King, Jr. Performing and Cultural Arts Complex in Columbus, Ohio, where he increased total annual contributions from $75,000 to more than $700,000. He is a former marketing consultant for numerous national corporations. In addition, John led community and fundraising efforts that raised more than $1 million for various charitable organizations.

John earned two degrees in marketing and management from Franklin University in Columbus, Ohio. He is married to Tammarra, and has one daughter, Jordan.

Charles Brooks Perry
President & Chief Executive Officer
Pinkney-Perry Insurance Agency, Inc.

Charles Perry is one of the founders and is currently president and chief executive officer of the Pinkney-Perry Insurance Agency, established in 1961 in the state of Ohio.

Charles has served on numerous boards and committees. He served more than 11 years as chairman of the Minority Enterprise Input Committee, a subsidiary committee of the National Minority Supplier Development Council. Likewise, he served as chairman of the Cleveland Mayor's Business Minority Advisory Ad Hoc Committee. Charles was also a board member of the Minority Enterprise Legal Defense and Education Fund. He is the proud recipient of several accolades and awards for his distinguished public service as well as honors in the field of insurance.

Charles has been married to his wife, Sylvia, for 47 years. They have three children and five grandchildren. He is an avid golfer who also enjoys singing with the Olivet Institutional Baptist Church male chorus and the Heritage Chorale in Cleveland, Ohio.

George A. Phillips, executive director of the Cuyahoga Metropolitan Housing Authority (CMHA), works closely with CMHA's board to strengthen the agency's management team and streamline operations. He works to inspire the 1,100 employees to follow their primary mission, which is serving the housing needs of the more than 52,000 persons involved in CMHA's countywide housing programs. Recently, the agency received national recognition for its social service programs; it now has the lowest vacancy rate in nearly ten years.

George has a reputation as a no-nonsense leader who is intensely focused on providing clean, safe, and affordable housing for the county's working poor, the underemployed, and the unemployed.

George worked at the Chicago Housing Authority for 11 years before joining CMHA. During that time, he earned steady promotions through the ranks to serve as director of housing management. In this capacity, he oversaw daily operations of the 40,000-unit public housing program.

A 2002 graduate of Cleveland State University's Leadership Academy, George is recognized in *Who's Who in Public Service* and holds numerous certifications from national housing organizations.

George resides in Cleveland, Ohio with his family.

George A. Phillips
Executive Director
Cuyahoga Metropolitan
Housing Authority

First elected to the Senate in 1998, State Senator C.J. Prentiss is in her third term representing the 21st Senate District. In December of 2004, she was elected Senate Minority Leader. She previously served eight years as a state representative (1991-1998), and a six-year term as an elected member of the State Board of Education (1985-1990).

Prentiss is president of the Ohio Legislative Black Caucus Foundation. She chairs the elementary and secondary education committee of the National Black Caucus of State Legislators (NBCSL), serves on the NBCSL executive committee, and is the NBCSL's financial secretary.

Some of Prentiss' many awards include the NBCSL Legislator of the Year Award, the NBCSL Roundtable Award, the Cleveland State Civic Achievement Award, the AAWA Woman of the Year Award, the Ohio Hunger Task Force Legislator of the Year Award, and the Greater Cleveland AIDS Taskforce "A Voice Against the Silence" Award.

She received her bachelor of arts degree in education and master of education degree from Cleveland State University. She holds a post-graduate certificate in administration from Kent State University and is a graduate of the Weatherhead School of Management's Advanced Management Program.

The Honorable
C.J. Prentiss
Senator, 21st District
Ohio Senate

Everett Prewitt
President
Northland Research Corporation

E verett Prewitt is an author and president of Northland Research Corporation, a firm that has provided real estate consulting services since 1982.

An alumnus of Leadership Cleveland, Everett is a former Army officer and a Vietnam veteran. He is chairman of the board for the East End Neighborhood House, and vice chairman of the Greater Shaker Square Development Corporation. Everett is also a trustee emeritus at Meyers College.

Everett was president of both the Cleveland Association of Real Estate Brokers and the Cleveland Area Board of Realtors, where he received the Realtor of the Year award. He also received the Award for Civil Service from the Citizen's League of Greater Cleveland. His novel, *Snake Walkers*, won first place for best fiction at the Los Angeles Black Book Expo-2005.

Everett received his bachelor of arts degree in business administration from Lincoln University in Pennsylvania and his master of science degree in urban studies from Cleveland State University. He received the Distinguished Alumni Award from both universities.

A native of Cleveland, Everett is a proud graduate of Glenville High School.

Dr. Pamela Lynne Redden
Great Lakes Regional Director
Alpha Kappa Alpha Sorority, Inc.

D r. Pamela Lynne Redden is the Great Lakes regional director of Alpha Kappa Alpha Sorority, Inc. She was named 2003 Woman of the Year by the National Coalition of 100 Black Women, Greater Cleveland chapter. Pamela has been featured in *Ebony* and *Jet* magazines, and she is a frequent Woman's Day speaker and workshop presenter. She co-hosts the Universal Sisters' Seminar, an annual Cleveland program celebrating black women, and often appears in health seminars on NBC and ABC affiliates.

Pamela is a board certified physician of internal medicine. She has been engaged in private practice, and has served as examiner at the Regional Transit Authority, medical director at Cleveland Job Corps and NEPRC, and was elected the first woman chief of staff at Huron Hospital. She is currently an internist at Northeast Ohio Neighborhood Center.

Pamela received her bachelor of arts degree from Fisk University and her medical degree from Howard University School of Medicine.

A native of New York City, Pamela is the proud mother of Schuyler and Cameron, a 2005 graduate of Hampton University. She is a lifelong member of St. John A.M.E. Church.

The Honorable Zack Reed became a member of Cleveland City Council on December 11, 2000. Reed views the improved quality of life for Mount Pleasant residents as being tied to three main issues: economic development, education, and public safety.

Reed has helped with $50 million in improvements, including a redevelopment plan for Kinsman Road and a number of new housing initiatives. In addition, Reed has been actively involved in the reconstruction of A.J. Rickoff School, the first new school to be built in the city of Cleveland in more than 20 years. Other notable improvements to Ward 3 during Reed's tenure include the reconstruction of Carol McClendon Park, formerly Bisbee Park, and significant improvements to parks and recreation centers in Ward 3.

The majority whip and chair of the council's public safety committee, Reed also sits on several other committees.

Outside of City Hall, Reed has established the Zack Reed Scholarship Fund for Cleveland Municipal School Students. He represented the United States on a trip to Geneva, Switzerland for the Young Leaders American-Swiss Foundation Conference 2004.

Reed is a graduate of John F. Kennedy High School.

**The Honorable
Zack Reed**
Councilmember
City of Cleveland

Myron F. Robinson is the president and chief executive officer of the Urban League of Greater Cleveland. His 36 years of experience with the Urban League movement began shortly after graduating from Youngstown State University with a degree in sociology. Myron has served as president of Urban Leagues in Madison, Wisconsin; Newhaven, Connecticut; and Greenville, South Carolina.

Since 1991, Myron has revolutionized the Urban League of Greater Cleveland's community programming. In 2004, under his strategic guidance, the Urban League of Greater Cleveland purchased and renovated its new headquarters. It became the only African-American service-based organization to own real estate in Cleveland.

Myron is presently on the boards of the State of Ohio Governor's Workforce Policy Board, John Carroll University, KeyBank, University Hospital Health System, and the Greater Cleveland Workforce Investment Board.

In addition to his undergraduate work, Myron completed the National Urban League Executive Development program at Harvard University, and has done graduate work at both the University of Pittsburgh and the University of Wisconsin.

Myron and his wife, Brenda, are the parents of two, and the proud grandparents of four. They reside in Cleveland.

Myron F. Robinson
President & Chief Executive Officer
Urban League of Greater Cleveland

Clarence D. Rogers, Jr.
Commissioner
Public Utilities Commission of Ohio

Clarence D. Rogers, Jr. was appointed commissioner of the Public Utilities Commission of Ohio in 2001. Previously, he was interim general manager and executive deputy general manager at the Greater Cleveland Regional Transit Authority. Rogers served two terms as chairman of the Ohio Turnpike Commission.

Rogers' legal career has included serving as assistant U.S. attorney and as Cleveland's chief police prosecutor. He was a partner in Ohio's first black incorporated law firm, where he was chief litigator. The American Arbitration Association and the Federal Mediation and Conciliation Service certified him as a labor arbitrator.

Rogers has received numerous awards and honors including the Kent State University Outstanding Alumnus Award, several UNCF Appreciation Awards, and being named in *The Best Lawyers in America®*.

He is a member of the Cleveland Bar Association, the National Bar Association, and the NAACP. Rogers has served on the boards of trustees of the Greater Cleveland Regional Transit Authority, the Urban League, Cleveland Children's Museum, and the National Minority College Golf Scholarship Fund.

Rogers received a bachelor of science degree from Kent State University and a juris doctorate from Howard University School of Law.

Davida Russell
President, Local 744 & Northeast District
Ohio Association of Public School
Employees/AFSCME Local Four

Davida Russell is the union president of the Ohio Association of Public School Employees for the transportation department at the Cuyahoga County Board of Mental Retardation and Developmental Disabilities (CCBMR/DD). As the union president and state executive board member of the Northeast District OAPSE/AFSCME, she represents more than 38,000 members across Ohio.

Davida is also an executive board member of the Cleveland AFL-CIO. In this position, she has represented public employees in Sao Paulo, Brazil at the URBIS 2002 International Fair and Congress of Cities, where she received an award from the Ambassador of Italy for her outstanding work. She actively holds leadership positions in the Cleveland Coalition of Labor Union Women and AFSCME United Political Area Committee.

Davida is a member of East Mount Vernon Missionary Baptist Church and a graduate of Cleveland State University's Labor Relations Certificate program. She is a graduate of the prestigious Leadership Cleveland Class of 2004.

Davida resides in Cleveland Heights with her husband, Carl Russell, and two daughters, Domonique Nicole and Brittany Lynne Russell.

The Honorable Shirley Strickland Saffold began her career in the practice of criminal law with the Legal Aid Society of Cleveland, Public Defender's Office. In 1987, she was elected judge of the Cleveland Municipal Court, and in 1994, she successfully campaigned and was elected to the Cuyahoga County Court of Common Pleas.

Saffold is active with many organization and civic groups, most of which advocate equality for women and human rights for African Americans. Over the past eight years, she has also advocated what she terms "the rights of the abused and neglected children of the world."

Saffold is a member of the National Bar Association, the American Judges Association, the Association of Municipal/County Judges of Ohio, and the National Association of Women Judges. She is the first African-American woman to be elected president of the American Judges Association.

Judge Saffold is a member of Mount Zion Congregational Church and an active member of Alpha Kappa Alpha Sorority, Inc. She received her bachelor of arts degree from Central State University in Wilberforce, Ohio in 1973, and her law degree from Cleveland-Marshall College of Law in 1976.

**The Honorable
Shirley Strickland Saffold**
Judge
Cuyahoga County
Court of Common Pleas

Sabra Pierce Scott is a native of Cleveland and a lifelong resident of Glenville. In 1977, she graduated from Laurel School, and she earned a bachelor of arts degree in American history from Case Western Reserve University in 1982.

Upon graduation from Case Western Reserve University, she began setting the foundation for her future work as a member of Cleveland City Council, a task she began in November of 2001.

To groom herself for this position, Pierce Scott worked as a neighborhood planner with the City of Cleveland's Department of Community Development. Notable projects under her direction include the former Rock Glen Townhouses, now known as Omni Vue, and the Glenville Plaza. In 1986, she was appointed administrative assistant to Cleveland City Council, and she served as administrative assistant to two council presidents. Additionally, she joined Bank One as a branch manager in 1994 and earned officer status in 1995.

Pierce Scott has received numerous awards and honors including the State of Ohio Minority Business Initiatives Award, the Sister to Sister Entrepreneurial Excellence Award, and the Community Re-Entry Right Relationship Award.

**The Honorable
Sabra Pierce Scott**
Councilmember
City of Cleveland

Hilton O. Smith
Corporate Vice President
Turner Construction Company

Hilton O. Smith, an ordained minister, is corporate vice president of Turner Construction Company, where he has served for more than 30 years. His duties include managing the company's corporate affairs, minority and woman-owned business, equal employment, and educational programs. Smith also led Turner's efforts in awarding more than $11 billion to thousands of minority and woman business enterprises.

Smith has been recognized as one of the leading corporate executives in America with more than 100 awards. He has received keys to the cities of Cleveland, Ohio; Dallas, Texas; Chattanooga, Tennessee; Toledo, Ohio; Miami, Florida; and Kansas City, Missouri. Some of his other honors include the Congressional Record Recognition by Congressmen Louis Stokes, Edolphus Towns and Senator George Voinovich; the National Urban League's Herbert Wright Medal for National Distinguished Community Service; and the U.S. Department of Commerce's Distinguished Supplier Diversity Executive Award.

Smith received his bachelor of arts degree from St. Augustine's College. He completed the labor relations program at Cornell University and the urban theological program at Yale University. He also received an honorary doctor of humane letters from David Myers University.

The Honorable
Shirley A. Smith
Representative, Tenth District
Ohio House of Representatives

The Honorable Shirley A. Smith was reelected to the Ohio House of Representatives in 2004, representing House District Ten in Cleveland. A dynamic leader, Smith remains an ardent champion for the disadvantaged and disenfranchised throughout Ohio. In her fourth term, she has crafted several important pieces of legislation, including measures that would create a Capital Case Commission to study the use of the death penalty in Ohio (H.B. 260) and amend current expungement laws (H.B. 317).

Smith presently serves on the juvenile and family law and the financial institutions, real estate, and securities committees and is ranking minority member on the health committee. She was also appointed to the joint legislative committee on health care oversight and the state criminal sentencing advisory committee. Additionally, Smith holds executive positions with the House Cuyahoga County Democratic Delegation, the Women's Democratic Caucus, the Ohio Legislative Black Caucus, and the National Black Caucus of State Legislators.

A Cleveland native, Smith holds a bachelor of arts degree and an associate of arts degree from Cleveland State University and Cuyahoga Community College, respectively. She is a mother and grandmother and an avid golfer.

The Honorable Judge Angela R. Stokes was born and raised in the Greater Cleveland community and comes from a family of distinguished public servants. Judge Stokes is the daughter of retired U.S. Congressman Louis Stokes and niece of the late Carl B. Stokes, former U.S. ambassador and mayor of Cleveland.

Judge Stokes graduated with honors from the University of Maryland, College Park, receiving her bachelor of arts degree in psychology. Likewise, she received her juris doctorate from the Howard University School of Law in Washington, D.C. She was first elected judge of the Cleveland Municipal Court on November 7, 1995, to an unexpired term, and was reelected in 1999 to a full six-year term that will expire on January 1, 2006.

During her term of service on the Cleveland Municipal Court bench, Stokes was instrumental in establishing Project HOPE (Holistic Opportunities and Preventative Education), which is the Cleveland Municipal Court's program for prostitution offenders.

A member of Faith Fellowship Church in Macedonia, Ohio, Judge Stokes also attends classes at its Hosanna Bible Training Center.

**The Honorable
Angela R. Stokes**
Judge
Cleveland Municipal Court

A graduate of John Adams High School and John Carroll University, the Honorable Pauline Tarver, one of seven children, grew up in Hough. Moving to the southeast side of the city, she worked in her councilman's ward office and The Rape Crisis Center before joining the Cleveland Branch of the National Association for the Advancement of Colored People (NAACP). During her 22 years as executive director, she also served as a liaison between community organizations, corporations, and local and state governments.

After passing the bar in 1992, Pauline began practicing law, specializing in criminal misdemeanor, personal injury, domestic relations, bankruptcy, and probate. She also served as an acting magistrate in East Cleveland Municipal Court.

Early in 2003, Pauline realized, despite some very strong opposition, it was time to get serious about politics. It was her first attempt and after a lot of hard work and long hours campaigning, she was elected to the Cleveland Municipal Court on November 4, 2003.

**The Honorable
Pauline H. Tarver**
Judge
Cleveland Municipal Court

Rosalind Thompson
Executive Vice President,
Human Resources
Jo-Ann Stores, Inc.

Rosalind Thompson is the executive vice president of human resources for Jo-Ann Stores, Inc. She joined the company in 1992.

Jo-Ann Stores, Inc. is headquartered in Hudson, Ohio. The largest retailer of fabrics and craft supplies, Jo-Ann's has more than 800 stores in 48 states, with more than 22,000 employees. Rosalind is a member of the executive committee and has four direct reports.

Rosalind volunteers on the board of directors of United Way. She serves as alumni chair of Leadership Cleveland, as the board chair of The Center for Families and Children, and with Cuyahoga Community College. Rosalind is also an active member of The Links, Inc. and Jack and Jill of America.

Rosalind grew up in Milwaukee, Wisconsin, and lived in Chicago, Minneapolis, Oakland, and Columbus before moving to Cleveland. She holds a bachelor of arts degree in sociology from Carroll College in Wisconsin.

Rosalind and her husband of 21 years, Wendell, live in Orange Village, Ohio. They have two children, Adrienne and Cameron. Adrienne is a sixth-grade English teacher at Hawken School, and Cameron is a junior at University School.

Dr. Jerry Sue Thornton
President
Cuyahoga Community College

Dr. Jerry Sue Thornton is president of Cuyahoga Community College, the oldest and largest community college in Ohio. She is responsible for fulfilling the college's mission of providing high-quality, accessible, and affordable educational opportunities and services each year to 60,000 students from Cuyahoga County and northeast Ohio.

Since being named president in 1992, Dr. Thornton has formed productive partnerships for the college with local school districts, colleges, and universities. She has also formed partnerships with private industry and institutions such as NASA, Playhouse Square, and the Rock & Roll Hall of Fame and Museum.

Thornton serves on several corporate, nonprofit, and foundation boards. These include the National City Corporation, Applied Industrial Technologies, American Greetings, RPM International, Inc., United Way Services of Greater Cleveland, and the Cleveland Foundation.

Among Thornton's awards are the Urban League's Corporate Excellence Award 2000, the 1999 Black Professional of the Year Award from the Black Professional Association, and the Spirit of Women Award from the National Council of Negro Women, Inc.

Judge George W. Trumbo served on the Cleveland Municipal Court from 1982 until 1997. Prior to his appointment and subsequent election, he was a referee and director of criminal arraignment in the Cuyahoga County Common Pleas Court from 1959 to 1982.

Trumbo served as president of the Cleveland Public Library board of directors. He was the first African-American president of the Shaker Heights Kiwanis chapter. He is a past president of the Northern Ohio Municipal Judges Association and a member of the Judicial Council of the National Bar Association.

A 33rd-degree Freemason, Trumbo is a member of the Champion Lodge of Elks and the Ecclesiastes Lodge-120. He also served in the legal department and the civil liberties department of the Imperial Council.

A longtime member of Mt. Olive Baptist Church, Trumbo is an honorary trustee, past director of the junior church, and a Sunday school teacher.

Trumbo received an honorable discharge from the U.S. Navy and graduated from The Ohio State University and the Case Western Reserve University School of Law.

The father of five and a grandfather of three, Trumbo is married to Judge Sara J. Harper, retired.

**The Honorable
George W. Trumbo**
Judge, Retired
Cleveland Municipal Court

Earle B. Turner is clerk of the Cleveland Municipal Court. He has served as coordinator of the Mill Creek Development and as chairman of the Browns Stadium Committee.

Turner's professional memberships and affiliations are extensive. He served on the board of trustees for Hiram House and on the Northeast Ohio Area-Wide Coordinating Agency, the Citizens League of Greater Cleveland, and the Cuyahoga County Democratic Committee. He has been involved with the El Hasa Temple-Excelsior Lodge-11 and the Bezalel Consistory-Number 15. He has also served as a board member of the Rock and Roll Hall of Fame and Museum and as chairman of the Southeast YMCA.

Some of Turner's awards include a certificate presented to him by Congressman Louis Stokes for Youngest Councilman Elected in the City of Cleveland in 1975. He was also recognized as Most Outstanding Councilman of the Decade in 1979, and was presented the Phenomenal African-American Man Award in 2003.

Turner holds a bachelor of arts degree in political science and business administration from Central State University.

Born in Cleveland in 1953, Earle is married to Marcia Turner and has four children, Shiloh, Christina, Lacora, and Kierra.

Earle B. Turner
Clerk
Cleveland Municipal Court

Andrew A. Venable, Jr.
Director
Cleveland Public Library

Andrew A. Venable, Jr. is director of the Cleveland Public Library. He manages the third-largest public research library in America, a metropolitan library system with more than 750 employees providing books, information, and service at a main library complex.

The Ohio Library Council named Andrew Librarian of the Year for 2001. Professionally, he is active in the American Library System, Urban Libraries Council, Ohio Library Council, and the Cleveland Area Metropolitan Library Association.

Andrew received a master of science degree in library science from Case Western Reserve University in 1978, and a bachelor of science degree in business administration from Virginia State University in 1968. Likewise, he completed the program for senior executives in state and local government at Harvard University's John F. Kennedy School of Government in 2001.

Andrew is a member of Olivet Institutional Baptist Church and Alpha Phi Alpha Fraternity, Inc. He is a life member of the NAACP and active in community organizations.

A native of Staunton, Virginia, Andrew is the proud father of one daughter and one son. He is the grandfather of three.

The Honorable
Robert J. White, III
Councilmember
City of Cleveland

As a young man, Councilman Robert J. White, III received the opportunity to better himself through a scholarship program. Today, he works diligently to offer the same advantages to the people of Ward 2. Since joining Cleveland City Council, White has worked with the Union Miles Development Corporation (UMDC) to provide services to residents as well as improve community and economic development opportunities.

White has worked with the UMDC to create a reading room for children, and has instituted snow removal and grass cutting programs for seniors and the physically challenged.

In addition, White has worked to make the Mill Creek housing development, a project that began prior to his term of service, a reality. Mill Creek has 217 market rate homes and prompted the Regional Transit Authority (RTA) to build the Mill Creek Station. Before becoming a councilman, White worked as an insurance agent, a teacher, and a legal intern.

He attended Bates College in Lewiston, Massachusetts where he earned a bachelor's degree in political science and education. White also attended The Penn State Dickinson School of Law.

Davil W. Whitehead is vice president, corporate secretary, and chief ethics officer of FirstEnergy. The real estate, facilities, security, and enterprise records management departments all report to Whitehead.

Previously, Whitehead was regional vice president for the northern region of FirstEnergy's Illuminating Company subsidiary, with responsibility for customer account services, customer support services, and external relations. Before the 1997 merger of Ohio Edison and Centerior Energy that formed FirstEnergy, Whitehead was regional vice president of Centerior's central region, with responsibility for most aspects of the company's operations in the Cleveland area. He also served as director of governmental affairs for Centerior and was general counsel for The Illuminating Company.

Whitehead is involved in many professional and civic organizations in the Greater Cleveland area. He is a director of the Cleveland State University Foundation and a member of First Tee of Cleveland. He serves as vice president of the board of park commissioners for Cleveland Metroparks, and is a board member of United Way of Greater Cleveland and Cleveland Scholarship Programs, Inc.

Whitehead received his bachelor of arts degree and his law degree from Cleveland State University.

David W. Whitehead
Vice President, Corporate Secretary
& Chief Ethics Officer
FirstEnergy

Earl Williams was elected to a four-year term in 2003. He currently serves as a staff attorney with the Cuyahoga Metropolitan Housing Authority, and has previously been an assistant Cuyahoga County public defender and an assistant Cuyahoga County prosecutor. He served as a registered principal with an investment banking firm, and is currently an industry arbitrator with the National Association of Securities Dealers.

Williams is a member of the economic development, community life and health, and safety and public works committees. He is also a member of the Shaker Heights Citizens Committee and a member and former officer of the Shaker Schools PTO. Williams volunteers his time as president of the board of directors of the Mt. Pleasant NOW Development Corporation, where he directs a multi-million dollar economic and community development investment program for the Kinsman Road area.

Williams holds a bachelor's degree in communications from Ohio University, and a law degree from Cleveland State University's Cleveland Marshall School of Law.

The Honorable
Earl Williams, Jr.
Councilmember
City of Shaker Heights

Sonali Bustamante Wilson
Chief Legal Counsel
Cleveland State University

Sonali Bustamante Wilson is the chief legal counsel and secretary to the board of trustees of Cleveland State University. She has been affiliated with the university since 1996.

Sonali holds a bachelor's degree from Boston University, a master's degree in government studies from Harvard University, and a law degree from Georgetown University Law Center.

Previously, Sonali was a law clerk for Ohio Supreme Court Justice Herbert R. Brown. From 1988 to 1994, she was an appellate litigation associate with the Cleveland office of Arter & Hadden and served on the board of trustees of the Cleveland Bar Association.

Active in social and community service, Sonali recently served as president of the Cleveland chapter of The Links, Inc., and on the board of trustees of the Cuyahoga County Board of Mental Retardation and Developmental Disabilities. She is the legal advisor to the Greater Cleveland alumnae chapter of Delta Sigma Theta Sorority, Inc., and a member of several other organizations.

A native of Cleveland, Sonali is married to Dr. N. Stephen Wilson, and they are the proud parents of Martine, Joy, and Julian.

Artha Woods
Cultural Activist

Artha Woods was born in Atlanta, Georgia, and raised in Cleveland. She attended Cleveland public schools, graduated from Central Senior High School as valedictorian, and attended Case Western Reserve University School of Education on a scholarship. The first black woman hired by the Ohio Bell Telephone Company as an elevator operator, she retired as a supervisor after working for Bell for 41 years.

Artha ran for Cleveland City Council in 1971 and retired from City Council as the clerk of council.

Artha's special interest has been furthering the cultural development of black womanhood. With Jon McCullough, she founded the country's first modeling and charm school for black women. Likewise, she established the Starlight Cotillion for girls graduating from Cleveland public schools, and offered students from a cotillion class a scholarship to college.

Artha is currently writing a book about her exciting and interesting life, which has been referred to as the "Trilogy of Triumph."

A park in Ward 6 in the Buckeye-Woodland area was named after Artha Woods at the request of the residents. She is a member of Antioch Baptist Church.

Cleveland's
MOST INFLUENTIAL

Gail E. Wright is a program manager for Battelle, a global science and technology enterprise. Wright manages the small business technology transfer and commercialization program, the NASA Glenn Garrett Morgan Commercialization Initiative (GMCI). She also manages its youth outreach project, Inspiring Today's Youth for Tomorrow's Opportunities (ITY), which introduces urban-based youth to innovation and technology-based career opportunities. As president of her own development and marketing company, Wright Alternatives, she specializes in program development and the promotion of unique music, film and art projects.

Wright has 20 years of experience in business, technology, and law. She is a National Technical Association Achiever of the Year, a *Crain's Cleveland Business* Woman of Note, and one of the Minority Business and Professionals Network's 2005 Fifty Influential Minorities in Business.

Wright holds a bachelor of arts degree from Princeton University and a law degree from Cleveland Marshall College of Law. She is a member of the Small Business Technology Council, the National Technical Association, the International Economic Development Council, the National Association of Black Journalists, the Museum of Contemporary Art, and a sponsor of the Rona R. Carter Scholarship Program.

Gail E. Wright
Program Manager
NASA Glenn GMCI
Battelle

KeyBank

STRENGTHENING OUR COMMUNITIES

Key recognizes, appreciates and values its reputation as a trusted source of banking and financial products, and as an important contributor to the stability of the diverse communities we serve. As a leading business in Cleveland, Key benefits by helping to improve the quality of life and economic vibrancy of the places our customers, employees and shareholders live and work. Therefore, the company is committed to supporting the area's economic revitalization, providing extensive urban outreach and offering financial education.

Through the outreach and innovation of Key's Community Development Bank, many people in Cleveland's neighborhoods are achieving their first steps toward economic independence. Our loans and investments in low- and moderate-income (LMI) neighborhoods enable small businesses to come to life and for people to achieve dreams of home ownership, education and wealth creation.

Community Reinvestment

As one of the nations' top 10 banks in community development, Key is proud of earning six consecutive "Outstanding" ratings since the inception of the Community Reinvestment Act in 1977. Key's performance is not merely satisfying a requirement. It signifies the company's efforts to consistently push beyond what is required by offering a breadth of targeted products and programs that benefit the communities in which it does business.

Much of Key's community development lending targeted businesses and organizations located in LMI communities across the country, helping to stabilize and revitalize these areas. During the four-year exam period, Key provided throughout its retail footprint:

> Real estate financing for affordable housing and other community development loans in excess of $1.4 billion;
> $8.8 billion in small business loans;
> $500 million in investments;
> $18 million in contributions; and
> Over 200,000 hours of community services.

Urban Initiatives

After working hard to better understand the business needs existing in Cleveland's urban communities and seeking input from LMI individuals and community leaders, we recognized that one of the most immediate needs is convenient, safe access to money, particularly paychecks. Specifically, we wanted to offer an alternative to the exorbitant rates often charged for paycheck access.

KeyBank Plus / Financial Education

Underscoring its strong commitment to urban revitalization, KeyBank now offers KeyBank Plus check-cashing services in 20 Cleveland KeyCenters. Those using KeyBank Plus services are not required to open a checking or savings account with Key – a marked departure from previous banking practices. With KeyBank Plus check cashing, individuals can cash approved payroll or government checks and purchase money orders at a discounted rate.

Additionally, Key's *Learn and Earn* financial education curriculum – provides free financial education classes to individuals in Cleveland's communities. Key has committed to building wealth in the communities they serve by offering help with long-term financial goals and economic literacy through one-on-one coaching and classes.

Participants in the program have access to dozens of free classes on budgeting, using checking accounts and credit cards, and other financial basics. Entrepreneurs can get help, too, with classes on how to develop business plans and understand cash flow, among others. As well, KeyBank and national nonprofit One Economy Corporation have partnered on the creation of **Money Made Easy** (www.thebeehive.org/moneymadeeasy), a financial literacy website that helps consumers manage their money. Money Made Easy offers a complete financial education curriculum that consumers can follow at their own pace.

The free courses and coaching are available at Key's Buckeye Plaza KeyCenter at 11461 Buckeye Road which has a 40-seat classroom, 9-station computer lab and private offices for one-on-one coaching. Classes are also held at Cudell Improvement, Inc., 11650 Detroit Avenue, on the West side of Cleveland.

KeyBank

Through this innovative approach to the urban community, Key is providing historically underserved consumers with access to new services, financial education and core banking products. Together, the elements of this strategy can move consumers from check cashing to financial security and self-sufficiency.

Philanthropy

Key's fiscal expertise as a leading financial institution helps communities and individuals prosper. Economic self-sufficiency results from sound financial education and workforce development. At Key, economic self-sufficiency involves two main thrusts – workforce development and financial education. *The Key Foundation* seeks to encourage candidates for grants to recognize the importance of diversity and, accordingly, makes contributions that demonstrate a sincere commitment to individual diversity. Beneficiaries of Key Foundation grants experience educational programs, providing job training and teaching workforce and life skills necessary to secure employment and earn a living.

Diversity

At Key, we are developing a workforce that reflects the diversity of our customers and communities. We go beyond compliance to commitment. We offer training, mentoring programs and partnerships to our employees, vendors and to our communities.

Key continues to be a trailblazer in adopting vendor relationships with minority and women-owned businesses as a part of its overall business strategy. Today, Key's company-wide *Supplier Diversity* strategy is designed to continue the development of those strategic relationships with minority and women-owned businesses (MWBEs), thus reflecting our commitment to the communities we serve, our clients and our shareholders.

Key's *Supplier Diversity* business strategy is:

> a strategic corporate business imperative
> a part of Key's overall sourcing strategy
> a plan to provide meaningful opportunities through fair competition, and a way to build economic wealth in the communities we serve

CEO Commitment

Key Chairman and CEO, Henry Meyer, is a strong advocate of the *Supplier Diversity* strategy. In a recent CEO Briefing on Supplier Diversity sponsored by the Northern Ohio Minority Business Council and the Commission on Economic Inclusion, Meyer stated, "The powerful attributes of inclusion, diversity and respect, that we aspire to infuse within the Key organization, have powerful outcomes. We have found that they improve business performance; help to understand our customers; drive important investments in people; and support job creation and economic development in communities here at home and around the U.S. In short, we're moving to make diversity truly part of the Key "brand" and our reputation." For Key, building and growing relationships with MWBEs is truly a strategic business imperative and a competitive advantage.

Key's expenditure with MWBEs has surpassed $100 million since 2001, when it launched a concerted effort to expand its supplier diversity business strategy. Key is committed to increasing its total MWBE spend from six to eight percent in 2005, moving toward a corporate scorecard goal of 10 percent by year-end 2006. Currently, Key has approximately $1.7 million in contracts with Cleveland-area minority-owned firms (MBE), and an additional $1.6 million in women-owned companies (WBE) in Cleveland.

Key works diligently to not only identify new opportunities to engage MWBE's but also reevaluates existing relationships to increase the level of business and support the expansion of capabilities.

Through the Northern Ohio Minority Business Council, Key launched the "Partner's First Module". The module is designed to engage partnering majority firms, in this case, Kelly Services, Office Max/Boise and Sherwin Williams, with Key in a formal mentoring program with selected MBEs. The goal is to provide insight, education and strategies that will result in the growth of these firms.

Key is ranked 13th on *DiversityInc Magazine's* Top 50 companies for diversity, a distinction owed in part to Key's strategic supplier relationships.

When neighborhoods are filled with people who support themselves through meaningful work and then wisely manage what they earn, everyone wins. We are proud to support, promote and celebrate the strength of our diverse neighborhoods.

KeyBank

Jeffery J. Weaver
Executive Vice President &
Group Head of Portfolio Management
KeyCorp

Erskine Cade
Senior Vice President & Director,
Government Relations
KeyCorp

Jeffery J. Weaver is executive vice president and group head of portfolio management at KeyCorp. He is responsible for the development and implementation of economic capital optimization strategies for Key's credit portfolio.

Weaver was most recently managing director and regional portfolio manager for the U.S.A., Europe, and Australia loan books for TD Securities (USA), LLC in New York. Previously, he was managing director and head of transactions of corporate finance and select industries.

Before joining TD Securities, Weaver worked for the Bank of New York in its trade and multinational banking division. He held positions of increasing responsibility at the Bank of New York, JP Morgan, and Citicorp Investment Bank.

Weaver serves on the Cornell University Council, Cornell University Alumni Trustees Nomination Committee, and is a past director-at-large of the Cornell Alumni Federation. He is also involved in various philanthropic, civic, and cultural endeavors.

Weaver holds bachelor of arts degree in economics and government from Cornell University, where he also earned his master of business administration degree in finance. He resides in Shaker Heights, Ohio with his wife, Tracey, and their two children, Kyle and Trent.

Erskine Cade is presently senior vice president and director of government relations for KeyCorp. In this capacity, he is responsible for advocating and advancing Key's position to members and committees of the state legislatures and their staffs, departments, regulatory agencies, commissions, and other special interest groups.

Cade started his career with The Standard Oil Company of Ohio in retail marketing, holding a variety of positions in this area. As retail sales manager, he was in charge of sales for the Greater Cleveland Metropolitan area.

A native of Birmingham, Alabama, Erskine received a degree in business administration from West Virginia State College. He earned an executive master's degree in business administration from the Weatherhead School of Management at Case Western Reserve University.

In addition to serving on several boards, Erksine has chaired the American Association of Blacks in Energy, and the Government Relations Committee for United Way Services. He is a member of the National Black MBA Association, the National Black Caucus of State Legislators corporate roundtable, and Omega Psi Phi Fraternity, Inc. He is also board chair of A Cultural Exchange and is a Leadership Cleveland alumnus.

Paul N. Harris
Executive Vice President
KeyCorp

Robin Cottingham
Senior Vice President &
Chief Administrative Officer
KeyCorp Global Treasury Management

Paul N. Harris is executive vice president, secretary, and general counsel of KeyCorp. His responsibilities include managing Key's law group, where he oversees the legal affairs of the corporation, its affiliates, and major lines of business and support groups. In addition to serving as secretary of the corporation, Paul serves as a director of KeyBank, N.A. and a member of KeyCorp's management committee and executive council.

Paul joined KeyCorp in 2003, and was elected corporate secretary in May of 2003. He previously served as partner-in-charge of the Cleveland office of Thompson Hine LLP.

Paul received a bachelor of arts degree from the University of Chicago and a law degree from Stanford Law School. He is a member of the American Society of Corporate Secretaries and the Cleveland Bar Association.

Active in the Cleveland community, Paul is a trustee and immediate past president of the board of trustees of the Friends of the Cleveland School of the Arts. A trustee of Hawken School, The Cuyahoga Community College Foundation, and The Children's Museum of Cleveland, he is a member of the Cleveland-Marshall College of Law Visiting Committee.

Robin C. Cottingham is senior vice president and chief administrative officer of KeyCorp's global treasury management group. She is responsible for managing strategic planning and implementation, knowledge management, and alliance management for global treasury management.

Previously, Robin served as director of product management responsible for the development and delivery of cash management, international, B2B e-commerce, and commercial deposit products throughout KeyCorp. She also served as senior vice president responsible for leading quality planning, quality control, and continuous improvement initiatives for KeyBank N.A., and as senior vice president of the community banking group for the Greater Cleveland District.

Robin joined the former Society National Bank in 1979 as a management trainee. She attended Baldwin Wallace College where she earned a bachelor's degree in business finance and received an executive master of business administration degree.

An alumna of Delta Sigma Theta Sorority, Kappa Kappa chapter, Robin serves on the Hiram College board of visitors, and was inducted in the Garfield Society of Hiram College in 2005. Additionally, she serves on numerous civic and professional committees.

Robin and her family reside in University Heights, Ohio.

KeyBank

John W. Moody, Jr.
**Executive Vice President
& Regional Credit Executive
KeyBank, N.A.**

Fred A. Cummings
**Managing Director,
Equity Research Department
KeyBank/McDonald Financial Group**

John W. Moody, Jr. is a proven credit executive with 28 years of experience in marketing and credit. He is currently executive vice president and regional credit executive for middle market lending in Northeast Ohio with KeyBank, N.A. He is responsible for managing credit standards in Northeast Ohio's middle market lending units, community development/KCDC, and the public sector nationally.

Previously, he served as senior vice president and credit administration executive for the Cleveland District, community finance, private banking, and the KeyCorp Development Corporation.

In the community, Moody serves as chairman of the City of East Cleveland Financial Planning and Supervision Commission. He is a member of Blacks in Management; a past president and program director of the Northern Ohio Chapter of Robert Morris Associates; and a past trustee of the Cleveland Citywide Development Corporation.

Moody received a bachelor of arts degree in accounting with a minor in finance from Howard University. He attended the Stonier Graduate School of Banking at Rutgers University, and received a certificate in commercial lending from the Colgate Darden School at the University of Virginia.

Since joining McDonald & Company in June of 1989, Fred Cummings has been promoted to managing director in the equity research department. He now leads the financial institution's research group and is responsible for covering 23 banks and thrifts, including all the large banks in Ohio and Michigan for KeyBank/McDonald Financial Group.

Cummings also publishes several widely followed statistical reports on the region's banks and thrifts. He was recognized as one of *The Wall Street Journal's* 1998 All-Star Analysts, ranking first in stock picking and second in estimate accuracy. He was named among 30 Young Leaders of the Future in *Ebony*, and as one of the Future Forty Leaders of Greater Cleveland by *Kaleidoscope Magazine*.

Cummings' professional societies include the Cleveland Society of Security Analysts and the Bank and Financial Analysts' Association. He is a member of the board of directors for INROADS/Northeast Ohio and New Directions, and a trustee for The Ohio Foundation of Independent Colleges and Western Reserve Academy.

A graduate of Western Reserve Academy, Cummings received a bachelor of arts degree from Oberlin College. He is married and has two children.

KeyBank

Karen Currie-Knuckles
Director of Human Resources
KeyCorp

Jacqueline Dalton
Senior Vice President
Program Manager
KeyBank, N.A.

Karen Currie-Knuckles is the director of human resources for the investment and capital markets businesses of KeyCorp. She provides human resources leadership to the executive management team and 3,800 employees. Her primary accountabilities include developing and implementing a human resources strategy that aligns with the business vision and strategy. Karen is also responsible for employee relations, recruitment and retention, compensation, and succession planning.

Karen joined KeyCorp as the human resources manager for McDonald Investments, and her role was expanded to include the asset management and private banking businesses.

Before joining KeyCorp, Karen was human resources manager for LTV Steel Corporation. She also worked at Eaton Corporation and Technicare Corporation.

Karen has an undergraduate degree in business administration from Cleveland State University with a major in accounting. She also has an executive master of business administration degree from Case Western Reserve University.

Karen is on the board of directors of the Northeast Ohio Human Resources Planning Society and serves on the Securities Industry Association's human resources committee.

A Cleveland native, Karen is married, has four children, and resides in Solon, Ohio.

Jackie Dalton is senior vice president, program manager in consumer product management at KeyCorp. In this role, she manages Key@Work, a workplace banking program focusing on the delivery of financial products and services to the employees of Key's small business and commercial banking clients.

Previously, Jackie was district retail leader for KeyBank's Cleveland District. She also played a major role in Key's service quality initiative.

Jackie began her career as a part-time teller and then joined the management associate program. She became a senior vice president in 1999 and was promoted to district retail leader in the Idaho district. She played a significant role in leading the Idaho and Utah teams towards Key's corporate vision and high performance management strategies.

Jackie earned a bachelor's degree in business administration from Cleveland State University, and a master of business administration degree, with a concentration in accounting, from Case Western Reserve University, Weatherhead School of Management. She is a Certified Public Accountant.

Jackie currently serves on the boards of the Cleveland Scholarship Program, Minority Organ Tissue Transplant Education Program, and Health Legacy of Cleveland, amongst others.

KeyBank

Wesley Gillespie
Senior Vice President
Business Banking
KeyBank

As a business banking team leader, Wesley Gillespie's role is to profitably manage and grow the business banking portfolio for KeyBank in the Greater Cleveland District. His role includes recruiting, business development, training, strategic planning, and implementation. Gillespie's team of 13 people is primary responsible for attracting, retaining, and servicing new and existing business banking clients. He is also a member of the Greater Cleveland District Leadership Team for KeyBank.

Prior to joining Key ten years ago, Gillespie was an officer for a large financial institution in Youngstown, Ohio. Raised in Harlem, New York, he earned his bachelor's degree in organizational communication and economics from Youngstown State University.

Gillespie is very involved in his community, and serves as a trustee and executive committee member of Shoes and Clothes for Kids, and a trustee for Boys & Girls Clubs of Cleveland. He truly believes that "to whom much is given, much is required." Giving back to the community is a part of his personal vision statement.

Gillespie currently resides in Cleveland Heights with his wife, Desiree, and their daughter, Selena. He is a member of Providence Baptist Church in Cleveland.

David M. Elbert
Senior Vice President &
Chief Consumer Lending Officer
KeyBank, N.A.

David M. Elbert is senior vice president and chief consumer lending officer of community development banking at KeyBank National Association. He graduated from Clarion State University, receiving a bachelor of science degree in business administration. He is in the process of obtaining a master of business administration degree from John Carroll University.

David has been employed at KeyBank since 1988. He is responsible for the strategic leadership of the community development banking consumer lending group's mortgage and consumer sales activity nationwide. He manages profitability, conducts sales training and marketing seminars, assists with product development and staffing, and adheres to The Office of the Comptroller of the Currency (OCC). KeyBank has received five consecutive Outstanding ratings with the OCC.

Under David's leadership, Key redesigned its flagship low and moderate mortgage lending product (HomeAssist). This HomeAssist Product has been a role model for community development banking across the country.

David is a trustee of the Epilepsy Foundation, board member and matching gift chairman of The College Fund (UNCF), a Cystic Fibrosis committee member, and a member of Urban Bankers.

David lives in Solon, Ohio with his daughter Aliah.

Quentin McCorvey
Vice President
Philanthropic Investments
KeyCorp and Key Foundation

Quentin McCorvey is an administrator, strategist, and community leader with wide range of experiences in governmental, health-care, and nonprofit sectors. He has developed a strong record in communications and community affairs, strategic planning, relationship management, budgeting, program and policy development, and analysis.

Quentin earned a bachelor of arts degree in political science from Jackson State University in 1990. He later earned a master's degree in public administration from Cleveland State University in 1997.

Quentin serves as the vice president of philanthropic investments with KeyCorp and the Key Foundation. He is responsible for measuring the benefits of corporate and foundation grants and recommending optimal uses of funds, in line with the corporation and foundation's focus on economic self-sufficiency.

Quentin is a graduate of the 2002 leadership classes of both Cleveland Bridge Builders and Leadership Ohio, and was inducted into the *Crain's Cleveland Business* Forty Under 40 Club in 2002. He was also inducted into the *Kaleidoscope Magazine* 40/40 Club, Class of 2003.

Quentin is married to Kelli, and they have two small boys, Quentin Jr. and Kyle.

N. Michael Obi
Senior Vice President
Director, Performance Management Business Banking
KeyBank, N.A.

As senior vice president and director of performance manage-ment, Michael Obi is responsible for ensuring the alignment of people, products, processes, and technologies to deliver sustainable client and revenue growth for the business banking segment.

Obi's 15 years of corporate banking background involves diverse leadership roles at KeyBank, where his roles have included national sales director for the business-to-business e-commerce division, vice president, and sales process manager. Prior to joining KeyBank in 1998, he was the vice president and senior finance manager at Bank of America, assistant vice president and decision support manager at Wachovia Bank, and financial analyst at SunTrust Bank.

Obi currently serves on the board of trustees at the Center for Employment Training in Cleveland and the Lyric Opera Cleveland. Additionally, he is the board co-chairman for the Urban League's Multicultural Business Development Center and a member of the advisory board for the National Association of Black MBAs in Cleveland.

Obi obtained both his bachelor's degree in accounting, and his master's degree in business administration at the University of North Florida's Coggin School of Business in Jacksonville, Florida.

Renee Holcomb Hardwick
Senior Vice President, Senior Sales Manager
Financial Advisor
McDonald Investments Inc.

Renee Holcomb Hardwick is a senior sales manager for McDonald Financial Group (MFG).

Most recently, Renee served as a regional manager for the Bank Channel Investment Program. She also coordinated the coaching, mentoring and development of MFG financial advisors and retail bank relationship managers as part of a national initiative to integrate investment and insurance sales at Key.

Renee began her career at Key as a corporate banking trainee and progressed to commercial banking officer, team sales leader, and senior relationship manager. She also served as senior vice president-sales and client manager for MFG, formerly Key PrivateBank.

A Series 7, 9, 10 and 66 licensed financial advisor, Renee holds a bachelor's degree in business administration from Dyke College and a master of business administration degree in finance from Cleveland State University. She also holds a State of Ohio Life, Accident & Health Insurance License.

Renee is a member of Antioch Baptist Church and The Links, Inc., and serves on the board of directors of the Cleveland Pops Orchestra and Health Legacy of Cleveland.

Renee and her husband, Jerome R. Hardwick, reside in Cleveland Heights.

Poppie Parish
Vice President & Officer
KeyBank, N.A.

Poppie Parish is vice president and officer of corporate minority and women's business enterprise development for community development banking for KeyCorp. Parish's primary responsibilities involve assisting minority- and women-owned businesses in competing more effectively as suppliers and contractors for KeyBank.

Parish's experience in supply chain management and supplier diversity were instrumental in solidifying Wendy's International, Inc. and FirstEnergy Corp. as leaders in the area of minority and women business development. She has more than 30 years of diverse business experience.

A Cleveland State University graduate, Parish served as executive board member of the Columbus Regional Minority Supplier Development Council. Likewise, she was a committee chairperson of the National Minority Supplier Development Council, and an executive board member and treasurer of the Cleveland Regional Minority Purchasing Council.

Parish has served as a member of several boards and committees. She serves on the board of the Northern Ohio Minority Business Council, the supplier diversity advisory board for Kent State University, and the advisory board of Firm Foundations Community II.

A native of Cleveland, Parish and her husband Alford, an entrepreneur, reside in Bedford Heights and are the parents of three adult sons.

Corporate Spotlight

Emmanuel T. Glover
Vice President &
Cleveland East Area Retail Leader
KeyBank

Emmanuel T. Glover is vice president and Cleveland East area retail leader in KeyBank's Cleveland District. Emmanuel is responsible for the sales and operations of 16 banking centers with combined deposits and credits outstanding of $1.6 billion. He is also responsible for driving a high performing, client-focused sales culture by coaching and developing 170 sales and service professionals to achieve balance sheet growth, generate revenue growth, and achieve profitability.

Emmanuel has 14 years of banking experience. In addition to his current position of area retail leader, he has held leadership roles as a business development team leader and commercial lending officer.

Emmanuel holds a master of business administration degree and project management training from Baldwin Wallace College, and a bachelor of business administration degree from Eastern Michigan University. He is currently working on a second master of business administration degree at the University of Virginia.

A member of Mt. Zion of Oakwood Village, Emmanuel was inducted into the *Kaleidoscope Magazine* 40/40 Club in 2003, and is a lifetime member of the National Black MBA Association.

His hobbies and interests include sports, movies, music, and traveling.

Shawn Card
Associate
KeyBanc Capital Markets

Shawn Card is an associate in the mergers and acquisitions group of KeyBanc Capital Markets. In this capacity, he focuses on buy-side and sell-side merger and acquisition transactions, corporate divestitures, and financial advisory assignments for public and private companies across a wide range of industries.

Previously, Card served as a senior financial consultant at Wells Fargo, where he worked with the CFO of a subsidiary of Wells Fargo, Servus Financial Corp., in generating and implementing ideas to grow the company. In this capacity, he helped manage the securitization of $540 million in student loan assets.

Before joining Wells Fargo, Card was an associate financial consultant at Pricewaterhouse Coopers (PwC) in the financial advisory services group, serving clients in a broad range of industries. He participated in numerous engagements involving economic damages calculations for commercial litigation disputes and consulting engagements, as well as forensic accounting investigations.

Card graduated from Morehouse College with a bachelor of arts degree in finance. He received his master of business administration degree from the Tuck School of Business at Dartmouth College.

A native of Boston, Massachusetts, Shawn is married to Erica.

Cheryl Willis
Vice President, Area Retail Leader
KeyBank

Margot James Copeland
Executive Vice President-Director Civic Affairs
Executive Vice President-Director Corporate Diversity
KeyCorp

Cheryl Willis is a vice president and area retail leader for KeyBank, overseeing branch system management and sales. As an area retail leader, she has done an exemplary job in turning around her centers, whose performances lead the Northern Ohio market.

Prior to rejoining KeyBank, Cheryl was a vice president in private banking with JP Morgan, where she provided banking and investment services to the bank's premier clients. During her early years with JP Morgan, she was a vice president and multiple branch manager. Her innovative management style and results-based accomplishments made her a recognized leader at the bank. However, Cheryl was no stranger to KeyBank, where, early in her 30-year banking career, she gained valuable experience in retail, credit, private banking, and sales.

Cheryl has served on several nonprofit boards, including Leadership Geauga and Jack and Jill of America. Community giving has always been very important to her. She has volunteered for many initiatives, including the Red Cross, MOTTEP, Habitat for Humanity, the United Way, and KeyBank's Building a Stronger Foundation for the Future.

Margot James Copeland is executive vice president-director of civic affairs and corporate diversity for KeyCorp, one of the nation's largest bank-based multi-line financial services companies. In this role, Margot serves as chair of the Key Foundation and is responsible for managing the company's annual $20 million philanthropic investment program and workforce diversity initiatives. She is the former president and chief executive officer of the Greater Cleveland Roundtable and has served as senior director for Leadership Cleveland.

Former Mayor Michael R. White appointed Margot vice chairperson of the 1996 Bicentennial Commission and subsequently to the Cleveland Millennium Commission. *New Cleveland Woman* magazine named her one of the "100 Most Powerful Women in Cleveland." Additionally, she has been featured in *Crain's Cleveland Business* as a "Cleveland Woman of Influence" and recognized by *SBN* magazine as a "Master Innovator."

Margot is active in community organizations including the Thomas White Foundation, Kenneth Scott Foundation, and The Great Lakes Museum of Science, as well as many others.

Corporate Spotlight

Erbert Johnson, CPA
Senior Vice President
Director, Public Finance
KeyBanc Capital Markets

Erbert Johnson has more than 25 years of business experience. Currently, he holds the position of senior vice president/director of KeyBanc Capital Markets. He is responsible for advising public entities in Ohio and nationally on raising capital through bond offerings for facility expansion and ongoing operations. He holds the General Securities Registered Representative Licenses (Series 7 and Series 63).

Before accepting his position at Key, Johnson served as the top financial officer at the largest school districts in Ohio and Wisconsin for ten years. Previously, he held positions of increasing responsibility in financial services after beginning his career as an auditor at KPMG Peat Marwick.

Johnson is a Certified Public Accountant (CPA) and holds a bachelor's degree in business administration with a major in accounting from the University of Wisconsin at Madison.

A past chairman of the Milwaukee Public Debt Commission, Johnson currently serves on the Cleveland Hearing and Speech Center board. He is also a member of the Cleveland State University-Maxine Goodman Levin College of Urban Affairs visiting committee.

Johnson is married with two children. He enjoys bike riding and wine collecting.

Michelle S. Rochon
Senior Vice President
Talent Acquisition and Employment Services
KeyCorp

Michelle S. Rochon is senior vice president of talent acquisition and employment services at KeyCorp. In her role, she leads a team of talent acquisition managers and specialists that have responsibility for sourcing, attracting, assessing, and selecting top talent to fill positions at Key. Michelle's goal is to build a talent acquisition culture at Key.

Michelle joined KeyCorp as a vice president and manager in organization development in 1999. She was promoted to senior vice president in 2001 and has held various managerial positions in organization development.

Prior to joining Key, Michelle worked at General Electric. She supported, and was promoted to, increasingly responsible roles in human resources and lines of business including sales, distribution, and finance.

Michelle is an active member of the Cleveland Chapter of the National Black MBA and a board member (at large) for the Cleveland Rape Crisis Center.

Michelle holds a bachelor's degree in marketing from Notre Dame College of Ohio and a master's degree in organization development and analysis from Case Western Reserve University.

Michelle resides in Beachwood, Ohio and is the proud parent of three adult children.

KeyBank

Corporate Spotlight

Jannie M. Blunt
Vice President
KeyBank/McDonald Financial Group

Mary A. Fox
Vice President
District Operations Leader
KeyBank

As vice president of KeyBank/McDonald Financial Group, Jannie Blunt earned her trusted advisor status as the primary contact through relationship management of 200 clients, with an aggregate balance of $131 million. Under her leadership, an integrated team of specialists structure financial plans that provide for the creation, growth, and preservations of wealth for families and businesses.

Jannie began her career with KeyBank in the personal trust division. Over the years, she has held positions of increasingly challenging responsibilities in the area of personal relationship management.

In 1995, Case Western Reserve University awarded her a master's degree in business. She holds the designations of certified trust and financial advisor, registered representative Series 7 and 66, and Ohio licensed insurance agent.

Jannie has focused her energy on numerous community services and board activities throughout the years. She currently serves on the boards of The Nature Center at Shaker Lakes, Family Transitional Housing, The Club at Key Tower, and the Wedgewood Golf Association.

A New Orleans native, Jannie is a member of Antioch Baptist Church and a blessed mother and grandmother. She resides in University Heights, Ohio.

Mary Fox is vice president and district operations leader for 36 KeyCenters in the Cleveland District of KeyBank. She is responsible for ensuring operational procedures are in compliance, assisting employees with complex issues, maintaining client satisfaction, and supporting the sales process and revenue generation.

Mary joined Society Bank as a branch bookkeeper in 1968. She earned several promotions and participated in the management associate training program in 1977. She was elected an officer of the bank and branch manager in 1980 and was eventually elected vice president in 1989.

Mary holds a bachelor of science degree in business administration from Baldwin-Wallace College. She has also completed courses at the American Institute of Banking and various in-house training classes offered by KeyBank.

Mary has served as second vice president of the board of directors for the Girl Scouts of Lake Erie Council and chaired its fund, development, and diversity committees. A recipient of the Girl Scouts' top honor, the Thanks Badge, Mary received the YWCA's Women of Professional Excellence Award in 1999.

Mary serves on the board of trustees and is a choir member at Mt. Pleasant United Methodist Church.

UniversityHospitals HealthSystem

University Hospitals of Cleveland

CORPORATE SPOTLIGHT

Karen L. Ashby, M.D.
Obstetrician/Gynecologist
MacDonald Women's Hospital

Karen L. Ashby, M.D. is an obstetrician and gynecologist at University Hospitals of Cleveland's MacDonald Women's Hospital and assistant professor of reproductive biology at Case Western Reserve University. She serves as director of the OB/GYN clerkship program and is a liaison for family practice residents.

Dr. Ashby received her bachelor's degree from Princeton University, where she graduated cum laude. She earned her medical degree from Case Western Reserve University and completed a residency in internal medicine at Cornell University. She then completed her OB/GYN residency program at Mt. Sinai Medical Center in Cleveland. While at Mt. Sinai, Dr. Ashby was the OB/GYN student clerkship director.

Dr. Ashby has co-authored journal articles and has presented at major scientific meetings. She is a highly requested lecturer on such women's issues as hormone replacement therapy and menopause.

Edward N. Burney, M.D.
Director of Glaucoma Service
University Hospitals of Cleveland

Edward N. Burney, M.D., is a professor of ophthalmology at Case Western Reserve University, the director of ophthalmology at the Cleveland Veterans' Administration Medical Center, and the director of glaucoma service at University Hospitals of Cleveland.

In 1983, Dr. Burney began his residency in ophthalmology at University Hospitals Health System, the Veterans Administration Medical Center, and MetroHealth System, where he served as administrative super chief. Upon graduation, he joined the UHHS staff as a general ophthalmologist. Dr. Burney completed a glaucoma fellowship at the Wilmer Eye Institute of The Johns Hopkins University, and has served as subsection chairman of the Glaucoma Section of the National Medical Association for three years.

Dr. Burney has been named to Northeast Ohio's "Top Doc's List," listed in the *Best Doctors in America, 6th Edition*, and was awarded *American Legacy Magazine's* Professional Achievement and Project Focus Healthcare Awards. In addition to other honors, he was inducted into the Cleveland Educators and Alumni Achievers Hall of Fame.

Dr. Burney earned a bachelor's degree from Ohio Dominican College, graduating first in his honors pre-med class, and a doctor of medicine degree from Case Western Reserve University.

Jannifer Harper, M.D., a member of the administrative leadership team at University Hospitals of Cleveland, plays a key role in physician oversight of credentialing, risk management, case management, and preparedness for the Joint Commission on Accreditation of Healthcare Organizations. Additionally, she is involved in quality improvement programs and patient safety.

Her career includes nearly 20 years of leadership experience in medicine. She began her career in 1984 as a general internist with Ohio Permanente Medical Group, where she held positions of increasing responsibility until being named regional chief of medicine in 1993. After serving for two years in this capacity, Dr. Harper accepted an appointment to vice president and medical director for CIGNA HealthCare for the North Central Region. In 1999, Dr. Harper was promoted to vice president and regional medical director for CIGNA HealthCare's Midwest Region.

Prior to joining University Hospitals of Cleveland, she served as medical director for The Medical Group of Ohio and OhioHealth Group.

Dr. Harper holds a doctor of medicine degree from Case Western Reserve University School of Medicine and is board certified in internal medicine.

Jannifer Drake Harper, M.D.
Vice President and
Associate Chief Medical Officer
University Hospitals of Cleveland

Howard R. Hall, III, Ph.D., Psy.D. is a pediatric behavioral psychologist at Rainbow Babies & Children's Hospital.

Dr. Hall holds two doctorate degrees in psychology; a Ph.D. in experimental psychology from Princeton University, and a Psy.D. in clinical psychology from Rutgers University. He completed an internship at Rutgers Medical School, and post-doctoral and fellowship studies in the area of substance abuse prevention at Rutgers University and Case Western Reserve University.

A special medical interest of Dr. Hall is to study the effect of hypnosis on children. He has reported successful results helping children overcome pain, chronic coughs, anxiety, headaches, sleep problems, and bed-wetting at Rainbow Babies & Children's Hospital.

For the past two decades, Dr. Hall has also conducted and published pioneering work on the effects of hypnosis on immune responses. His current research is on the Sufi (Islamic Mysticism) Middle Eastern paranormal rapid wound healing phenomena.

Dr. Hall is married with two daughters in college. A jazz pianist, Howard Hall is the band leader of Jazz Circle, an ensemble of a few University Hospitals employees who play in the UH atrium at lunchtime on Thursdays.

Howard R. Hall, III,
Ph.D., Psy.D.
Pediatric Behavioral Psychologist
Rainbow Babies & Children's Hospital

Carla M. Harwell, M.D.
Medical Director, Otis Moss, Jr.
University Hospitals Medical Center

Dr. Carla M. Harwell is the medical director of the Otis Moss, Jr. University Hospitals Medical Center and assistant professor of medicine at Case Western Reserve University.

The Otis Moss, Jr.~ University Hospitals Medical Center offers primary care services to many Fairfax community residents in Cleveland as well as the greater Cleveland community. Since completing her residency training, Dr. Harwell has served as medical director, with a special interest in reducing the health care disparities that exist in the African-American community.

A Cleveland native, Dr. Harwell joined University Hospitals of Cleveland in 1995 as an internal medicine resident. She holds a bachelor of science degree in biology, a bachelor of arts degree in psychology, and a medical degree, all from the University of Cincinnati.

During medical school, Dr. Harwell was a participant in the David Satcher Clerkship, a program for minority medical students that introduces them to University Hospitals. Not only did she return to Cleveland for her medical residency, but Dr. Harwell now also serves as director of that program.

Dr. Harwell serves on numerous boards and has been the recipient of several awards.

John J. Jasper, M.D.
General Surgeon
University Hospitals of Cleveland

John J. Jasper, M.D., is a board-certified general surgeon at University Hospitals of Cleveland, specializing in bariatric surgery. He also serves on the faculty at Case Western Reserve University and is the medical student clerkship director at Cleveland's VA Medical Center.

After receiving his medical degree from the University of Minnesota Medical School, Dr. Jasper completed his medical internship and residency at University Hospitals of Cleveland. Prior to embarking on his career in medicine, Dr. Jasper put his undergraduate degrees in electrical engineering and physics to good use in his work as an electrical engineer.

Besides bariatric surgery, Dr. Jasper's special interests include general, breast, and advanced laparoscopic surgery. He is a member of the American College of Surgeons.

Deforia Lane, Ph.D. is the director of music therapy at the Ireland Cancer Center at University Hospitals of Cleveland. She completed her bachelor's degree in vocal performance at the University of Cincinnati College-Conservatory of Music and began graduate studies at the Curtis Institute of Music. She attended Cleveland State University for her master's degree and earned her Ph.D. in music education from Case Western Reserve University. She holds board certification as a music therapist and faculty authorization from the American Music Therapy Association.

Dr. Lane has designed and implemented music therapy programs for diverse populations. Among the institutions that she has served as a consultant are the Ohio Department of Mental Health, the Mayo Clinic, and the National Department on Aging.

Dr. Lane is distinguished by her ability to empathize with her clients because of her personal struggle with cancer. She is married to Cleveland architect Ernest Luther Lane, and they have two sons, Curtis and Martin.

Dr. Lane lectures throughout the medical and educational communities. She has authored several articles in scholarly nursing journals, and Zondervan Publishers released her autobiography and a video entitled *Music as Medicine*.

Deforia Lane, Ph.D.
Director of Music Therapy
Ireland Cancer Center
University Hospitals of Cleveland

Dr. Lolita McDavid came to Rainbow Babies & Children's Hospital (Rainbow) as the medical director of child advocacy and protection in 1996. She is known throughout Ohio for her campaigns to prevent child abuse and special programming to educate parents on discipline and safety. Dr. McDavid coordinates the medical services in Rainbow's Child Protection Unit, serving at-risk children and families in Northeast Ohio.

From 1991 to 1995, she directed the Greater Cleveland Project of the Children's Defense Fund (CDF). The project was the first county-based advocacy effort in the country for the national Children's Defense Fund. Prior to her work with CDF, Dr. McDavid was head of general pediatrics at MetroHealth Medical Center.

Dr. McDavid is a member of the board of trustees of Miami University, the Cleveland Institute of Music, the March of Dimes, and the Center for Child Health Research of the American Academy of Pediatrics. She sits on two advisory boards of the Robert Wood Johnson Foundation and serves as a consultant to the Health Resources and Services Administration in the U.S. Department of Health and Human Services.

Lolita M. McDavid,
M.D., M.P.A.
Medical Director
Child Advocacy and Protection
Rainbow Babies & Children's Hospital

University Hospitals of Cleveland

Barby R. Smith, R.N., A.C.N.
Advanced Clinical Nurse
University Hospitals of Cleveland

Barby R. Smith is a registered nurse and advanced clinical nurse for University Hospitals of Cleveland and the service manager for the hospital's department of urology.

Ms. Smith began her career in healthcare as a licensed practical nurse with the Highland View Rehabilitation Hospital in Warrensville, Ohio. She worked in this capacity for ten years. Ms. Smith joined University Hospitals of Cleveland in 1969, where she now serves as an operating room nurse.

Ms. Smith earned her licensed practical nurse certification from Jane Adams School of Practical Nursing in Cleveland, and an associate of science degree in nursing from Cuyahoga Community College.

Ms. Smith is the chair of the Minority Nurse Forum and has presented conferences on African-American history and breast cancer at University Hospitals of Cleveland and throughout the community. She has served as a team leader for University Hospitals' Race for the Cure and United Way campaigns.

Ms. Smith is a professional photographer and jewelry designer. She is also an avid writer of poetry, fiction, and non-fiction manuscripts. She is a member of the Cleveland Council of Black Nurses, the Urological Nursing Organization, and the Jehovah's Witnesses.

Jackson T. Wright, Jr., M.D., Ph.D.
Director
Clinical Hypertension Programs
University Hospitals of Cleveland

Jackson T. Wright, Jr., M.D., Ph.D. is director of the clinical hypertension programs at University Hospitals of Cleveland and the Louis Stokes Cleveland Veterans Administration Medical Center. He also serves as program director of the General Clinical Research Center at Case Western Reserve University (Case), where he is also professor of medicine.

A native of Pittsburgh, Dr. Wright earned a bachelor of arts degree from Ohio Wesleyan University and was the first black to earn an M.D./Ph.D. (Pharmacology) from the University of Pittsburgh School of Medicine. His house staff training in internal medicine was performed at the University of Michigan. Prior to moving to Case and University Hospitals of Cleveland in 1990, he served on the clinical pharmacology faculty for ten years at the Medical College of Virginia.

Since the early 1990s, Dr. Wright has had a major or leadership role in nearly all major studies evaluating the effects of various treatment in reducing hypertension and cardiovascular complications in black populations. His hypertension research is published extensively in more than 220 articles, book chapters, and abstracts, and he serves on many national and international advisory committees.

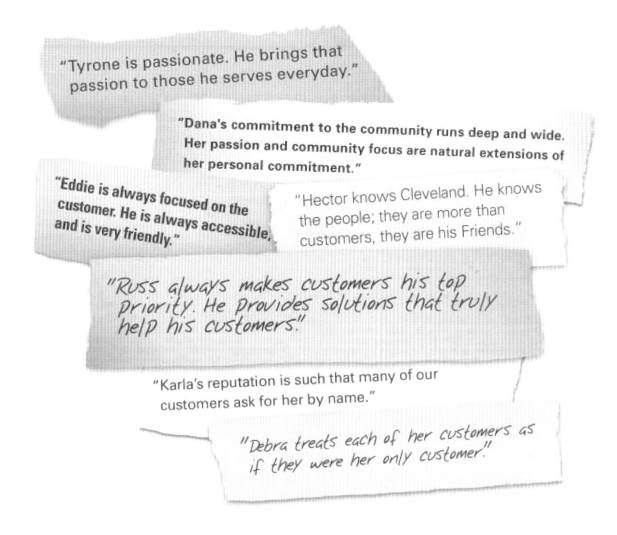

"Tyrone is passionate. He brings that passion to those he serves everyday."

"Dana's commitment to the community runs deep and wide. Her passion and community focus are natural extensions of her personal commitment."

"Eddie is always focused on the customer. He is always accessible, and is very friendly."

"Hector knows Cleveland. He knows the people; they are more than customers, they are his Friends."

"Russ always makes customers his top priority. He provides solutions that truly help his customers."

"Karla's reputation is such that many of our customers ask for her by name."

"Debra treats each of her customers as if they were her only customer."

WE COULDN'T HAVE SAID IT BETTER OURSELVES.

The Huntington associates being honored this year exemplify our core values in action. Their hard work and passion truly makes Cleveland a better place.

A bank invested in people.

 **Huntington**

huntington.com

Hector J. Allen
Vice President, Business Banking
Huntington National Bank

Dana M. Capers
Vice President of Community Development
Huntington National Bank

Hector Allen is vice president/community banking executive for Huntington. In his various positions at Huntington, his responsibilities have included assignments in community and government affairs, business banking and retail management. During his 25-plus years in banking, Hector's primary focus has centered around economic and community development objectives. He has been proactively involved in the Greater Cleveland community working extensively with Cleveland-area small businesses, not-for-profits, the local Community Development Corporation, and state and local government agencies promoting economic development.

Hector served a five-year term as president for the National Minority College Golf Scholarship Fund, an organization that provides golf scholarships at black colleges and universities. He is also a graduate of the Bank Administration Institute.

Hector has served on numerous community boards including the Beaumont School, United Negro College Fund, Hough Area Partners for Progress, Buckeye Woodland Community Development Corporation, Cleveland Action to Support Housing, Friendly Inn Settlement, The Cuyahoga Plan, Eliza Bryant, First Tee, United Way Associate Cabinet, United Way Allocations Panel, United Way Loaned Executive, Blacks In Management, and Urban Bankers.

Hector and his wife, Martha, and two daughters reside on the Eastside of Cleveland.

Dana M. Capers is vice president and community development specialist for Huntington National Bank, where she coordinates and manages community development initiatives for the Northern Ohio Region. Her responsibilities include working with the bank's lines of businesses to ensure the delivery of financial products and services to the low-to moderate-income community, maintaining dialogue with government officials and community leaders.

Committed to community involvement, Dana serves on the executive boards of the Cleveland/Cuyahoga County Workforce Investment Board, the Fairfax Renaissance Development Corporation, and Neighborhood Housing Services of Greater Cleveland. She is also a member of Abundant Grace Fellowship and Delta Sigma Theta Sorority, Inc., and is a graduate of the Cleveland Bridge Builders Class of 2005. She has been recognized as Cleveland Youth Council Member of the Year, a YWCA Woman of Professional Excellence, and as a member of the *Kaleidoscope Magazine* 40/40 Club.

Dana holds a master's degree in urban studies from Cleveland State University and a bachelor's degree in organizational communication from Ohio University.

She resides in Bedford Heights with her husband, Marty Capers, and daughter, Tara.

Huntington

Russell L. Edwards
Vice President, Retail Market Manager
Huntington National Bank

Karla M. Hatchett
Investment Officer, Institutional Sales
Huntington Capital Corp.

Russell L. Edwards is vice president, retail market manager of Huntington National Bank. In this position, Russell is responsible for 16 banking offices and more than 100 associates in the East Cleveland market. He leads his team of bankers in implementing retail and business banking strategy that maximizes the efforts to deliver outstanding customer service, sales results, as well as individual professional growth.

Russell is a graduate of Central State University in Wilberforce, Ohio with a bachelor of arts degree in political science.

A Cleveland native, Russell began his banking career as a collector with Bank One in 1991. In 1993, Russell joined Chemical Financial Services Corporation, later renamed Chase Financial Corporation, where he earned several promotions. In 1998, Russell pursued a sales career with Pitney Bowes Office Systems, and in 1999, he returned to banking with Firstar Bank. Recognized as one of Firstar's top branch managers, he was promoted to business banking officer in 2002. Russell came to Huntington National Bank in November of 2002.

Russell and his wife, Catherine, and two daughters, Taylor and Charisma, reside on the Eastside of Cleveland.

Karla Hatchett is an investment officer and a 25-year associate of Huntington Bancshares, Inc. Working with institutional investors, Karla's primary responsibilities include processing security trades, staying abreast of market conditions, maintaining confidential client information, and providing outstanding customer service.

Karla has served as a loaned executive to United Way. She is a supporter of and volunteers at the Renee Jones Empowerment Center and is a reading buddy for a children's reading program. Likewise, she has prepared and served meals for the needy and currently assists with a personal care program for shelters. Karla is also a member of the Church of Christ where she enjoys teaching Sunday school classes.

Karla graduated summa cum laude from Baldwin-Wallace College with a bachelor of arts degree in business administration. She also holds Series 7 & 63 licenses from the NASD.

Karla and her husband, Warren Hatchett, are the parents of Darnell and Crystal and grandparents to Starr and Damien.

Debra M. Keene
Assistant Vice President & Trust Officer
Private Financial Group
Huntington National Bank

Tyrone Price
Senior Staffing Manager
Huntington National Bank

Debra M. Keene is an assistant vice president and trust officer in the Private Financial Group of Huntington National Bank, with more than 25 years of experience in the financial services industry. Her current fiduciary responsibilities include the administration of trusts, estates, and investment management accounts for high net worth individuals and their families. Prior to Huntington, she worked at Key Bank as an officer for many years, with experience in retail services, operations, as well as trust.

Civic involvement for Debra has included tutoring, mentoring and assisting with AIDS awareness programs. She is a church board member and volunteers for a variety of community organizations.

Debra holds a bachelor of business administration degree with a major in marketing from Notre Dame College of Ohio. She is also a graduate of Cannon Personal Trust and Ohio Midwest Trust Schools. Debra and her nephew reside on the Eastside of Cleveland. She enjoys gardening, tennis and golf.

Tyrone Price is the senior staffing manager for Huntington National Bank, Northern Ohio region. In this position, he manages and recruits for all levels of positions. Tyrone is very involved within the Cleveland community; he currently sits on the Catholic Charities board, and networks with the City of Cleveland's One Stop job programs. Tyrone also volunteers his time mentoring children.

Tyrone is known throughout the city of Cleveland as a leader and someone who is committed to helping others achieve their goals in finding job opportunities.

Tyrone received a bachelor of arts degree from Baldwin-Wallace College in 1997. While attending college, he was twice named a pre-season All-American in football.

A native of Fremont, Ohio, Tyrone and his wife, Lisa Price, are the proud parents of three sons and one daughter. Both are highly active in their children's school and sports activities.

Eddie Strattonbey is vice president and general manager of Huntington's Main Banking Office in downtown Cleveland. He is responsible for the leadership of a team of professionals dedicated to serving individual and business clients in all aspects of financial services. This is accomplished by providing advice, products, solutions and outstanding service every day.

Eddie and his team have received numerous awards as one of Huntington's top performing banking offices.

A graduate of Whiting Business College, Eddie is a board member of East End Neighborhood House and board chairman of the Liberty Hill Baptist Church investment committee.

Eddie is a native of Cleveland, where he continues to reside with his wife Kim and daughter Kathryn.

Eddie Strattonbey
Vice President & General Manager
Huntington National Bank, Main Office

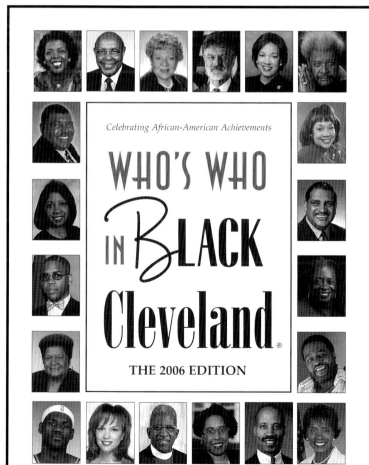

Order Additional Copies:

$24.95 Plus $8.00 S/H
A Great Gift Idea

Order Online:
www.whoswhopublishing.com

All Credit Cards Accepted

Or Call
(614) 481-7300

Please call to inquire about bulk purchases for youth groups, schools, churches, civic or professional organizations.

Last Year, These Tickets Turned Into Over 645 Million Dollars For Ohio's Public Schools.

For over 30 years, the Ohio Lottery has provided more than just fun.
We've helped Ohio and Ohioans in millions of ways.

Odds Are, You'll Have Fun.

CORPORATE SPOTLIGHT

Leon Bibb
Anchor, *Live On Five*
WEWS/NewsChannel5

The first African-American anchor in Ohio, Leon Bibb has delivered the news since he was 11, when he was a paperboy for Cleveland's newspaper. Now, he co-anchors *Live On Five* and narrates *Your Hometown*, short programs about the people and renaissance of the Northeast Ohio community.

A veteran journalist and broadcaster, Leon held several positions at WKYC-TV 3, Cleveland's NBC affiliate, after joining the station in 1979. Prior to that, Leon was a weekday anchor and reporter for WCMH in Columbus and a news reporter at WTOL in Toledo. He began his journalism career as a news reporter for *The Plain Dealer*.

Some of Leon's honors include an Emmy Award for *Cleveland Images*; induction into the Broadcasters Hall of Fame; the Distinguished Journalist Award from the Cleveland chapter of the Society for Professional Journalists; and a Bronze Star for his service in Vietnam.

In 1996, Governor Voinovich appointed him to the board of trustees at Bowling Green State University, where he is the current chairman.

A graduate of Bowling Green State University, Leon lives with his wife, Marguerite, in Shaker Heights. His daughters, Jennifer and Alison, are grown.

Danita Harris
Anchor, *Good Morning Cleveland*
WEWS/NewsChannel5

In 1998, Danita Harris came to NewsChannel5 and became a part of the *Morning Exchange*, where she did live feature reports. She was also seen on *Good Morning Cleveland*, doing her "Danita's Dish" segments.

Danita then moved to WJLA-TV in Washington, D.C., where she anchored the news on weekends and did entertainment reports during the week. Her love of the Cleveland area brought her back to WEWS in 2000, when she stepped into the anchor position for *Good Morning Cleveland* and *NewsChannel5 at Noon*. She also writes a monthly column for *Blessings Magazine*.

Before joining the *Morning Exchange,* Danita worked at Black Entertainment Television. A Chester, Pennsylvania native, she is a graduate of the University of Maryland, where she majored in broadcast journalism.

Danita is a board advisor for the Girls Club of Ohio, and an executive board member of the Northeast Ohio Region chapter of the Fellowship of Christian Athletes. Further, she is a member of Delta Sigma Theta Sorority, Inc. and the National Council of Negro Women, in addition to numerous other organizations. What is foremost in her life is her faith in God.

Jeff grew up outside of Cleveland in Mentor, Ohio. His fascination with lake-effect snow spawned his interest in weather, but it wasn't until later in his career that he discovered he was passionate about weather.

He attended the University of Toledo and received a bachelor's degree in broadcast communications in 1997. His first job was behind the scenes for seven years, working on everything from driving live trucks, to being a technical director for newscasts.

While working behind the scenes, he realized his love for weather and decided to go back to school. He attended Mississippi State University and finished his courses in the broadcast meteorology program.

In 2003, Jeff relocated to Lansing, Michigan at WLNS, where he worked as a weather anchor and reporter. When he was not filling in for the other meteorologists, he reported on the daily news.

He is proud to come back home to serve the community where he was raised. In his spare time, Jeff likes to play recreational sports and go running with his dog, Zach.

Jeff Mackel
Doppler 5000 Meteorologist
WEWS/NewsChannel5

Chris Miller joined NewsChannel5 in June of 2001 as a weekend sports anchor, and in 2003 was named sports director/main sports anchor at the station.

In 2003, Chris was the first sideline reporter for CSTV College Sports TV Network. Before coming to Cleveland, Chris served as sports director/main sports anchor at KGAN-TV (CBS) in Cedar Rapids, Iowa. There, he covered the University of Iowa and won the Associated Press Award for Best Sports Program for a 30-minute show during Midnight Madness.

In Iowa, Chris worked for two years as a regional sideline reporter for ESPN during the college football season, covering the Big Ten Conference.

Chris graduated from Indiana State University in 1996, majoring in radio/TV/film. His first job was at WTHI-TV (CBS) in Terre Haute, IN, where he was a sports reporter, producer, photographer, and fill-in anchor (he also ran the teleprompter for a while). Basically, Chris did everything but the plumbing.

Although he grew up in Winston-Salem, NC, and considers himself a Tar Heel, Chris, his wife Kalina, and their six children love calling Cleveland their home.

Chris Miller
Sports Director/Anchor
WEWS/NewsChannel5

Curtis Jackson
Weekend Anchor
WEWS/NewsChannel5

C urtis Jackson is the weekend anchor for NewsChannel5 at 6 p.m. and 11 p.m. He started his duties in March of 2005.

Before coming to WEWS, Curtis was the New York-based correspondent for *BET Nightly News*. While at BET, he was a finalist for the NABJ Salute to Excellence Awards for a series of reports on HIV rates in the southern states. The Kaiser Foundation awarded him a grant for his coverage.

Before joining BET, Curtis was the weekend anchor for WFXT in Boston. He anchored the station's coverage of the crash of TWA Flight 800 and the death of several firefighters in Worcester, Massachusetts.

On September 11, 2001, Curtis was sent to interview the victims' loved ones when two flights from Boston hit the World Trade Center towers in New York.

Curtis has also held anchor and reporting positions in Hartford, Connecticut and his hometown of Louisville, Kentucky.

In his spare time, Curtis enjoys playing with his son, Tre, and playing jazz standards and Stevie Wonder songs on the piano. He lives with his wife and son in the Cleveland area.

Debora Lee
Education Specialist
WEWS/NewsChannel5

D ebora Lee was born in Wheeling, West Virginia and attended colleges in both West Virginia and New Jersey. After more than a decade at WEWS, however, Deb proudly calls Cleveland her home.

She has won numerous local and national journalism awards including the National Headliner, a Cleveland Emmy, and a 2000 NABJ (National Association of Broadcast Journalists) award.

In her spare time, you may find Deb at an oldies concert, a local sporting event, or on a plane to the West Coast to visit her daughter Candace.

Tony Gaskins has been a reporter with NewsChannel5 since 1987. Before coming to NewsChannel5, Tony worked in Syracuse as a reporter, and he anchored the weekend news. He began his career in Harrisburg, Pennsylvania in 1976, as a reporter and weekend public affairs radio show host. In Syracuse, Tony anchored a weekday award-winning newscast before moving into television.

Tony won an Emmy award in 1989 for an Underground Railroad special. He tracked the path slaves followed from the South to Ohio and into Canada.

Tony attended Harrisburg Area Community College and majored in communications and photography. He enjoys biking, weight lifting, and reading, and he is a member of the Cleveland National Association of Black Journalists.

Tony Gaskins
Government Specialist
WEWS/NewsChannel5

Jonathan Costen is proud to call Akron home after working in four television markets, climbing the ladder to the Cleveland-Akron market.

He began his career on the assignment desk at WSB, a powerhouse radio station in Atlanta. After earning a bachelor's degree in journalism and political science from Georgia State University, Jonathan worked for television newsrooms in Augusta, Georgia; Chattanooga, Tennessee; Birmingham, Alabama; and Norfolk, Virginia.

In 1999, Jonathan came to NewsChannel5 to work in the Akron bureau. He provides live reports from the Summit County region each day for *Good Morning Cleveland*. He also reports from Cleveland.

Jonathan covers a variety of serious, breaking news stories for WEWS, but is also well known for human interest stories and his amazing sense of humor. He enjoys rehabilitating his charming Akron home.

Jonathan Costen
Akron Bureau Reporter
WEWS/NewsChannel5

Black United Fund of Ohio
"The Helping Hand That Is Your Own"

"We have a responsibility to lead
in our own growth and development."
- Black United Fund Co-Founder, Walter Bremond

History

Over 30 years ago, the founders of the Black United Fund organized the Brotherhood Crusade to gather financial resources to build a better community in the Watts section of Los Angeles. Rather than waiting for help from people or agencies outside of their community, neighbors pooled their money and time and created after school programs, small businesses, programs to feed the poor and care for the elderly.

Since then, the National Black United Fund has spread across the country, raised tens of millions of dollars, and empowered many thousands to change their lives for the better. Today, the National Black United Fund has 20 affiliates in 18 states from Oregon to Florida. Everywhere the mission is the same. Be "The Helping Hand That Is Your Own."

Our Mission

Black United Fund of Ohio's mission is to create, support and sustain African American social, economic, cultural and educational institutions through the enhancement of African American philanthropy. Black United Fund participates in community development by helping local leaders organize and structure the vehicles for accessing new charitable dollars and expanding opportunities for giving. Payroll deduction is a primary method.

What We Do

The Black United Fund of Ohio participates in payroll deduction campaigns at all federal, state, county, city government offices, as well as, The Ohio State University and the Columbus Metropolitan Library. Black United Fund of Ohio opens up new sites each year where workers can direct their tax-deductible contributions to organizations that serve their communities' distinct needs. Opportunities to give through payroll deduction kick off in the early Fall of each year.

Black United Fund of Ohio is also a federation of non-profit agencies that serve many critical human needs, such as low and moderate home ownership, independent schools, business development, programs for the homeless, alcohol and drug abuse prevention among others.

In 1980, after eight years of litigation, the National Black United Fund prevailed and won admission to the Combined Federal Campaign (CFC) for federal workers. This effort led to the admission of some 800 organizations to the CFC and set the precedent for formerly excluded local organizations to participate in municipal and state employee payroll deduction campaigns.

Support Black United Fund of Ohio!
To make a contribution or, to become a new site for employee deduction donations, please call (614) 252-0888.

Members agencies across the state include Africentric Personal Development Shop. Avondale Redevelopment Corporation, Central Ohio Minority Business Association, Central State University Foundation, Christian Community Development Corporation. Columbus Area, Inc, Fountain of Hope, Greater Linden Development Corporation, Isabelle Ridgway Care Center, Jireh Services, Inc, Just For Today, MiraCit Development Corporation, Mt. Vernon Avenue Area District Improvement Association, NCBC Human Services Corporation, Northwest Ohio Black Chamber of Commerce, Omega Community Development Corporation, Prince Hall Scholarship Foundation, Sankofa Youth Entertainment, Sonshine Christian Academy, Take It To The Streets, Urban Cultural Arts Foundation, Walnut Hills Redevelopment Foundation.

Photos: Top - Kindergarten graduates at Black United Fund of Ohio member agency, Sonshine Christian Academy. Right - Mayor Michael Coleman admonishes youngsters to do their best at the Black United Fund of Ohio's annual school supply give-away and back to school program.

Cleveland Browns
are proud to support
Who's Who in Black Cleveland!

CLEVELANDBROWNS.COM

Celebrating African-American Achievements

Jerry Butler
Director, Player Development
Cleveland Browns

Romeo Crennel
Head Coach
Cleveland Browns

Jerry Butler is in his seventh year with the Browns and fifth year as the team's director of player development. Butler coached the Browns wide receivers from 1999 to 2000.

The player development department provides a wide range of league-sponsored programs designed to meet the needs of players and their families that set a standard of excellence promoting growth and balance in all areas of their lives. Players are provided assistance in life skills training, continuing education, financial education, career internships, entrepreneurship training, and player assistance services. Butler earned the NFL Winton-Shell Award for innovation and commitment to player development for the 2003-2004 season.

Butler was one of the NFL's most productive receivers during his playing career. When he retired from the Buffalo Bills, he held several of the club's all-time receiving marks, including two which still stand – most receiving yards in a game and most touchdowns in a game. Buffalo's first-round draft choice in 1979, Butler received numerous accolades, including recognition as the AFC Offensive Rookie of the Year. He earned a Pro Bowl selection in 1980.

Butler and his wife, Paula, have two children, Jerry and Chrissy.

Romeo Crennel was named head coach of the Cleveland Browns on February 8, 2005, the 11th full-time head coach in franchise history. Crennel returns to Cleveland after serving as the Browns defensive coordinator in 2000. He recently crafted the defense for the New England Patriots, helping them to win a Super Bowl in three of the last four seasons (2001, 2003-04).

Recognized as one of the top assistant coaches in the NFL, Crennel's resume includes 35 years of coaching experience, including 24 years in the NFL. He began his professional coaching career in 1981 with the New York Giants. In 12 seasons (1981-92), the Giants qualified for the playoffs six times, won three division titles and two Super Bowl championships. Crennel then served as the defensive line coach for the Patriots (1993 to 1996), spent three seasons with the New York Jets (1997-1999), and a season as the defensive coordinator with the Cleveland Browns (2000).

A Lynchburg, Virginia native, Crennel earned his bachelor's and master's degrees from Western Kentucky. He and his wife, Rosemary, have three daughters, Lisa Tulley, Tiffany Stokes, and Kristin Cullinane.

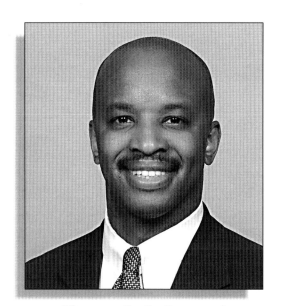

Kenneth A. Louard
Chief Legal Counsel
Cleveland Browns

Jacquelyn "Jakki" Nance, Esq.
President
The Cleveland Browns Foundation

Kenneth A. Louard is the chief legal counsel for the Cleveland Browns. In his current position, he negotiates, constructs, and reviews business contracts of various sizes, performs legal analysis, oversees litigation and other legal matters, and participates as a principal in vendor negotiations. Previously, he served as the director of business operations for the organization.

Louard moved to Cleveland in 1995 to become the chief operating officer of Lakefront Capital Investors, Inc., a minority-owned asset management company.

Previously, he served at Andrews and Kurth LLP and Dean Witter Reynolds, both located in New York City.

Committed to enhancing the communities in which he lives and works, Louard serves on the boards of Recovery Resources, the West Side Ecumenical Ministry, and the Northeast Conference for Community and Justice Inc. Likewise, he is on the boards of the Columbia University School of Social Work V. Benjamin and Agnes A. Louard Scholarship Fund and the Berea Chamber of Commerce.

Louard received a bachelor of arts degree from Harvard College and juris doctorate and master of business administration degrees from Harvard's Law and Business Schools.

He has two sons, Jamaal and Michael.

Jakki Nance serves as the president of The Cleveland Browns Foundation, the charitable arm of the Cleveland Browns. As its president, she is responsible for strategic planning, assessing community needs, and fundraising.

Nance is a member of Leadership Cleveland's Class of 2006, and serves as chairperson of the 2007 National Convention of Northeasterners, Inc., one of the oldest African-American women's social organizations in the country.

Nance is an active community volunteer, having chaired both the Heroes Luncheon for the Red Cross and Saks Fifth Avenue's Key to the Cure. She was selected as one of only 50 young African-American women nationwide to participate in The Links, Inc.'s inaugural class of the Scott-Hawkins Leadership Institute.

Nance continues her commitment to the community with a special interest in health and education. She is an active member of the Cleveland Clinic Taussig Cancer Center's National Leadership Advisory Board, where she is a committee chairperson. She serves on numerous other boards, and was a founding board member of the Cleveland Bridge Builders.

Nance resides in Moreland Hills with her husband Fred Nance and their two children, Melanie and Ricky.

Edmenson Suggs, Esq.
Director, Youth Development & Outreach
Cleveland Browns

Paul Warfield
Scouting & Career Planning Consultant
Cleveland Browns

A native New Yorker, Edmenson Suggs' diverse talents span industries from politics to law to sports. He tackles his daily responsibilities as the director of youth development and outreach with the same tireless energy and passion he utilized as a scholarship athlete at the University of Maryland.

After graduating, Suggs accepted a position with the United States Department of State. His daily responsibilities afforded him the opportunity to hone his understanding of politics and piqued his interest in the law.

In 1995, Suggs attended Rutgers Law School. After working in the legal profession in New York and New Jersey, he moved to Cleveland and accepted a position with Cleveland Municipal School District. As an athletic coordinator for Cleveland schools, he coordinated sports activities and served as the liaison with local professional sports teams to execute joint initiatives for the district's 72,000 students.

After two years with Cleveland schools, Suggs accepted his current position with the Cleveland Browns, where he is able to continue the work of effectuating change among young people through sports.

Suggs resides with his wife and his twin boys.

Paul Warfield is in his second season in the Cleveland Browns' front office as the scouting and career planning consultant. His responsibilities include college scouting, talent evaluation, and special projects. He previously worked for the Browns as director of player relations from 1985 to 1987.

Warfield starred for the Browns from 1964-1969 and from 1976-1977. He also spent five seasons with the Miami Dolphins. He led the Browns in receiving as a rookie and helped the Browns win the 1964 NFL Championship. Warfield played football at The Ohio State University and was enshrined in the Pro Football Hall of Fame in 1983.

During his football career, Warfield returned to college and earned a master of arts degree in telecommunications. He worked during the off-seasons in business and broadcasting.

Warfield has served the Boys and Girls Clubs of Cleveland for 15 years. He received the UNCF's Distinguished Volunteer Award in Cleveland, and was honored by the Black Media Workers of Cleveland and the United Way Services. He received The State of Ohio Governor's Award for excellence, achievement, and outstanding dedication to improving the quality of life for all Ohioans.

LeBron James
Guard/Forward
Cleveland Cavaliers

eBron James enters his third season as a guard/forward for the Cleveland Cavaliers. Last season, James earned All-NBA second team honors while averaging 27.2 points, 7.4 rebounds and 7.2 assists. He became only the fifth player in NBA history to post season averages of at least 27 points, seven rebounds and seven assists.

James was selected a starter to the Eastern Conference All-Star Team in 2005 and became the first Cavalier to ever win the NBA's Player of the Month Award in November and January of 2005.

An Akron native, James and his James' Family Foundation have made an impact in the Northeastern Ohio community. He is the Cavaliers co-captain of the All-Star Reading Team and annually distributes school supplies to students. Last summer, he launched the first King for Kids Bike-a-thon benefiting Akron youth, and in the last two years, he has teamed up with Nike to refurbish ten basketball courts in Akron. Each Thanksgiving, he donates meals in his hometown of Akron, and on Mother's Day, treats deserving mothers in Northeast Ohio to a spa treatment.

Eric Snow
Guard
Cleveland Cavaliers

ric Snow enters his second year as a guard for the Cleveland Cavaliers and his tenth season in the NBA. He ranked fifth in the league in assists-to-turnovers ratio and finished third on the team in assists. Twice in his career, Snow led his team to the NBA Finals (1996 and 2001) and over the past three seasons has missed just one game.

Through his Shoot 4 the Moon Foundation, Snow has made his mark through community service and philanthropy. He was the 2005 recipient of the J. Walter Kennedy Citizenship Award and also received the NBPA Community Contribution Award.

For the third consecutive season, Snow sponsored his "Full Court Fathers" program, which brings a father-son and father-daughter duo to every home game. He also donated $20 for every one of his steals and assists throughout the season. During the holidays, Snow provided 250 Thanksgiving meals to families in Canton and sponsored a winter coat drive with teammate Drew Gooden.

Born and raised in Canton, he and his wife DeShawn have three children, E.J., Darius and Jarren.

Drew Gooden enters his second year as a member of the Cleveland Cavaliers and his fourth season in the NBA. Acquired last summer from Orlando, Gooden put up career highs in nearly every statistical category, including averaging 14.4 points and a team-best 9.2 rebounds.

Gooden was the only Cavalier to play in every game this season and ranked eighth in the league in double-doubles with 37. In his three-year career at Kansas, he became only the second player to record at least 1,500 points, 900 rebounds, 100 blocks and 100 steals. As a junior, he led Kansas to the Final Four and was named a First Team All-American.

Last season, Gooden hosted a Halloween party at the Ronald McDonald House of Cleveland and at Thanksgiving, donated 250 meals to families in need. He sponsored a winter coat drive during January with teammate Eric Snow and construction is currently in progress for the Drew Gooden Reading & Learning Center in Cleveland's East End Neighborhood House. He has provided financial support to the East End Neighborhood House since his arrival in Cleveland.

Drew Gooden
Forward
Cleveland Cavaliers

Mike Brown was named the 17th coach in Cavaliers history on June 2, 2005. Brown becomes the second-youngest coach in the league behind New Jersey's Lawrence Frank.

Brown joined the Cavaliers after spending two seasons as the associate head coach of the Indiana Pacers. A 13-year veteran of the NBA, he is widely regarded as a defensive specialist. Prior to his time with the Pacers, he was an assistant coach for the San Antonio Spurs for three seasons, including the 2003 World Championship season.

The 35-year-old Brown began his NBA career with the Denver Nuggets in 1992, where he spent five seasons before spending three seasons with the Washington Wizards in various positions. As an assistant coach in the NBA, Brown's teams have compiled an overall record of 341-201 (.629).

Brown is a 1992 graduate of the University of San Diego (USD) with a degree in business. He played basketball two seasons at USD after spending two years at Mesa Community College. He and his wife, Carolyn, have two sons, Elijah and Cameron.

Mike Brown
Head Coach
Cleveland Cavaliers

Austin Carr
Director of Community and
Business Development
Cleveland Cavaliers

After a standout career with the Cleveland Cavaliers from 1971-80, Austin Carr rejoined the Cavaliers in the front office in 1991 as the director of community and business development. Carr is responsible for generating new business from northeast Ohio corporations, with a particular focus on smaller companies and minority organizations. In addition, Austin serves as an analyst for Cavaliers telecasts.

Austin was the first player chosen in the 1971 NBA Draft, after a brilliant college career at Notre Dame. He was on the NBA All-Rookie Team in 1972 and represented Cleveland in the 1974 NBA All-Star Game.

In 1981, the Cavaliers organization retired Austin's number, 34. The local media recently honored Austin as member of the Cavaliers' All-Time Starting Five, and Cleveland fans further honored him as part of the Cavaliers' All-Time Team.

Austin won the Walter Kennedy Citizenship Award after the 1979-80 season, which goes annually to the player or coach in the NBA who makes substantial contributions to the community. He continues his charitable activities with the United Black Fund, Junior Achievement, Ronald McDonald House, and the Cavaliers' All-Star Reading Team.

M. Campy Russell
Outer Market Events Specialist
Cleveland Cavaliers

M. Campy Russell is a Cleveland Cavalier legend. The nine-year NBA veteran played for the Cavs from 1974 to 1980 and in 1984, and was an All-Star in 1979 while with the New York Knicks. He was named to the Cavaliers' All-Time team and remains in the Cavs' all-time top ten in eight categories. He was the eighth pick of the first-round in the 1974 NBA Draft.

In 2002, Russell rejoined the Cavaliers as the team's outer market events specialist, a position involving sales, community relations, youth basketball programs, and directing the team's alumni relations. In 2004, he championed the Black Heritage Celebration, one of the most comprehensive multicultural celebrations in the NBA. He also has been the team's broadcast analyst for the last two years on the WUAB Channel 19 and UPN 43 Cavaliers pregame show.

Russell is an alumnus of the University of Michigan, graduating with a bachelor's degree in sports management and communications in 2000, and he is a member of the university's Hall of Honor.

He is the father of four daughters, Allex, Mandisa, Oyin, and Saki, and one son, Michael II.

Marvin Cross was appointed director of team security for the Cleveland Cavaliers in 2003. He is responsible for developing policy and procedures to ensure the safety of the team's players and operations. He was assigned to assist in the travel and security for the USA Basketball team at the 2004 Olympics in Greece.

Cross has more than 27 years of experience in law enforcement, serving as commander of community policing in the Cleveland Police Department, where he was responsible for the operations of 21 ward mini-stations. He also has more than 14 years of investigation experience involving criminal activity and hate crime incidents, while also working in partnership with the United States Attorney's Office, FBI and Justice Department.

Cross earned a bachelor of science degree in management from Myers University and graduated from the FBI National Academy in Quantico, Virginia. His dedication towards this city and state is shown in his role as the director of the Greater Cleveland Big Brothers/Big Sisters Blue Shadow Program and the director of Ohio's Law Enforcement Special Olympics Torch Run. He is married with two sons, Marvin, Jr. and Mike.

Marvin Cross
Director of Team Security
Cleveland Cavaliers

Bruce Wimbish joined the Cleveland Cavaliers in 2004 as corporate communications coordinator. He is responsible for gaining media exposure for the organization's community relations, marketing, and sales efforts and activities. He also assists with the team's Web site content, features, and photos.

Wimbish leads the committee responsible for the Cavaliers Black Heritage Celebration (BHC), one of the most comprehensive multicultural celebrations in the NBA. Going into its second year, the BHC has connected the Cavaliers with the community and is positioned to become a special event in the City of Cleveland.

Wimbish, a Columbus, Ohio native, joined the Cavaliers after an internship in their marketing department. Prior to that, he was a corporate sales intern with the NHL's Columbus Blue Jackets.

Wimbish is a graduate of the University of Cincinnati, where he received his bachelor's degree in business administration. He went on to The Ohio State University, where he received a master of business administration degree and has almost completed his master's degree in sports management. As an alumnus, he is active in events connected with the university, both in Cleveland and Columbus.

Bruce Wimbish
Corporate Communications
Coordinator
Cleveland Cavaliers

Bishop Floyd Eugene Perry, Jr.

Pastor of the Cathedral Church of God in Christ, located
2950 Martin Luther King Jr. Drive in Cleveland, Ohio.

Jurisdictional Prelate of the Ohio Southern Jurisdiction of
the Church of God in Christ.

A member of the Judiciary Board of the Church of God in Christ,
Inc. - Headquarters, Memphis, Tennessee.

Founder and President of the Church of God in Christ/Pentecostal
Connection (Ministerial Group) CPC.

Second Vice President of the Cleveland Branch NAACP

Cathedral Church of God in Christ
2940 Martin Luther King Jr. Drive
Cleveland, Ohio 44104
(216) 721-0572

Cleveland's

CORPORATE BRASS

"*A single bracelet does not jingle.*"

CONGO PROVERB

Michelle J. Berkley MSN, CNP
Clinic Manager
Cleveland Clinic Youth Wellness Center

Diane Bradford
Vice President,
Commercial Real Estate Group
Fifth Third Bank

Michelle J. Berkley is a Certified Nurse Practitioner for The Cleveland Clinic. She is the principle provider and clinic manager responsible for the day-to-day operations of the Cleveland Clinic Youth Wellness Center, an outreach project of The Cleveland Clinic.

Michelle has worked for The Cleveland Clinic for the past 12 years in several different areas. She worked as a registered nurse on a general medicine floor, as a case manager for home care, and as a client care administrator for an HIV/AIDS outreach project.

Michelle earned a master of science degree in nursing from Case Western Reserve University, and a bachelor of science degree in nursing from The University of Akron. She maintains board certification from the American Nurses Credentialing Center as an Adult Nurse Practitioner.

In addition to her clinical background, Michele has been an integral part of several start up projects in disadvantaged communities, including the AGAPE Program and the Youth Wellness Center. She was recently approved as a part of the National Health Service Corps.

Michelle recently received the Excellence in Nursing Award from the Cleveland Council of Black Nurses.

Diane Bradford joined the Fifth Third Bank team in February of 2004 as vice president in the commercial real estate group in the Northeast Ohio affiliate. Diane focuses on providing customized financing options for a variety of investment real estate projects, including land acquisition and development. Her focus also includes construction and renovation of residential housing, commercial buildings, retail development projects, and mixed-use property.

Prior to accepting the opportunity at Fifth Third, Diane's professional experience included five years of commercial banking. In addition, she has eight years of financial reporting and management experience working in the real estate development industry at Cleveland Housing Network and Associated Estates Realty Corporation.

Diane is also involved in organizations in the community, including Commercial Real Estate Women (C.R.E.W.) as a public relations manager, and the League of Women Voters.

Diane earned a bachelor of business administration degree from Cleveland State University and a certificate of non-profit management from Case Western Reserve University. She is continuing her education and currently enrolled in the master's degree program at Case Western Reserve University.

Michael Tuan Bustamante
Principal, Attorney at Law
The Project Group

Michael Tuan Bustamante is an attorney and principal of The Project Group. He has directed the firm's activities with respect to monitoring EEO compliance on the construction of the new Cleveland Browns Stadium, the Cleveland Hopkins International Airport, and Cleveland Division of Water Expansion Projects. On these engagements, Bustamante also played a key role in the analysis of contractual, budgetary, public, and corporate finance issues.

A member of the Ohio Bar, Bustamante has represented several minority- and female-owned businesses in private practice. He has also represented local and national nonprofit organizations and political campaigns.

In addition to his experiences as an attorney and consultant, Bustamante served as editor-in-chief of the *Call and Post* newspapers from 1993 to 1998. Being editor of Ohio's largest African-American weekly was an opportunity that provided him with a solid basis upon which to evaluate the social and political elements of the engagements on which he has been a participant. As a result, Bustamante's understanding of the diversity issue in the public and private sectors has resulted in public acknowledgement of his accomplishments in this area.

Raymond Curtis Cash, Jr.
Vice President
Ray's Sausage Co., Inc.

Raymond C. Cash, Jr. is vice president of Ray's Sausage Company, Inc., one of only three black-owned meat manufacturing companies in the United States. His father, the late Raymond C. Cash, Sr., started Ray's Sausage in 1952. Raymond, Jr. is responsible for the daily operation, marketing, and manufacturing of all of the company's products.

Currently, Raymond is a board member with the Mount Pleasant NOW Development Corporation and the Cleveland Housing Network. A past member of the Cleveland Business League, he received recognition from Who's Who in Business Professionals. In 1999, Cleveland State University recognized Raymond with an Outstanding Black Professional Award.

Raymond and his family appeared in *Ebony* magazine for their leadership role and business acumen. Over the past few years, he has participated in the United Black Fund Celebrity Cook-Off.

Raymond, a graduate of Fisk University in Nashville, Tennessee, holds a bachelor of arts degree in economics with a minor in psychology. He is a member of Omega Psi Phi Fraternity-Zeta Omega chapter, The Reindeers Club, and St. Timothy Baptist Church.

A native of Cleveland, Raymond is the proud father of Raymond, III, and Tiffany.

Mittie Olion Chandler
Director, Maxine Goodman Levin
College of Urban Affairs
Cleveland State University

Marcella Boyd Cox
Vice President of Marketing and Promotion
E.F. Boyd & Son Funeral Home

Mittie Olion Chandler is director of the Urban Child Research Center and an associate professor of urban studies and political science at Cleveland State University. She teaches courses in public policy and conducts research focusing on a range of issues, including minority business development, public housing, educational programs, and urban politics. Her chapter entitled "Black Clergy as Political Leaders," was recently published in *Black Churches and Local Politics*.

Mittie serves on the education committee of the Cleveland NAACP. Likewise, she serves on the boards of West Side Ecumenical Ministry, Empowerment Center of Greater Cleveland, Fairfax Renaissance Development Corporation, KidsHealth 2020, and Policy Bridge.

Mittie received a bachelor of arts degree from Michigan State University. Wayne State University awarded her a master of urban planning degree and a doctorate of philosophy in political science. She has been a member of Alpha Kappa Alpha Sorority, Inc. since 1969. She worships at Mt. Zion Congregational Church, United Church of Christ.

Mittie is a native of Detroit, Michigan and moved to Cleveland in 1985. She is the proud mother of Mae Evette, with whom she resides in Beachwood.

Marcella Boyd Cox is the vice president of marketing and promotion for the E.F. Boyd & Son Funeral Home in East Cleveland, Ohio. In this position, she manages public service events and marketing campaigns for the funeral home. Marcella is strongly involved as a community volunteer. She has found new ground in her efforts to promote the funeral industry through billboard and bus ads, a gospel show, and television commercials.

Marcella is a licensed funeral director and serves alongside her extended family in a business in its 100th year of service to the public. She serves in promoting various activities that benefit the African-American community, such as the Coalition of 100 Black Women, the National Council of Negro Women, and the Cleveland Chapter of Girl Friends, where she is a former national vice president. She is involved in Jack and Jill, and the National Funeral Directors and Morticians Association.

A native of Cleveland, Ohio, Marcella is the mother of two children, Timothy Francis and Ina Elisabeth.

Charles Domingue
Vice President &
General Merchandise Manager
Jo-Ann Stores, Inc.

Charles Domingue is the vice president and general merchandise manager for Jo-Ann Stores, Inc. He has total accountability for more than $500 million in revenue. Charles is involved in the strategic planning process driving the company's future growth.

Charles' career of more than 20 years is rich with successes in a number of pedigree retailers including May Department Stores, Target Corporation, and Sears. At each of these companies he received awards recognizing his superior financial results.

Charles serves on the board of the Cuyahoga Community College Foundation/JazzFest that touches 20,000 underprivileged students each year. He is also a member of New Community Bible Fellowship Church in Cleveland Heights. Formerly, Charles served on the board for the New York Home Textiles Show and as a mentor in the African American Network at Sears.

Charles received a bachelor of science degree in business administration from Washington University in St. Louis, Missouri.

A native of Baton Rouge, Louisiana, Charles is married to Denise, his wife of 28 years, and has two children, Kristen and Ryan.

His favorite quote is: "Based on results, you have exactly what you intended."

Ernest Germany, Jr.
Financial Analyst
Federal Bureau of Investigation

Ernest Germany, Jr. began his career with the FBI in September of 1980 as a clerk, assigned to the Cleveland division. Germany presently holds the position of financial analyst on the white-collar crime squad. He has earned two awards from the director of the FBI for outstanding work performance on both a HUD case and an interstate automobile theft ring case.

Germany was born in Cleveland, Ohio. After graduating from Collinwood High School, where he was featured in the High School Who's Who, he attended Cuyahoga Community College, where he acquired an associate of science degree. Germany holds a bachelor of business degree with a major in accounting from Cleveland State University. He is an active member of The Dayspring Holiness Church of God.

Germany is married to the former Denise A. McCoy of Toledo, a teacher in the Cleveland public school system. They have two daughters, Adriana and Nia, and one son, Earnest III. Germany has three sisters, Yvonne Jackson, Vendelia Germany, and JoAnn Germany. He is the youngest of four children born to Ernest Germany, Sr. and Corean Germany.

Giesele Robinson Greene, M.D.
Associate Medical Director
Great-West HealthCare

Walter J. Griffin
Director of Information Technology
Jo-Ann Stores, Inc.

Giesele Robinson Greene, M.D. is an associate medical director for Great-West HealthCare, a subsidiary of Great-West Life. She is responsible for insurance related medical decisions for more than 350,000 persons in ten states. A board-certified internist, geriatric specialist, and associate clinical professor of medicine at Case Western Reserve University College of Medicine, Dr. Greene practiced medicine in greater Cleveland for 18 years prior to assuming her current position.

Active in the community, Greene sits on the boards of Benjamin Rose, Health Legacy of Cleveland, and other organizations. She is the general chair for The 75th Great Lakes Regional Conference, Alpha Kappa Alpha Sorority, Inc., hosting 1,500 sorority members in downtown Cleveland, April 27-30, 2006.

Born and raised in Chicago, Illinois, Dr. Greene is a graduate of Howard University College of Medicine and has been married to James E. Greene, D.D.S. for more than 28 years. A long-time Sunday school teacher at St. Andrew's Episcopal Church, she is the proud mother of three children and is also proud of her niece and two nephews whom she and James are raising.

Walt Griffin is director of information technology for Jo-Ann Stores, Inc., located in Hudson, Ohio, with retail stores in 48 states. Walt is responsible for the computer technology and the vast technology infrastructure of the stores as well as voice and data communications that support the Jo-Ann business model.

An avid motorcyclist, Walt uses his hobby for the greater good. He has received numerous honors and awards for his volunteerism from a variety of community organizations. Walt leads his fellow motorcyclists as they make significant contributions to MDA, United Way, Zelma George Homeless Shelters, and the COPS & KIDS Program—dedicated to helping sick and underprivileged children live normal lives.

In 2003, he was nominated for the Cleveland Browns Quarterback Club by the COPS & KIDS Program as Volunteer of the Year for the region.

Walt is very well known in his company and in the community as an individual who will always get things done and help others.

Cleveland's
CORPORATE BRASS

Kathryn M. Hall
**University Director,
Equal Opportunity & Diversity
Case Western Reserve University**

Constance T. Haqq
**Director of Communications
& Community Relations
Northeast Ohio Regional Sewer District**

Kathryn M. Hall is the university director of equal opportunity and diversity at Case Western Reserve University. She began her employment at Case in April of 2004. Prior to her employment at Case, Hall worked for 13 years at Cuyahoga Community College as the director of diversity and community outreach.

Hall is a Certified Diversity Professional and holds a master's degree in psychology with emphasis on diversity management from Cleveland State University. She earned certification from the NTL in Washington, D.C. with specialization in diversity management. Hall received her undergraduate degree from Baldwin-Wallace College in political science and sociology.

A past board president of the YWCA of Greater Cleveland, Hall serves on the City of Cleveland Community Relations Board, the United Black Fund board, and the board of Sankofa Fine Arts Plus. She volunteers with the New Life Community Center and the Ohio Classic.

Constance Haqq joined the Northeast Ohio Regional Sewer District in June of 2005, as the director of communications and community relations. Her charge is to oversee the organization's internal and external communication and public outreach programs.

She is the former executive director of the Nordson Corporation Foundation in Westlake, where she held strategic positions in corporate and nonprofit environments. Before going to Nordson Corporation, Constance had an 11-year career as a managing director of INROADS/Northeast Ohio.

Constance has served on volunteer boards including the St. Ignatius board of regents, the Mt. Pleasant Development Corporation, Karamu House, Inc., and Ohio Boys Town. She currently serves on the board of Business Volunteers Unlimited, In Counsel with Women, and Ursuline College's Accelerated Learning Program.

A graduate of John Adams High School in Cleveland, Constance is also an alumna of Leadership Cleveland. She holds degrees from Tufts University and the Case Western Reserve University School of Applied Social Sciences.

Constance is currently a resident of Shaker Heights, Ohio.

Roderick Ingram
Deputy Director
Office of Marketing Services
Ohio Lottery

Roderick Ingram was named deputy director of the office of marketing services on January 19, 2005. As deputy director, he oversees the bureaus of advertising and creative services, business development, the *Cash Explosion® Double Play Show*, merchandising, promotions, and sponsorships. Ingram joined the Ohio Lottery in October of 2002 as advertising manager, and later served as director of sponsorships and promotions. He most recently held the position of deputy director of business development, and he continues to manage chain accounts and seeks new business opportunities.

Prior to joining the Ohio Lottery, Ingram spent 17 years at NewsChannel 5 in Cleveland. His last position at NewsChannel 5 was director of station operations and business development. Ingram holds a bachelor's degree in finance and a master of business administration degree from Cleveland State University, specializing in marketing and innovations management.

Ingram and his wife, Angela, live with their three children, Rod Jr., Evan, and Shelby, in Orange Village.

Linda L. Johnson
Executive Vice President,
Statewide Operations
Medical Mutual

Linda Johnson is the executive vice president of statewide operations for Medical Mutual. She is responsible for all administrative functions for claims processing and customer service for the company's accounts in Ohio and nationwide.

Johnson joined Medical Mutual in 1993 as vice president of statewide operations. She was promoted to executive vice president of statewide operations in 2000, and is responsible for managing a $37 million budget and more than 700 hundred employees. The operations division is responsible for the Claims Distribution Center, all administrative functions associated with claims processing, customer and provider service, and member appeals. The division is also responsible for service accreditation, regulatory compliance, systems development and maintenance, operations training programs, and quality assurance.

Johnson began her career with Blue Cross & Blue Shield of West Virginia in 1973 as a claims processor. She rose to the position of supervisor in 1977 and progressed through various management positions until promoted to vice president of statewide operations in 1988.

She and her husband, Phillip, reside in Solon and have four children and two grandchildren.

Kandace Jones
Regional Director
Platform Learning Inc.

Sharon Jones
Executive Vice President,
Clinical/Operations
VNA Healthcare Partners of Ohio

Kandace Jones is the regional director for Platform Learning Inc., overseeing the operations of more than 30 after-school programs for students. She lives by the quote, "Be the change you wish to see in the world," and strives to provide students with the support to be successful in school and in life.

Kandace has a broad background in marketing. As an assistant brand manager for P&G, she led large teams of marketing, sales, product development, consumer research, finance, and product supply in the launch of 11 new products.

In addition, Kandace also spent two years in marketing and promotions in the recording industry, most notably co-founding her own record label, Underground Elevation, LLC. She also recently founded Elevation Properties, LLC, the company housing her real estate investment properties, with plans to teach inner city youth the importance of owning property.

To her credit, Kandace earned her master of business administration degree from FAMU. She is also a member of Delta Sigma Theta Sorority, Inc., and will soon begin coursework toward her doctorate of philosophy in international education.

Kandace was recently married to Dr. Kevin S. Jones.

Sharon Jones is the executive vice president, clinical/operations for the Visiting Nurse Association Healthcare Partners of Ohio, a leading home health care agency located in Cleveland.

Sharon has 27 years of experience in home health care, including 20 years at a senior management level. Her responsibilities include labor relations and corporate-wide agency operations to support delivery of services and programs. She coordinates corporate risk management, compliance, and quality improvement activities, and is a member of the executive committee responsible for strategic planning and financial management of the corporation.

A committed professional and community volunteer, Sharon serves on numerous boards, including the Institute for Educational Renewal and the Eliza Jennings Senior Care Network. She is a board member and treasurer for the Ohio Council for Home Care and the Visiting Nurse Associations of America. Likewise, she serves on the National Association for Home Care & Hospice's Voluntary Home Health Agency advisory board. Sharon has received several awards, including Woman of Professional Excellence and Volunteer of the Year.

Sharon has published and presented locally and nationally on several topics relating to home health, technology, and nursing.

Anthony D. Kinslow
Vice President, Human Resources
Case Western Reserve University

Leslie Lester
Chief Financial Officer
Ray's Sausage Co., Inc.

Tony Kinslow has served as the vice president for human resources at Case Western Reserve University since June 16, 2003. At Case, Kinslow develops human resources policies and programs covering all aspects of human capital management.

Tony's experience includes stints at California Institute of Technology (Caltech), Vanderbilt University, and Vanderbilt's affiliate hospital, Metropolitan Nashville General Hospital. He has worked in human resources for more than 13 years.

Tony holds a bachelor of arts degree in economics from California State University Sacramento, a master of arts degree in international relations from University Southern California, and a juris doctorate from Vanderbilt School of Law. He is admitted to the Tennessee and Mississippi Bar Associations. He is a member of the Society of Human Resources Management, and the College & University Professional Association.

Tony retired from the military with the rank of lieutenant colonel after 23 years of service with the Air Force and Air National Guard.

Tony, born in Nashville, Tennessee, is married to Ms. Carla L. Alexander of Cedartown, Georgia. He has three sons, Craig, Anthony, and Nickolas.

Leslie Lester is the chief financial officer and coordinator for Ray's Sausage Co., a meat manufacturing company specializing in sausage and souse meat. Ray's has national distribution.

Leslie is an honored member of Strathmore's *Who's Who in Leadership and Achievement*, and she is featured in Manchester's *Who's Who in Executives and Professionals*. Leslie is an affiliate of the Hazard Analysis Critical Control Point (HACCP) and the Ohio Association of Meat Processors. She is also a member of the Advisory Committee Board for Meat and Poultry for the Ohio Department of Agriculture.

In 1994, Leslie received a bachelor of science degree from Wilberforce University, and, in 2004, she received her certificate in massage therapy.

Leslie's hobbies are travel, golf, and shopping.

Randell McShepard
Director of Community Affairs
RPM, Inc.

Randell McShepard currently serves as director of community affairs for RPM, Inc., a $2.5 billion specialty coatings/paint company headquartered in Medina, Ohio. Randell is responsible for coordinating external affairs and community partnerships for the company, in addition to managing the corporate philanthropy program.

Prior to joining RPM, Randell worked in the nonprofit community for 15 years, and he has an extensive background as a strategic planning consultant. He is active on several boards including Baldwin-Wallace College, the Sisters of Charity/St. Ann Foundation, the United Way, and the Ohio Community Service Council. He also serves as chairman of the City of Cleveland's Workforce Investment Board.

Randell was born and raised in Cleveland and is a proud alumnus of Baldwin-Wallace College (undergraduate) and Cleveland State University (graduate).

Dr. André K. Mickel
Director, Post-Doctorate
Residency Program in Endodontics
Case School of Dental Medicine

Dr. André K Mickel is a practicing board certified endodontist and is the director of the Post-doctorate Residency Program in Endodontics at Case School of Dental Medicine, where he earned his doctorate of dental science degree and endodontic specialty degree.

In 1996, Mickel became the first African American and the youngest director of an endodontic residency program in the United States. *Cleveland Magazine* selected him as one of Cleveland's "Fifty Most Interesting People" for his innovative clinical relaxation techniques to reduce root canal patient's anxiety and perception of pain.

In 2001, the American Association of Endodontists gave Mickel the Osetek Educator award, given to the most outstanding young endodontic educator in the world.

Mickel, a deacon and Sunday school teacher at Antioch Baptist Church, has served on numerous professional and civic boards. He has served as a president of five organizations, including the Cleveland chapter of Alpha Phi Alpha Fraternity, Inc., in which he holds a life membership.

Mickel cherishes his life with his "Crown of Jewels," Dr. Sabrina Mickel, and their two sons, Andre and Alexander, both eight years of age.

Duane Miller
Deputy Director
Office of General Services
Ohio Lottery

Duane Miller was named deputy director of the office of general services in June of 2001. In this capacity, Miller oversees a variety of agency support functions. Chief among them are the Bureaus of Agent Licensing, Vehicle Fleet Administration, Office Services, Warehouse Operations, and the Customer Call Center.

Miller started at the Ohio Lottery in June of 1998 as the Cincinnati region assistant manager. Prior to joining the Lottery, he held various management and sales positions in such well-known companies as Johnson & Johnson, Carter Wallace, and Bic.

Miller earned a bachelor's degree in economics from Kent State University in June of 1984. He is currently a master of business administration degree candidate at David Meyers University.

Chris Miree
Vice President,
Central Regional Manager
Fifth Third Bank

Chris Miree is the vice president, central regional manager, for Fifth Third Bank's Northeastern Ohio affiliate. As manager of Fifth Third's central region, Miree is responsible for all retail operations, business development, and coordination of bank activities for 13 banking center and Bank Mart® locations in Cuyahoga County.

Miree began his career with Fifth Third Bank in August of 2002 as a banking center manager in Cincinnati, Ohio. He relocated to Cleveland in January of 2005, when he was promoted to central region manager in Northeastern Ohio. Prior to working at Fifth Third Bank, Miree had six years of retail banking experience.

Miree received his bachelor's degree in public administration from Ohio University in 1995. He also has a master's degree in political science from Ohio University.

Chris and his wife, Jane, reside with their three children, Shayna, Christopher, and Sean in North Royalton.

G. Dean Patterson, Jr.
Assistant Vice President for Student Affairs
Case Western Reserve University

For more than 28 years, G. Dean Patterson, Jr. has worked in the field of higher education to help institutions of higher education better understand the needs of all students regardless of their culture or ethnicity. Currently, he is the assistant vice president for student affairs at Case Western Reserve University.

Previously, Patterson held a clinical faculty appointment at Frances Payne Bolton School of Nursing. He taught seminars in the Medical School of Case Western Reserve University, and was a clinical instructor for psychology at John Carroll University and Case. Patterson was a pioneer in the area of family centered care.

Patterson is quite accomplished in the field of higher education, and an award-winning creative artist. His philosophy is that institutions of higher education have the responsibility to help students do more than just meet their desire to make their place in this world, but more importantly, to go forth with the responsibility of making this world a better place.

Anthony Peebles
Vice President
Public Funds Group
Fifth Third Bank

Anthony Peebles is the vice president and sales manager of the public funds group for Fifth Third Bank, Northeastern Ohio. His primary focus is providing treasury management and investment advisory services, as well as financing solutions, for government entities and not-for-profit institutions.

Anthony serves on the visiting committee of the Levin College of Urban Affairs at Cleveland State University. He is vice chair of the Gateway Economic Development Corporation and serves on the advisory board of the Cleveland Bridge Builders Leadership Development Program. Anthony is a member of The 100 Black Men of Greater Cleveland and a life member of Kappa Alpha Psi Fraternity, Inc.

Anthony served as the 88th president of the City Club of Cleveland. He is also past president and co-founder of the Urban Financial Services Coalition.

Anthony holds a bachelor of arts degree in political science from Duke University and a master of business administration degree from Baldwin-Wallace College.

A native Clevelander, Anthony is the husband of attorney Tracy Martin-Peebles and the proud father of two daughters, Madison and Olivia. They are members of Mt. Zion Congregational United Church of Christ.

Craig Platt
Information Technology Director
Global Customer Relationship Center of Excellence
General Electric Company

Craig Platt is an executive with the General Electric Company (GE), where he works as the information technology director, leading the Global Customer Relationship Center of Excellence in the consumer and industrial business. He drives business growth and productivity by providing information technology solutions to critical business processes related to sales and customer services.

Based in Cleveland, Platt provides the vision and strategy for a global team with members in India, Hungary, and the Americas. His GE career spans 21 years, and he also serves on the business development team, leading the due diligence activities for information technology.

Platt is the recipient of GE's 2001 Global Diversity Symposium Icon Award for e-Business. He serves as a business partner on the East Cleveland School District continuous improvement team, and is active in GE Volunteers and the GE African American Forum.

A native of Steubenville, Ohio, Platt received a bachelor's degree from the University of Cincinnati in mathematics, and is also a certified Six Sigma Black Belt.

Craig and his wife, Theresa, reside in Richmond Heights, and are the proud parents of four sons, Marlon, Desmon, Jolon, and Craig.

Emilie Poua
Manager of Multicultural &
International Tourism
Convention & Visitors Bureau of Greater Cleveland

Emilie Poua is the manager of multicultural and international tourism at the Convention & Visitors Bureau of Greater Cleveland (CVB). With the numbers of international and multi-culture/minority visitors constantly increasing, the CVB has redeveloped their strategy for international marketing, with an added emphasis on multicultural tourism opportunities.

Emilie is a native of Paris, France and is very proud of her Spanish and African heritage. She graduated from the University of Marne La Vallee with a bachelor of arts degree in applied foreign languages, and a minor in business. Since her arrival in Cleveland in 1999, she has worked at the CVB in various positions such as database marketing coordinator and visitor information assistant. Emilie sees Cleveland as a wonderful city full of multicultural heritage. She has been working closely with various local organizations to help promote various multicultural initiatives and events in Cleveland.

Emilie credits her parents for her strong self-determination. She is a member of *Kaleidoscope Magazine*'s 40/40 Club and the Cleveland Advertising Association. Emilie enjoys volunteering for Dress For Success Cleveland, cooking, and traveling.

Rockette Richardson
Vice President of Community Development
Sky Bank, Greater Cleveland Region

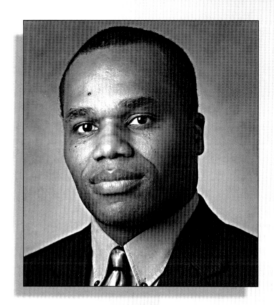

Ronald Richeson
Manager, Treasury
Invacare Corporation

Rockette Richardson is vice president of community development for Sky Bank's Greater Cleveland region. Her primary responsibilities are business development in the areas of affordable housing, home ownership, economic revitalization, and small business in Sky's greater Cleveland marketing area. Before joining Sky Bank in July of 2003, Richardson was the corporate relations manager for Bank One's northeast Ohio region.

Richardson currently serves on the board of trustees of Shoes and Clothes for Kids. She is a former board member of the Greater Cleveland Committee on Hunger, the Akron Urban League, and East Akron Neighborhood Development Corporation. In addition, she served on the policy committee of the Cuyahoga County Early Childhood Initiative and on Summit County United Way's 2001 and 2002 corporate campaign cabinets. She was a member of the 2003 LeadDiversity Class, a leadership development program of the Cleveland chapter of the National Conference for Community and Justice. Further, Richardson was inducted into *Kaleidoscope Magazine*'s 40/40 Club in 2000.

A native of Texas, Richardson received her bachelor of arts degree in religion from Princeton University in 1978. Her interests include reading and travel.

Ronald Richeson is the manager of the treasury for Invacare Corporation, the global leader in the manufacture and distribution of innovative home care and long-term care medical products. Ron has extensive experience in corporate treasury functions. His responsibilities include managing the working capital, debt, derivatives, foreign exchange, and risk management strategies for the corporation.

Ron's team at Invacare has successfully negotiated various financings totaling in excess of $1 billion, thereby positioning the corporation to meet its internal and acquisition growth objectives. He is also responsible for domestic and international bank relationships and cash management systems.

Prior to joining Invacare, Ron worked in a similar role at British Petroleum.

A graduate of Virginia State University, Ron holds a master of business administration degree in finance from Trinity University. He is a member of the Northeast Ohio Treasury Management Association and the Association for Financial Professionals, and he is a Certified Treasury Professional (CTP).

Ron and his wife, Colleen, have two children, Marques, currently attending Harvard Law School, and Jonathan, age ten. The Richesons reside in Brunswick Hills.

Frank Robinson, Jr.
Chief, Risk Management Office
NASA Glenn Research Center

Gina L. Routen
Director, Department of Personnel
& Human Resources
City of Cleveland

Frank Robinson, Jr., the chief of the risk management office, joined the National Aeronautics and Space Administration's Glenn Research Center (GRC) in January of 1986.

Frank is responsible for management of safety, reliability, and mission assurance for NASA GRC's aerospace programs. He is also the director for the Assurance Technology Center which supports NASA headquarters. In his previous assignment, he was project manager for the Thermal Energy Storage Experiment, which flew on the space shuttle in 1996.

Frank is a past president of the National Technical Association. He is the founding chairperson of the Consortium of African American Organizations (CAAO) in Cleveland. The CAAO consists of 24 African-American organizations who work to bring economic and networking opportunities to Cleveland.

Frank earned a bachelor of science degree in electrical engineering from The Ohio State University and received a master of science degree in engineering management from Cleveland State University.

Frank is married to Sandy Lynn Robinson, who is also an OSU graduate and is presently dean of Health Careers and Sciences at Cuyahoga Community College. They have two children, Daanicia and Frank III.

Gina L. Routen, director of personnel and human resources at the City of Cleveland, joined the Campbell administration in July of 2003. She provides direction and vision to the department responsible for recruitment, hiring, education and training, employee benefits, labor relations, EEO concerns, and more. Gina is widely respected in the human resources community, having served in the field for more than 20 years. She has served in both private and public sectors, and in the academic arena.

In July of 2004, Director Routen and the City of Cleveland were honored at the sixth annual Cleveland HR Star Conference. Gina was chosen for exhibiting diversity and excellence in her field, and for being a woman of vision.

Gina earned a bachelor's degree in business administration from Baldwin-Wallace College, and was awarded a master's degree in labor relations and human resources from Cleveland State University.

She is the proud mother of Janelle Routen and is equally proud to be "Gigi" to her beautiful granddaughter, Jasmine.

Stephen L. Thomas
Managing Principal
V Consulting Group, LLC

Treva Thomas
Vice President
Private Client Services
FirstMerit Bank

Stephen L. Thomas currently serves as managing principal for V Consulting Group, LLC (VCG), a strategic business and technology-consulting firm launched in late 2003. Stephen works with the other principals of the firm to show organizations and companies of various sizes how to effectively utilize technology for operational and revenue growth along with encompassing risk mitigation throughout.

Prior to VCG, Stephen spent the last five years guiding the information technology and vendor management services for DeepGreen Financial, an Internet-only financial company. Stephen has more than 20 years of experience in information technology, with ten-plus years in leadership positions, including consulting to National City, SBC, NASA, LTV Steel, and the federal government.

Stephen has served on several boards including The Western Reserve Historical Society–African-American Archive Association, the National Black Engineers (NBE), and The National Society of Black Engineers (NSBE). He is currently the interim president of the National Alliance of Market Developers, Cleveland chapter.

Stephen holds a bachelor of science degree in computer information systems from the University of Dayton, and a master of business administration degree from the University of Phoenix, in addition to various professional certifications.

Treva Thomas joined FirstMerit Bank as vice president and operations manager for private client services in January of 2004. In this capacity, she is responsible for the policy and procedural operations for the private banking group.

Before joining FirstMerit, Treva served as vice president and senior project manager with KeyBank and McDonald Financial Group. Her background includes more than 15 years in banking.

Treva began her banking career with National City Bank, and was appointed branch manager and commercial lending officer in 1994. Since that time, she has held several other positions of increasing responsibility.

Treva received her bachelor of arts degree from Howard University and a master of business administration degree from Baldwin-Wallace College.

An active member of Alpha Kappa Alpha Sorority, Inc.'s Alpha Omega Chapter, Treva is involved in several community service projects and committees. She is also an active member of Mt. Zion Church of Oakwood Village and has served as a member of the finance ministry and children's ministry.

Treva resides in Twinsburg with her two children, who are twins, Jalyn and Jordan.

May L. Wykle, Ph.D., R.N.
Dean & Florence Cellar
Professor of Nursing
Case Western Reserve University

May L. Wykle, Ph.D., R.N., FAAN, FGSA is dean and Florence Cellar Professor of Nursing at the Frances Payne Bolton School of Nursing at Case Western Reserve University. Recognized nationally as an expert in the field of aging adults, she is the recent past president of the Honor Society of Nursing, Sigma Theta Tau International, and presently serves on the advisory board for Johnson & Johnson's "Campaign for Nursing's Future."

Wykle has been a faculty member at Case since 1969 and was named director of the University Center on Aging and Health in 1988. She has done extensive research in geriatric mental health, family care giving, minority caregivers, and caring for patients with dementia. Further, she has initiated educational programs internationally in Europe, Africa, and Asia. She is a fellow in the American Academy of Nursing and the Gerontological Society of America, and has received numerous other honors, awards, and appointments.

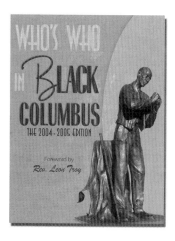

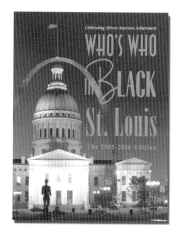
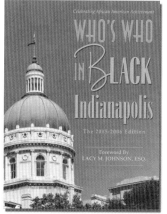
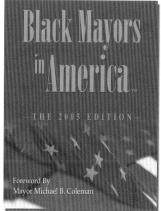

Emily Davis
Television Community Affairs Director
WOIO CBS 19/WUAB 43

For more than three decades, Emily Davis has been both a pioneer and powerhouse in Cleveland television. After attending John Carroll University and Cuyahoga Community College, she began her career at WJW-TV in 1972.

Emily joined WOIO-TV in 1987 as an assistant to the general manager. Two years later, she became the executive producer for *Shaker Square*, a community affairs show. In 1991, the newly named community affairs director premiered two new shows, *Legislative Review* and *Viewpoints*. Currently, she is the executive producer of *Around the Block.*

Emily's 32-year career is full of accomplishments. She is now the most well known community affairs director in the city, and she holds that title for two television stations, WOIO and WUAB-TV. Active in the Cleveland Cavaliers All-Star Reading Team initiative, she spearheads the stations' partnership with the team. For nearly a decade, she has done similar work with Cleveland's Case Elementary School.

Emily has received honors from The Salvation Army, the Cleveland-Citizens FBI Academy, Swim for Diabetes of Greater Cleveland, the American Red Cross, United States Congress, and The Alliance for the Mentally Ill.

Ulysses Glen, Sr.
Publisher & Editor
East Side Daily News

Ulysses Glen, Sr. is the publisher and editor of *East Side Daily News*, a weekly publication that serves a regional area in the southeast side of Cleveland. He has been the publisher of the newspaper since its inception on July 10, 1980. His 25-year tenure is the longest of a publisher in the Cleveland area.

Glen has served as president of the Greater Cleveland Minority Publishers Association. He is one of the founding members of the Neighborhood Community Press Association of Greater Cleveland, and a former two-term president.

A former amateur and professional boxer, Glen has served as judge and referee. He is also a judge for the Ohio Athletic Commission and the World Boxing Organization, judging fights in North America, South America, and Europe.

Glen graduated from Glenville High School. He received a bachelor's degree in sociology from Cleveland State University, and a master's degree in journalism from the Graduate School of Journalism at Kent State University.

He is the father of two sons, Ulysses, Jr. and Warren, and the grandfather of two grandsons, Ulysses I and Warren, Jr.

Bob Lanier is chief executive officer and publisher of *Black Pages*, a minority business publication serving Ohio since 1991. *Black Pages* publishes four annual directories in Ohio: Greater Cleveland, Akron, Greater Columbus, and Toledo. *Black Pages* has been recognized as an advocate for minority business and community involvement in numerous publications including *The Akron Beacon Journal, The Plain Dealer, The Reporter, Call & Post,* and *The Columbus Pos*t.

Lanier is co-founder of the Black Pages Publisher Association (BPPA), a national association of *Black Pages* publishers throughout the United States, with 61 members. He is currently serving as the BPPA's parliamentarian. Some of his other local and national affiliations include the Northern Ohio Minority Business Council, the 100 Black Men of Greater Cleveland, the Akron Minority Health Initiative, and the Urban Leagues of Cleveland and Akron.

Lanier is a native of Albany, New York. He enjoys golfing, working on his computer, and reading. He is married to Linda Lanier and is the proud father of Jessica LeAnne Lanier.

Bob Lanier
Chief Executive Officer & Publisher
Black Pages

John Lenear is vice president of advertising and the editorial page editor of the *Call & Post.* His opinions impact public policy, although he prefers to work behind the scenes.

After attending college at Wayne University, Lenear started his communications career as a disc jockey and then news director at WJMO. Additionally, he was a radio network correspondent for CBS, and co-hosted a weekly program on a local PBS affiliate.

Throughout his career, Lenear developed considerable business skills. In the 1960s, he started Metro Communications, a cable television and marketing company. He sold the cable end of the business to his partner in 1979 and the remaining portion in 1995.

Lenear has worked as a community relations consultant to the U.S. Justice Department, and consulted with the Harlem Commonwealth Council. Likewise, he worked as a personal assistant to Irving Kahn, chairman and CEO of the Teleprompter Corporation, the forerunner to Time Warner Cable.

Lenear was also chairman of the Cleveland Cable Television Commission, which created the specifications for the Cleveland Cable Television Franchise.

John and his wife are the parents of four adult children.

John H. Lenear
Vice President, Advertising
Call & Post **Newspapers**

Cleveland's
MEDIA PROFESSIONALS

Celebrating African-American Achievements

Mother Love
Co-Host
dLifeTV

The multi-talented and "even more fabulous" Mother Love is co-host of *dLifeTV* on CNBC every Sunday night. Mother Love is a published author, veteran of television and radio talk shows, film actress, advice columnist, motivational speaker, and stand-up comic. She recently was the recipient of the Eli Lilly 2005 Lilly for Life Award for Excellence in Journalism, and the Urban Leadership International 2005 Urban Angel Award for her excellence in community service and philanthropy leadership.

Since her diagnosis of type two diabetes in 1990, Mother Love has lost more than 100 pounds and has improved her diabetes management through healthy lifestyle changes. She speaks to audiences across America on health and motivational issues.

An accomplished author, Mother Love has penned two advice-based books, *Listen Up Girlfriends* (St. Martin's Press) and *Forgive or Forget: Never Underestimate the Power of Forgiveness* (HarperCollins). Her advice column, "Tell Mother Love," is featured in the Cleveland *Call & Post.* Mother Love, her husband and manager Kennedy Rogers, and their son reside in Los Angeles, California.

Richard A. Johnson
Publisher & Chairman
Kaleidoscope Magazine, LLC

Richard A. Johnson is the publisher and chairman of *Kaleidoscope Magazine*, LLC. *Kaleidoscope Magazine*, launched in 1992, highlights the spectrum of African-American achievement and celebrates Greater Cleveland's diversity. Johnson serves as executive producer for the magazine's weekly television and radio shows, and also oversees the company's publishing and public relations division, which designs and prints collateral materials for corporations and nonprofit organizations.

Johnson has served as the national publisher of magazines such as *Real Men*, the 100 Black Men of America magazine, and the Thurgood Marshall Scholarship Fund's magazine, *The Scholar*. Prior to the establishment of Kaleidoscope, he was with Fenix Enterprises.

Johnson is a graduate of Cleveland State University, where he earned a bachelor of arts and sciences degree. He is actively involved in a myriad of civic and community organizations.

A. Grace Lee Mims is hostess/producer of *The Black Arts* and *Arts Log* on WCLV-FM. She created *The Black Arts*, which features black composers and performers of classical music, in 1976.

Grace teaches voice at the Cleveland Music School Settlement and is considered an authority on the Negro spiritual. A soprano, she has recorded "Spirituals" with piano and "A Spirit Speaks" with her family's jazz-folk ensemble, The Descendants of Mike and Phoebe.

Grace graduated from Hampton University with high honors and received her master's degree in library science from Western Reserve University. In 1999, she was awarded an honorary doctorate of music from Cleveland State University. Her many other honors include national, regional, and local Hampton Alumni awards for initiating and chairing the Cleveland Hampton Scholarship Fund for 35 years. Grace also serves on the boards of the Cleveland Institute of Music and the Cleveland Arts Prize.

A native of Snow Hill, Alabama, Grace graduated as valedictorian of Snow Hill Institute, founded by her grandfather. She is the widow of Howard A. Mims, Ph.D., for whom Cleveland State University's African-American Cultural Center is named.

A. Grace Lee Mims
Hostess/Producer
WCLV-FM

Jeff Phelps is president and CEO of Jeff Phelps' Video Productions Inc. and Phelps Media Group, in addition to being the producer/director of the highly acclaimed cable television show *Another Look*. Since its inception, Jeff has sought to educate, inform, and entertain through the power of media. His vision, tenacity, and creativity are also the genesis of several other productions, including *Another Look at the MOVIES*, *Cleveland Beats News & Views*, *Black Political Agenda*, and *Another Look on the RADIO*.

In 2003, Jeff was named a Phenomenal African-American Man, an honor for which he received congressional recognition. That same year he was an inductee of Men With A Mission, an organization celebrating outstanding African-American men in Cleveland. Most recently, Jeff was featured in the inaugural edition of *Who's Who in Black Cleveland®*, a directory of some of the city's most influential and prominent people.

As a member of the NAACP, SCLC, The Association for the Improvement of Minorities, and the National Football League Alumni Association, Jeff is committed to greatness and making a difference. His motto is "seize the day."

Jeff Phelps
President & Chief Executive Officer
Jeff Phelps' Video Productions Inc.

Stephanie Phelps
Founder
Sisters Turning Pages

As vice president of Phelps Media Group and founder of Sisters Turning Pages, Stephanie Phelps is poised to expand her commitment to women through philanthropy and a number of other projects. Stephanie holds a degree in mass communications and journalism from Kent State University. She is listed in Strathmore's *Who's Who in Public Relations*, and is a member of the Press Club of Cleveland.

Stephanie has established a unique niche in Cleveland's media. She is host of the long-running *Another Look*, which airs on Adelphia Cable and Village Television. Stephanie began as a traffic reporter and newscaster for WJMO radio, then was creator, producer and host of *Woman to Woman*, a public affairs program which still airs, some 20 years later, on WZAK radio, where it began.

When not in front of the camera, Stephanie works for the Department of Children and Family Services, where she is responsible for the day-to-day public relations functions for the agency's recruitment department.

Stephanie is a member of Olivet Institutional Baptist Church. She is married to Jeff Phelps and they have two sons.

Richard "Zoom" Scott
Producer & Technician
WJW/Fox 8 News

Richard "Zoom" Scott is one of the most talented individuals in television. He works full-time at Fox 8 and is executive producer of the cable television show *Urban Flix*, which airs on Village Television. Zoom has won multiple Emmy Awards for shows such as *Neighborhood*, the longest-running public affairs show in Cleveland's television history. He has 24 years of experience in the industry and still loves every minute of it.

Zoom is a member of the United Black Fund Associate Board of Greater Cleveland. He serves as co-chair of the Celebrity Soul Food Cook-Off. He is a member of Emanuel Baptist Church and serves on the pulpit committee. Zoom pledged Alpha Phi Alpha Fraternity, Inc. and has ties to several chapters. He loves fashion and is the executive producer of the Cool, Smooth, and Jazzy Hair and Fashion Show. He also coaches his son's basketball team.

In 1982, Zoom received a bachelor of fine and professional arts degree from Kent State University. A native of Alliance, Ohio, Zoom has been married to April R. Scott for 13 years and they have a son, Demetrius Corteze Scott.

Brenda M. Ware-Abrams is a renowned Gospel announcer broadcasting on WABQ 1540 AM, and the hostess of an inspirational service on public access television. She was inducted into the National Broadcaster's Hall of Fame in 1996, the first African-American woman from Cleveland to receive this honor.

Abrams is the founder and chief executive officer of Gospel Inspiration, Inc. Her commitment and dedication has earned her the title of "Cleveland's Sweet Inspiration." She is a member of the Olivet Institutional Baptist Church.

A precinct committee person since 1972, Abrams is actively involved in numerous community projects. She serves on many boards, organizations, and committees, and has received numerous honors and accolades for her achievements.

A native West Virginian, Abrams appeared on her father's broadcast on WOAY AM for 13 years before moving to Cleveland. She has been broadcasting on WABQ since 1975.

Abrams is the wife of Arthur Abrams, Jr., and the mother of Arthur III, Melbia, and Katherine, and the grandmother of seven. She has been employed for 17 years as a compliance officer and executive assistant to the executive director of Community Action Against Addiction, Inc.

Brenda M. Ware-Abrams
Gospel Announcer
WABQ 1540 AM

Branson Wright joined *The Plain Dealer* as a sports reporter in 2000, becoming the Cavaliers beat writer during the 2001-2002 season. He is a 1989 graduate of the University of Cincinnati.

Wright has been published in several national magazines, including *ESPN The Magazine*, and he is often seen on ESPN and heard on national sports radio shows. He covered minor league baseball and the Continental Basketball Association in Grand Rapids, Michigan before coming to Cleveland. He also worked in North Carolina and for *The Lima* (Ohio) *News*.

Wright, born in Cincinnati, is the father of Pasha and Brandis and the husband to Lori, a native of Pittsburgh and a graduate of DePaul University.

Branson Wright
Sports Reporter
The Plain Dealer

Reverend Tyrone F. Davis
Pastor
Greater United Faith Baptist Church

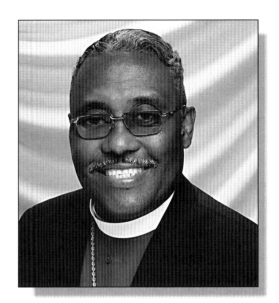

The Most Reverend J. Delano Ellis, II
President & Chief Executive Officer
Pentecostal Church of Christ

The Reverend Tyrone F. Davis is the pastor of Greater United Faith Baptist Church in Cleveland, Ohio. To his credit, his is a married, licensed, and ordained Baptist minister.

Reverend Davis is the former secretary of the Baptist Ministers Conference of Cleveland and Vicinity, Inc. He currently serves on the board of directors of the Southern Christian Leadership Conference's Cleveland chapter. Additionally, he is a member of the Mt. Pleasant Ministerial Alliance, the Pilgrim Baptist-Ministers Night Conference, and the NAACP Cleveland chapter.

Davis has certificates in religious studies, drug counseling, and community service, in addition to food service and hospitality management. He is enrolled at American Baptist College in Cleveland, and will receive a theology degree in 2007.

His favorite quotation is from the Reverend Dr. Martin Luther King, Jr., "True peace is not merely the absence of tension, it is the presence of justice."

J. Delano Ellis, II is president of the Pentecostal Church of Christ and is responsible for the spiritual growth of more than 800 members.

Recognized as a leading spiritual authority, Bishop Ellis has been called by media representatives worldwide to provide insight into religious and social topics, and is one of the leaders to be called during times of national crisis. He has served as Civil Air Patrol chaplain, currently serves as American Cadet Alliance chaplain, and is founder of two international organizations: Joint College of African-American Pentecostal Bishops and United Pentecostal Churches of Christ.

Ellis received a bachelor of arts degree from Howard University, a master of religious education degree from Nazarene Seminary, a doctorate of sacred theology from C.H. Mason Bible College, and a doctor of philosophy degree from Stafford University.

A Philadelphia, Pennsylvania native, Bishop Ellis is husband to Reverend Sabrina Ellis and proud father of Jesse, David, the Reverend Lillian Hanna, Jessica, Jasmine, and one adopted daughter, Victoria Winfield.

Cleveland's
SPIRITUAL LEADERS

Rev. Leatrice J. W. Emeruwa, Ed.D.
Founding Minister
Williams Center of Truth

Reverend Wardell Harris
Pastor & Founder
Greater Harvard Avenue C.O.G.I.C.

As founding minister of Williams Center of Truth, the Reverend Leatrice J.W. Emeruwa teaches scriptural meta-principles for spiritual growth.

A Central High School graduate, her degrees are from Howard, Kent State and Akron universities. An English/reading administrator in the Cleveland public schools, she retired from Cuyahoga Community College as professor emerita of English/reading.

Rev. Emeruwa was a Poet-in-the School and "culture pioneer" during Cleveland's 1970s Black Arts movement. She is an Ohio Arts Council prize-winning poet with published poetry and essays, who also performs poetry and tells tales.

A founding member and past president of Howard University Alumni Club of Cleveland, Emeruwa is a 2005 Outstanding Volunteer Alumna honoree. She holds life memberships in Sigma Gamma Rho Sorority, Inc.; the National Council of Negro Women; the NAACP (Golden Heritage); and the National Sorority of Phi Delta Kappa, Inc.

The only preacher/ poet in Cleveland, she counts as blessings her son, Earl Chima, daughter, Vanessa Turner, and granddaughter, Erika.

Elder Wardell Harris is the pastor and founder of the Greater Harvard Avenue Church of God in Christ. Greater Harvard Avenue is a dynamic urban community church established to address the spiritual, physical, and social needs of the community. Harris was ordained as an elder in 1983, and in 1986, he founded Greater Harvard Avenue Church of God in Christ.

Harris attended Philander Smith College, where he majored in business administration. He graduated from Grace Christian College in 1980 and received a certificate in theology from Moody Bible Institute. He also attended Ashland Theological Seminary.

Harris serves as chairman of the state ordination board, chair of the state trustee board, dean of education, and a member of the executive board of the National Conference of Pastors and Elders. Further, he is a member of the National Council of Pastors and Elders-Church of God in Christ.

Harris is also a civic leader and serves as a board member of Cleveland for Juvenile Justice and the vice president of the Miles-Lee Minister's Alliance.

Elder Harris is married to Ora L. Harris and they have two children, Stephen and Antoinette Harris.

Cleveland's
SPIRITUAL LEADERS

Celebrating African-American Achievements

Bishop Clifford L. Kimbrough, Jr.
**Jurisdictional Prelate for Ohio Northwest
Ecclesiastical Jurisdiction
Church of God In Christ, Inc.**

Bishop C. L. Kimbrough, Jr. is the jurisdictional prelate for the Ohio Northwest Ecclesiastical Jurisdiction in the Church of God In Christ, Inc. He has operated in this esteemed position for the past four years, and he oversees approximately 36 churches throughout the state of Ohio, including his local assembly, Jonas Temple Church of God in Christ, in Cleveland.

Although a native of Canton, Ohio, Kimbrough has been serving in the Cleveland area for more than 15 years as the administrative assistant to his predecessor, the late Bishop Robert L. Chapman. His recent relocation to Cleveland enabled him to become a great supporter of social services in the area. He is currently a partner with the Northeast Neighborhood Development Center in hopes of building affordable housing.

Kimbrough received a bachelor of arts degree, with honors, from Walsh University and is currently working on a master of arts degree at Ashland University.

Kimbrough is married to Catherine "Lady Loretta" Kimbrough, and is the proud father of four children, Clifford, III, Monica, Camon and Chyvonne.

Reverend Tamarah Ann Maxwell
**Pastor
Eaglewing Missionary Baptist Church**

The Reverend Tamarah Ann Maxwell is the first female African-American Baptist pastor in Ohio. She has been a pastor for nine years.

In addition to being a preacher, Maxwell is a well-trained gospel singer. She has performed at the former Mayor White's office and at many prestigious events. She recently traveled to New York City to record her first album, which is soon to be released.

"Pastor Tammy" uses her ministry to reach the old and young in the community, with real, down to earth teachings. She is a dynamic speaker who always leaves a great impression. She has evangelized in New York, Washington, Michigan, and West Virginia.

Pastor Tammy was trained under the teachings of her father, the late Reverend Henry O. Maxwell, Sr., who pastored the same church for more than 35 years. Upon his passing, his protégé accepted the call to ministry. She also attended John Carroll University.

Pastor Tammy is a single mother with two children, Crystalyn and Zachary.

Bishop Prince J. Moultry
Pastor
The InTouch Christian Center

Richard A. Muhammad
Minister
Muhammad Mosque #18

Bishop Prince J. Moultry is bishop and pastor of the nondenominational The InTouch Christian Center. He was elevated to the office of bishop by a unanimous vote of the 28 elders.

Moultry is known for his work with gangs, ex-felons, and others, assisting them with finding and keeping jobs through his ministry programs. He is chaplain for the City of East Cleveland Jail, as well as chief executive officer of The Greater Cleveland Jail Diversion Program.

Moultry received the FBI Leadership Award of Excellence for his "Adopt-A-Corner" program, which moved drug dealers off of street corners and replaced them with positive men from the community.

A singer, songwriter, and musician, Moultry recently released two CDs, *Never Forget* and *Go Tell It On the Mountain*. Many people read his weekly "Bishop Speaks" column in the Cleveland edition of the *Call & Post* newspaper.

Moultry sees his life as the song "I Don't Feel No Ways Tired," as he continues to show it every day in his actions with his staff, in meeting people where they are, and assisting them to become empowered to climb to higher ground.

Minister Richard A. Muhammad is the Cleveland representative of the Honorable Minister Louis Farrakhan at Muhammad Mosque #18. In this position, he serves as pastor, community leader, and motivational speaker. He is also the president of the Center for Self-Improvement, Inc., which is an organization designed to improve the conditions of urban communities by helping citizens avoid the traps which prevent most minorities from achieving success.

Minister Richard's experience has granted him the ability to address professional audiences and speak the current lingo of the youth. His presentation is so motivating and full of life that it has inspired many audiences, whether in a Muslim mosque, Christian church, university, or corporate boardroom. Whether he is in a lecture hall, barbershop, classroom, or pulpit, his most apparent feature is his zest and lucid articulation of the message of the Honorable Minister Louis Farrakhan.

A native of Boston, Massachusetts, Minister Richard is the husband of Thombra Muhammad and the proud father of four sons and two daughters.

Bishop Floyd Eugene Perry, Jr.
Pastor
Cathedral Church of God in Christ

Reverend Dr. Earl Preston, Jr.
Senior Pastor
Morning Star Baptist Church

Bishop F. E. Perry serves at the Cathedral Church of God in Christ in Cleveland, Ohio. He is also the jurisdictional prelate of the Ohio Southern Jurisdiction of the Church of God in Christ. As jurisdictional prelate, Perry is the overseer of a number of churches statewide.

Perry had leadership roles in the local NAACP and with the Urban League. Often, he speaks to school audiences about the drug problem and the need for tougher drug law enforcement. Currently, he is the second vice president of the NAACP's Cleveland branch.

Perry serves on the judiciary board of Church of God in Christ, Inc., the third most powerful board in the national church. He chaired the church's second largest convention, the UNAC-5 Convention, comprised of five auxiliaries. Previously, he served as vice president of the church's National Publishing Board.

Bishop Perry is the founder and president of the Church of God in Christ/Pentecostal Connection, a group of pastors united in giving assistance to the community.

A Shaker Heights resident, Perry is married to the former Jonelle Haynes and has one daughter, Lanelle, and two sons, Mark and Courtney.

The Reverend Dr. Earl Preston is the senior pastor at Morning Star Baptist Church. For the past 27 years, he has developed community outreach ministries. Reverend Preston was also the founder of the nationally known Prestonian Choral Ensemble, and an orator in the inauguration service of the first black mayor of Cleveland.

Preston has been featured in Strathmore's *Who's Who Registry of Business Leaders* and in *Who's Who in Religion*. He has been honored by *Church Magazine*, the Gospel Hall of Fame, and by Cleveland mayors Stokes, Perk, Kucinich, Voinovich, and White.

A past chairman of the National Convention of Gospel Choirs and Choruses, Preston's civic and fraternal affiliations include the Interdenominational Ministerial Alliance, Omega Psi Phi Fraternity, and the Cleveland Police Department Chaplains, with whom he holds the rank of captain.

Preston received his master's degree from Ashland Theological Seminary in 1980. In 1983, Trinity Theological Seminary awarded him a doctorate in ministry. He also studied at Lincoln College, Oxford, England in 1987.

A native of Cleveland, Reverend Preston travels and lectures on the histories of gospel music and the black church.

Pastor K. Selessie Simmons I
Senior Pastor
Greater Faith Baptist Church

Reverend Gwendolyn H. Snell
Interim Pastor
Good Shepherd Lutheran Church

Pastor K. Selessie Simmons I, the senior pastor of Greater Faith Baptist Church, preaches and teaches the infallible Word of God. He ignites and provokes the Joshua Generation to apply the principles of God's Word to their daily life. He encourages the Moses Generation to pour out wisdom, teaching the Joshua Generation to take back the inheritance that is theirs through the blood of Jesus Christ.

Simmons is the founder of Reapers of Promise Ministries, Inc. Their mission is to empower every individual who seeks answers to the difficulties of everyday life. They seek to develop and build the minds and hearts of individuals that they prosper in faith, family, and finances, as their soul prospers. The focus is to liberate the disenfranchised.

Simmons is a native of Philadelphia, Pennsylvania who has furthered his studies in Christian counseling at the Philadelphia Biblical University and Moody Bible College.

He is the husband of Kim Simmons and the father of four sons, Jarmarr, Irvin, Kevin II, Keith, and one daughter, Kaiyana.

The Reverend Gwendolyn H. Snell was called to be the transformation pastor at Good Shepherd Lutheran Church in Cleveland, Ohio. In this call, she will work along with a transformation team to change each ministry.

Reverend Snell was newly elected to the National African American Lutheran Association as the corresponding secretary. She was a contributing writer to *What Can Happen When We Pray*. In addition, Snell co-hosts a local cable talk show called *Sisters Speak*. A kidney transplant recipient, she received a 2004 Volunteer Award from the Minority Organ Transplant and Tissue Education Program.

Snell received a bachelor of arts degree from Capital University, a master of arts degree from Marygrove College, and a master of divinity degree from Trinity Lutheran Seminary.

A native of Detroit, Michigan, Reverend Snell enjoys cooking and entertaining family and friends.

Reverend Dr. Rodney S. Thomas
Pastor & Founder
Imani Temple Ministries

Reverend Dr. Taylor T. Thompson
Pastor
St. John AME Church

The Reverend Dr. Rodney S. Thomas is the pastor and founder of Imani Temple Ministries in Cleveland, Ohio. The son of a pastor, he delivered his first sermon at age 16. Before being led by the Holy Spirit to found Imani Temple Ministries, Rev. Thomas was senior pastor of St. James AME and St. Paul AME churches in Cleveland, and Zion AME Church of Delaware, Ohio. He was assistant pastor of St. Andrews AME Church in Memphis, Tennessee.

Thomas graduated, cum laude, from LeMoyne-Owen College with a degree in sociology and criminology. He received a master of divinity degree from Methodist Theological School of Ohio, and an honorary degree in divinity from Monrovia College, Liberia.

A native of Memphis, Tennessee, Thomas has received numerous honors and recognition for outstanding leadership and achievement in civic, religious, and community organizations. He holds board membership for the NAACP, The Free and Accepted Masons, AME Church Cleveland Ministerial Alliance, Greater Cleveland Methodist Ministerial Alliance, Senior Outreach Services, and Alpha Phi Alpha Fraternity, Inc.

Rev. Thomas enjoys activities with his children, Rodney and Raven. He likes to walk, read, and golf.

The Reverend Dr. Taylor Thompson is pastor of the historic St. John African Methodist Episcopal Church in Cleveland. For 175 years, St. John AME has ministered to the spiritual, social, political, and economic needs of the community.

Dr. Thompson has served as a member of the World Methodist Council executive committee and the National Pan-Methodist Commission on Cooperation and Union. He is past president of the Faith Community Alliance of Greater Cincinnati, the Metropolitan Area Religious Coalition of Cincinnati, and the Interdenominational Ministerial Alliance of Greater Cincinnati.

Currently, Thompson is president of the AME Ministerial Alliance of Greater Cleveland, a member of the Methodist Ministerial Alliance of Cleveland, and a member of the United Supreme Council AASR-PHA as a 33rd Degree Mason.

A native of Pittsburgh, Pennsylvania, Thompson was educated in Pittsburgh Public Schools. He earned a bachelor of science degree in management from the Massachusetts Institute of Technology, a master of divinity degree from the Pittsburgh Theological Seminary, and a doctor of ministry degree from the United Theological Seminary in Dayton, Ohio.

Dr. Thompson is married to Dr. Barbara J. Hunter Thompson.

Bishop Roberta Vines
Pastor
Confirmed Word Faith Center

Reverend Marvin J. Walker
Pastor
Second New Hope Baptist Church

Bishop Roberta Vines was born in Five Points, Alabama on June 19, 1934 to sharecroppers. She attended school in Selma at Selma University and R.B. Hudson High School. In later years, her family migrated to Cleveland, Ohio, and from there, she spent ten years in Pasadena, California, from 1970 to 1980. There, she studied pastoral leadership at Confirmed Word Faith Center under the teachings of Pastor Earl Johnson.

Roberta returned to Cleveland in 1981 and started Confirmed Word Faith Center of Cleveland, Ohio as the pastor, and she later received the honor of bishop. Vines and her congregation have attended many praise giving conventions with churches from Alabama to California. Currently, the church provides a food give-a-way station for the people in the Cleveland community, and also serves dinner on occasion after Sunday services.

For the past 12 years, Bishop Vines has traveled to Western Africa and ministered to the people in some of the villages, bringing the word of God, food, clothing, toys, transportation, and more recently, a clean water system. She has real compassion for God's people in the United States as well as Africa.

The Reverend Marvin J. Walker is the pastor of the Second New Hope Baptist Church. Second New Hope is an 81-year old Cleveland landmark in the East 116th Street area.

Walker serves as the recording secretary of the Baptist Pastor's Council of Cleveland. He is also the treasurer of the Baptist Minister's Conference, a member of the United Pastors in Mission, and a trustee of the Buckeye Area Development Corporation.

A product of the Cleveland Public School System, Walker is a 1968 graduate of East Tech. He has attended Cuyahoga Community College and Warren Bible School. In addition, he served the City of Cleveland for 31 years in the Cleveland Police Communication Department as a chief dispatcher.

Walker has received many certificates from the National Baptist Convention, USA, Inc., where he serves on the faculty.

The husband of Mary Liggins, Walker is the proud father of two children, Brian and Arica Taylor, and he has one granddaughter, Autumn.

Alexis E. Afzal
Executive Director
Alex Community
Development Corporation

Alexis E. Afzal is executive director of Alex Community Development Corporation (Alex CDC), a nonprofit organization which encourages economic development in the areas of small business development, workforce development, and financial literacy education.

Alexis founded Alex CDC in 1998 after holding a senior position with a local CPA firm which specialized in consulting services for small businesses. This followed her career as a regional vice president with the nation's largest financial services company.

Alexis is esteemed a whiz in career, business, and financial planning for individuals, families, and business enterprises. Under her leadership, Alex CDC was appointed by the U.S. Small Business Administration in 2003 to direct the Cleveland Women's Business Center. The Center provides training, counseling, and technical assistance to women and other emerging entrepreneurs who want to start or expand a business. In 2004, Alexis was honored by the American Business Women's Association for her contribution to women in business.

Alexis received her bachelor of business administration degree from Cleveland State University. She is a Certified Public Accountant, a Registered Investment Representative, a Registered Investment Principal, and a Licensed Insurance Professional.

Tanya M. Allmond
Executive Director
Northeastern Neighborhood
Development

Tanya M. Allmond is the executive director and chief fundraiser of Northeastern Neighborhood Development. She has brought $72 million in grants to the community, providing more than 650 new homes, 375,000 square feet of new commercial space, and management and technical assistance to more than 500 small businesses.

Professionally, Tanya is on the Shorebank Enterprise Group board of directors, the board of NHS, and a member of the Carnegie Mellon University Black Alumni Association. Additionally, she is a 2003 graduate of Leadership Cleveland.

Tanya is the founder and current board president of the Black Professionals Association Charitable Foundation, a board member of AAA, and a member of the Greater Cleveland Delta Life Development Center Foundation board of directors. She is a life member of the NAACP, and a member of Delta Sigma Theta Sorority, Inc. and Olivet Institutional Baptist Church.

Tanya received a bachelor's degree at Carnegie Mellon University, and studied business administration and management at the Wharton Graduate School of Finance of the University of Pennsylvania. She is certified by the National Development Council and holds numerous leadership awards.

For more than 25 years, Jesse O. Anderson has been a dedicated advocate for persons with disabilities. To his credit, he has represented the City of Cleveland on the Greater Cleveland Regional Transit Authority board of trustees for more than 16 years.

In 2002, Jesse received the Citizen of Distinction Award presented as a part of the City of Cleveland's first Disability Awareness Day. He was chosen as an Ohio delegate to the White House Conference on Handicapped Individuals, and he chaired the City of Cleveland's International Year of Disabled Persons.

Jesse served on the council for the Ohio Rehabilitation Services for 15 years. He is also the founder and past president of the Disabled Rights Task Force, Inc., and a former officer of the Easter Seals Society of Cleveland and Ohio. Additionally, he is a board trustee for the Disability Network of Ohio-Solidarity, Inc., and for the Legal Aid Society of Cleveland.

Jesse is active in the American Public Transportation Association and the Conference of Minority Transportation Officials. A self-employed realtor and financial accountant, he holds a degree in business management from Dyke College.

Jesse O. Anderson
Trustee
Greater Cleveland
Regional Transit Authority

Edna D. Connally is principal of the John D. Rockefeller Fundamental Education Center. In this position, she and her staff educate the students to become life-long learners; work towards sustaining a successful, fulfilling, and prosperous future; and experience all that life has to offer.

Edna is a Pogue fellow with the Pogue Institute for School Leadership and Management. She also volunteers with Race for the Cure and Crafting for Girls.

A member of Antioch Baptist Church, Edna is also a member of the Greater Cleveland chapter of Delta Sigma Theta Sorority, Inc., Jack and Jill of America, the Ohio Association of Secondary School Administrators, and the Cleveland Council of School Administrators.

Edna received a bachelor of arts degree from Bowling Green State University and a master's degree from Cleveland State University. She is presently working on a master's degree in pastoral counseling at Ashland University.

A native of Cleveland, Edna is the wife of James and the proud mother of Jauron, Sauniell, and Ilyaun.

Edna D. Connally
Principal
John D. Rockefeller F.E.C.

William Harrison Dillard
Retired
Olympic Gold Medalist

William Harrison Dillard was born on July 8, 1923. As a baby, he was diagnosed with a condition known as rickets, which prevented him from walking until he was 16 months old. As a result of his thin frame, Dillard was nicknamed "Bony Babe" by his schoolmates. This was shortened to "Bones" when he entered East Tech High School.

In his senior year at East Tech, Dillard became the city and state champion in the high and low hurdles. Consequently, he earned a scholarship to Baldwin-Wallace College in nearby Berea, Ohio.

He was abruptly called to duty in World War II, serving 16 months stateside and 16 overseas. Upon his return to Baldwin-Wallace, he resumed his athletic career that led to his winning 14 national championships and four Olympic gold medals: two in 1948 and two in 1952.

Dillard served on the boards of the American Lung Association; the Cleveland Church Federation; the Cedar Avenue YMCA; and the Cleveland Sports Commission. A former 27-year Cleveland Board of Education employee, Dillard was the first African-American head of its business department, a position he held for 12 years.

Kenneth Dwayne Hale
Director
High Tech Academy

Kenneth D. Hale is director of High Tech Academy, an option school established between the Cleveland Municipal School District and Cuyahoga Community College that prepares high school students for technological careers and higher education. Since 2000, more than 500 high school students have strengthened their academic skills, attended college classes, and earned college credit before graduating from their high schools.

Kenneth guided the design, development, and implementation of the successful educational model where students are challenged by high standards and a rigorous curriculum. With the generous support of National City Corporation and NASA, the Academy has become a national model for linking secondary and higher education with leading businesses.

Kenneth is also a free-lance writer, and president/CEO of Empower Communications, Ltd., a grant writing and fundraising consulting company.

He has earned prestigious awards from Cuyahoga Community College, City Year, and The Phenomenal Foundation.

A Cleveland native, Kenneth enjoys mentoring and coaching youth, and is a member of Hope Alliance Bible Church and Alpha Phi Alpha Fraternity, Inc.

Kenneth and his wife, SeMia, are the proud parents of four children, Kelvin Dyrell, Kenia Danelle, Kelton Darnell, and Kiera Danielle.

For 37 years, Solomon Harge, executive director of the Consumer Protection Association, has focused on education, advocacy, and economic empowerment for individuals in need. Harge serves the following organizations: the Consumer Federation of America; Dominion East Ohio, advisory committee; and the United Way Services' Agency Executives. In 1959, he founded Greater Cleveland Toastmasters 2825, which was the first African-American Toastmasters organization in Cleveland, and one of the first to include women among its members.

Harge has also served on the boards of Sunny Acres Foundation and Community Guidance, Inc. He was board president of First Church of Religious Science and served on the consumer advisory councils of the United States Underwriters Laboratories, Ford Motor Company, Ameritech, and AT&T. Harge has also been a member of the Supreme Court of Ohio and the Board of Commissioners of Grievances and Discipline, and he served as the chairman of the Civil Service Commission.

Harge and his wife, Dorothy, have two children, Felicia and Solomon, Jr., and a granddaughter, Nakia.

Solomon Harge
Executive Director
Consumer Protection Association

Amelia Jenkins is the multi-cultural outreach coordinator for the Alzheimer's Association Cleveland Area Chapter.

Since 1980, the association has supported families affected by Alzheimer's disease in Northeast Ohio. African Americans have the highest rate of Alzheimer's disease and are the least represented in clinical studies or potential treatments. Through outreach efforts, Amelia seeks to raise awareness in underserved communities about support services provided by the association.

Amelia began her career in health care administration with Blue Cross and Blue Shield of Northeast Ohio, where she received her license to market health and life insurance in the State of Ohio. In addition, she has worked with various Medicaid and Medicare managed care health plans.

Amelia is a trustee of the American Sickle Cell Anemia Association and member of The Hospice of Western Reserve African-American outreach committee. She has a degree in marketing from Cleveland State University.

Amelia resides in Maple Heights and is the mother of three adult children and the grandmother of eleven grandchildren. She enjoys traveling, event planning, volunteering for community interest, and reading.

Amelia D. Jenkins
Multi-Cultural Outreach Coordinator
Alzheimer's Association
Cleveland Area Chapter

Yolanda Lamar-Wilder
Founder & President
Women Entrepreneurs Of America, Inc.

Yolanda Lamar-Wilder is founder and president of Women Entrepreneurs Of America, Inc. Women Entrepreneurs Of America is a nonprofit membership-based women's organization whose mission is to "empower and support" women in business and provide resources to those who want to start their businesses.

Prior to starting Women Entrepreneurs Of America (formerly known as WEA, Inc.), Lamar-Wilder created her own employment service, Labor U.S. of A. Employment Agency, Inc. in May of 2000. In addition to her current duties, Lamar-Wilder also manages her own consulting company, Wilder Consulting Services, Ltd.

In 2000, the National Council of Negro Women, Inc. honored Lamar-Wilder for her articles in *The Cleveland Monitor*, and she was asked to join the National Council of Negro Women, Inc. She currently serves on the executive committee as the public relations chair for the Western Reserve Section. Lamar-Wilder also serves on the executive boards of the Consortium of African-American Organizations and the City of Cleveland Workforce Investment Board, where she also serves on the economic committee.

Raised in Gary, Indiana, Lamar-Wilder now lives in Cleveland. She has two sons and one daughter, along with six grandchildren, all in Indiana.

Willetta Andrea Milam
President & Founder
HELP RESOURCES, Inc.

Willetta Andrea Milam is president and founder of HELP RESOURCES, Inc., a nonprofit community-based organization that advocates for both senior citizens and youth. HELP RESOURCES has two very important components in its mission. Most of its members and staff volunteer time to mentor youth who have family histories involving drugs, alcohol, and violence. The mentoring program operates year-round, helping youth with social and academic nurturing.

Willetta is also a school board member of the Cleveland Municipal School District. She was appointed to the school board in 2003 by Mayor Jane Campbell, who reappointed her to a four-year term in July of 2005.

A native of Youngstown, Ohio, Willetta received her bachelor of arts degree in social sciences, with a concentration in political science, from the University of Pittsburgh at Bradford in 1983. In 1988, she received her juris doctor degree from the Antioch School of Law. Willetta has received many honors and awards and has held many positions both in Ohio and Washington, D.C.

She is the proud mother of three children, Bruce Jr., Michael, and Krystal.

On December 6, 1984, Yvonne Pointer's 14-year-old daughter, Gloria, was abducted, raped and murdered. To date, her murder remains unsolved. Since the death of her daughter, Yvonne has worked entirely throughout the community both locally and nationally as an advocate for child safety. For her efforts, she has received numerous honors, including induction into the Women's Hall of Fame, appearing on the *Oprah Winfrey Show*, and receiving the 2001 Essence Award, to name a few.

In 1991, the Gloria Pointer Scholarship was established in Cleveland, Ohio to help students pursuing higher education goals. In 2003, the Gloria Pointer Teen Movement was established in Ghana, West Africa. Both scholarships are funded through proceeds from Yvonne's book, *Behind the Death of a Child*.

A Cleveland native, Yvonne is employed by the City of Cleveland in the Department of Community Relations as a project director. Her hobbies include traveling and writing, and her articles have appeared in both local and national publications.

Yvonne is the mother of two, Raymon and Denyelle, and the proud grandmother of three, Iyana, Raymon, Jr. and Cheneille.

Yvonne Pointer
Community Activist, Author
& Motivational Speaker

Tonia Kates Stewart, Ph.D., is the executive director of a local nonprofit agency, Cleveland MOTTEP (Minority Organ Tissue Transplant Education Program). MOTTEP's mission is to increase awareness, through education and advocacy, about organ and tissue donation, disease prevention and wellness in the Greater Cleveland African-American community.

Stewart received all three of her degrees from Bowling Green State University. She began her career in higher education and has held positions at Bowling Green State University, where she was associate vice president for student affairs, and at Kent State, where she was director of development. Currently, Stewart is a full-time lecturer at Case Western Reserve University teaching courses in non-verbal communication and multicultural communication.

Stewart serves on several local boards and is a member of the Western Reserve chapter of The Links, Inc.

A graduate of the Cleveland Public Schools, Stewart's passions are her two children, Ben, a junior at Wright State, and Aliece, a freshman at Bowling Green State University.

Tonia Kates Stewart, Ph.D.
Executive Director
Cleveland MOTTEP

Alton Tinker
Councilman
City of Bedford Heights

Alton Tinker is a councilman for Ward 3 in the City of Bedford Heights, Ohio. He chairs the building and housing committee and serves as a member of numerous other committees. Additionally, he is vice president and credit officer for Keybank's community development underwriting group. He makes credit decisions on community development loans.

Alton is founder of the Society of Urban Professionals, a 1,200-member networking group. He serves on the board of trustees for Lutheran Housing Corporation, where he is the treasurer of the board, and on the advisory board of the Million March Movement.

Alton has been the president of the Cleveland chapter of the National Black MBA Association since 2003. Under his leadership, the Cleveland chapter won Chapter of the Year in 2003 and 2004. He has received recognition in numerous publications.

Alton earned his master of business administration degree with a concentration in finance from Cleveland State University. He earned his bachelor of science degree in industrial engineering from Southern Illinois University.

Born in Jamaica, he is married to Lynnette and is the proud father of two children, Justin and Jaylyn.

Hazel L. Williams
President
Black United Fund of Ohio

Hazel L. Williams is the president of the Black United Fund of Ohio (BUFOhio), an independent, nonprofit fundraising federation and economic development organization with 25 member agencies across Ohio. BUFOhio serves critical human needs including alcohol and drug abuse prevention and treatment, programs for the homeless, business development, and several other programs.

BUFOhio provides member agencies access to additional funding sources through payroll deduction campaigns at all federal, state, county, and city government offices, The Ohio State University and private sector businesses. Williams hosts BUFOhio's weekly radio program, Black United Fund Presents.

BUFOhio is the Ohio affiliate of the National Black United Fund, a movement for self-help and self-sufficiency that began more than 30 years ago with the Brotherhood Crusade fundraising campaign in Los Angeles. Today, the National Black United Fund has 25 affiliates from Oregon to Florida that have raised millions of dollars for projects that serve critical human needs.

Williams is a graduate of Ohio Wesleyan University. Fluent in French, she studied international business at the École Supérieure de Commerce in Nantes, France, and was awarded the prestigious Huntington International Fellowship.

Nicole Yvonne Williams is an accomplished author, orator, and musician. She currently serves as communications director for Congresswoman Stephanie Tubbs Jones of the 11th Congressional District, Ohio. In this position, she coordinates all media for the Representative and serves as her speechwriter. Additionally, Nicole has served as spokesperson and consultant on various national political campaigns and community related programs.

Nicole attended Spelman College in Atlanta, Georgia where she majored in music. Named a Ray Charles Scholar, she graduated with departmental honors in 2000. She later received her master of arts degree in communications management from John Carroll University in University Heights, Ohio.

Nicole is active in a variety of organizations including the Beachwood Chamber of Commerce, The National Alumnae Association of Spelman College and Delta Sigma Theta Sorority, Inc. She is a 2002 graduate of Cleveland Bridge Builders and the National Conference for Community and Justice LeadDiversity programs.

A life-long member of Eastview United Church of Christ, she served on the board of the Western Reserve Association of the United Church of Christ.

Nicole Yvonne Williams
Communications Director
Congresswoman Stephanie Tubbs Jones

Ronald A. Winbush is executive director of Community Action Against Addiction, Inc. He is currently a member of the national board of trustees of the American Association for the Treatment of Opioid Dependency. A member of the Leadership Cleveland Class of 1994, Winbush has been involved in numerous civic and professional endeavors in the Greater Cleveland community for more than 30 years. He has also received many awards and honors for his dedication and commitment to various affiliations.

Winbush's former employment includes serving as assistant executive director of the American Red Cross, executive director of the Eliza Bryant Nursing Home, and positions with the City of Cleveland and the Murtis Taylor Multi-Service Center.

Winbush earned a bachelor's degree from Cleveland State University and a master's degree in social science administration from Case Western Reserve University. He is also a licensed independent social worker with the State of Ohio.

A Cleveland native, Ronald is the father of two children. He supports numerous public service organizations including the Midtown Corridor, the NAACP, 100 Black Men, the Million Man March, the Teen Father's Program, and the Southern Christian Leadership Conference.

Ronald A. Winbush
Executive Director
Community Action Against
Addiction, Inc.

Montrie Rucker Adams, APR
President
Visibility Marketing Inc.

Leon Anderson III
Chief Executive Officer
Sports and Spine Physical Therapy, Inc.

Montrie Rucker Adams, APR is president of Visibility Marketing Inc. and a principal with Corporate Image Group LLC. Montrie helps businesses communicate the right messages to key audiences. Through effective marketing communications and public relations campaigns, companies become more visible.

Montrie has contributed to several publications including the *Women of Color Devotional Bible* and *Kaleidoscope Magazine*, where she also served as editor-in-chief.

She serves on the boards of Continue Life Inc., the Public Relations Society of America (PRSA), and on the Cleveland Museum of Art's African-American Task Force. She is a lifetime member of the National Black MBA Association.

The National Council of Negro Women, Crain's *Cleveland Business'* Forty Under 40, The Phenomenal Woman Foundation, and *Kaleidoscope Magazine's* 40/40 Club have recognized Montrie's civic contributions. She is also an accomplished public speaker, having received the Distinguished Toastmaster Award from Toastmasters International.

Montrie earned a master of business administration degree from the University of North Carolina, a bachelor of arts degree from Baldwin-Wallace College, and accreditation in public relations.

Montrie and her husband, Todd Q., have two children, Tadj Josiah and Najah Mizan.

Leon Anderson is chief executive officer of Sports and Spine Physical Therapy, located in Beachwood. The goal of Sports and Spine is to resolve their clients' pain resulting from injuries, mechanical neck/back dysfunctions, or surgical procedures. The company provides individualized treatment programs for orthopedic conditions, emphasizing manual techniques.

Leon co-founded The "Let's Talk About…" Youth Enrichment Program, a nonprofit organization providing extended learning opportunities through partnerships with local communities. This program promotes lifetime learning, self-empowerment, critical thinking, and fun. Leon spends his spare time mentoring youth and coaching high school football.

Leon earned a bachelor of science degree from The Ohio State University, majoring in management information systems. He received his physical therapy degree from the University of Connecticut, and holds a master's degree in orthopedic manual therapy from The Ola Grimsby Institute.

Leon is currently vice president of the American Academy of Physical Therapy. He served as a subject matter expert for the American Physical Therapy Association's orthopedic clinical specialist exam, and is currently an on-site reviewer for the Commission on Accreditation in Physical Therapy Education.

Darlene Darby Baldwin
President & CEO
Midtown Scientific, Inc.

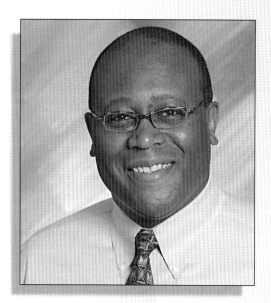

Cedric D. Beckett
President & Chief Executive Officer
Strong Tool Company

Darlene Darby Baldwin is the president and CEO of Midtown Scientific, Inc., a certified Minority Business Enterprise (MBE). Established in November of 2003, this business serves as a distribution channel and supplier to the scientific research community.

As a business owner and behavioral analyst who utilizes organizational development practices and methods to effectively promote change, Darlene holds the city's first African American-owned research distribution company. She partners nationally with numerous manufacturers and supplier, providing complete lines of scientific research products.

Darlene serves on the board of directors for the National Minority Health Institute and the Cuyahoga County Alcohol and Drug Services Board. Likewise, she is the board president for mentoring2Max and a member of the Alzheimer Association's Multi-Cultural Advisory Board.

A member of Warrensville Road Community Baptist Church, Darlene is a success story of the Cleveland Public Schools and a graduate of John Carroll and Case Western Reserve Universities.

Darlene is the beloved wife of Danny Baldwin and proud mother of three, twins Kalem and Khaliah Watts, and Vanessa Baldwin. It is Darlene's greatest hope that this business will help to fuel the local economy.

Cedric D. Beckett is the president and CEO of Strong Tool Company, a leading distributor of metal-cutting tools, abrasives, and industrial supplies to the automotive, aerospace, and medical industries in the Midwest. He is concentrating on expanding his company geographically in Ohio, Indiana, Michigan, and Alabama.

Beckett is a former vice president of Barnes Group, Inc., and former president of Barnes' industrial distribution business, Bowman Distribution, in Cleveland.

Beckett holds a bachelor's degree in mechanical engineering from Polytechnic Institute of New York, and a master's degree in operations management. Likewise, he holds a master of business administration degree in finance from Rensselaer Polytechnic Institute.

To his credit, Beckett is on the board of directors for E CITY (Entrepreneurs Connecting, Inspiring and Teaching Youth) and the Northern Ohio Minority Business Council. Previously, he served on the board of governors for the state of Connecticut Department of Higher Education, The Connecticut Science Museum, Big Brothers/Big Sisters, and INROADS.

Beckett received the 1998 Most Distinguished Alumni Award from Rensselaer Polytechnic Institute, and was chosen as one of *Crain's Cleveland Business* "Forty Under 40" in 2002.

Dargan J. Burns
President & Founder
Burns Public Relations Services

Kelly Chapman
President
Lightworld Enterprises

Dargan J. Burns, founder of Burns Public Relations Services, has engaged in public communications, marketing, and community relations for 45 years. His agency counsels top management in public communications and economic development.

A Hampton University graduate, Burns continued his academics at Harvard and Boston Universities. In 1952, he was the first African American to receive a master of science degree from Boston University's School of Public Relations and Communications.

Burns organized the Cleveland agency after seven years as director of public relations for the Karamu House and Karamu Theatre. He retained Karamu House and acquired former UN Ambassador Dr. Zelma George as his first new client.

Some of Burns' long-time corporate clients included Tops Friendly Markets, Inc., the Cuyahoga County Board of Commissioners, Wilberforce University, and Standard Oil Company (now BP/AMOCO).

Burns is a member of the Church of the Covenant and Omega Psi Phi Fraternity, Inc., and is legend emeritus of the National Alliance of Market Developers. He received the prestigious H. Naylor Fitzhugh Humanitarian Award in 2003.

Burns is the proud father of two sons, Dargan J. Burns, III and Cedric C. Burns, both entrepreneurs in Atlanta.

Kelly Chapman is president of the executive search firm Lightworld Enterprises, Lightworld Entertainment, and Lightworld Records. Previously, Chapman was a general manager for Ameritech.

The founder of Kelly Chapman Ministries, Inc., Chapman serves on the boards of Karamu House, Inc., The Girl Scouts of Lake Erie Council, and The Center for Families and Children. In addition, she worships at NewSong Church. Featured in *Money Magazine*, Chapman is the youngest person to establish a fund at the Cleveland Foundation.

Chapman is a member of Cleveland Bridge Builders, *Kaleidoscope Magazine*'s 40/40 Club and *Crain's Cleveland Business* "Forty Under 40."

Finally, she is an international recording artist with a critically acclaimed CD entitled *Real* and a corresponding book in production. Her song, "Heal Me," was selected as Black Entertainment Televisions' debut song for the hurricane Katrina commercials. Her music video, interviews, and performances air on major television stations worldwide.

Chapman received a bachelor of arts degree and a master of business administration degree from the J.L. Kellogg Graduate School of Management and Case Western Reserve University.

She resides in Cleveland Heights with her lovely daughter, Natalie.

Stephana Childs-Caviness
Founder & President
A Woman's Point, Inc.

Lonnie Coleman
President & Chief Executive Officer
Coleman Spohn Corporation

Stephana Childs-Caviness, the founder and president of A Woman's Point, Inc., matriculated from Case Western Reserve University with a major in communications. She held positions as a liaison to the Cleveland City Council under former Mayor Dennis J. Kucinich and as interim executive director of the Lorain County Urban League. She teaches anger management for Beech Brook as well as developing cable television shows.

A Woman's Point, Inc. began as a live radio talk show on WJMO and transitioned to cable television in 2004. One of Stephana's short-term goals is to produce a documentary on HIV/AIDS. She received her training from the producer and founder of Power NeTv. In addition, she received sponsorship from the United Black Fund of Greater Cleveland, Inc. for both radio and television. She believes that God has been the catalyst for her life's inspiration, strength, and success—"With God, all things are possible."

Stephana takes pride in her three children, Theophilus, Stephen, and Theana. She participates in various fundraising activities, but the one dearest to her is fundraising for breast cancer research—she is a six-year survivor.

Lonnie Coleman is president and CEO of Coleman Spohn Corporation, a mechanical contracting firm established in 1994 to install heating, ventilating, and air conditioning systems for the commercial and industrial construction market. Headquartered in Cleveland, Ohio, the company has a branch office in Toledo, Ohio.

Lonnie has been actively involved in the changing skyline of Cleveland. He has participated in the construction of such facilities as the Rock and Roll Hall of Fame, Jacob's Field, and the Stem Cell Research Facility of Cleveland Clinic.

Lonnie is involved in many professional and civic organizations in the Greater Cleveland area. He serves as president of the Presidents' Council, and a board member of Shore Enterprise Development Bank, The MetroHealth Hospital Foundation, and The Greater Cleveland Partnership, to name a few.

Lonnie's honors and achievements include receiving the Governor's "Minority Business of the Year" Award, among many others.

A Solon resident, Lonnie has been married for 36 years to Frances Y. Hurd, a native of Lima, Ohio. They are the parents of three children, Kelli, Kiana, and Christopher.

Lonnie's interests are economic development, minority business development, youth, golf, reading, and traveling.

William Christopher Daniel
Proprietor
World Waste Inc.

Call it dirty, call it disgusting. However you view it, just know that William Christopher Daniel, owner of World Waste Inc., has made other peoples' trash his treasure.

Growing up, Chris watched his dad run and operate Daniel & Son Rubbish Co. He often dreamed of running the operation with a larger vision, picking up garbage all over the world. This is how World Waste Inc. obtained its name. On January 1, 1990 his dream became a reality, and he aims not only to take over the city, but to take over the world.

Chris is known to be stern and hardcore in the business but says, "You have to, because this line of work is often overlooked and perceived to be a poor man's job." However, World Waste Inc. has an impressive client list which validates his hardcore work mentality.

Chris has never forgotten where he came from and where it all started. He prides his company on good customer service and discounted prices.

He hopes World Waste Inc. will be around for generations to come.

Vicki Dansby
President
Imagine That…Entertainment & Event Management

Vicki Dansby, president of Imagine That…Entertainment & Event Management, is a native of Cleveland, Ohio. She and her partner Duane Moody formed Imagine That . . . in 1998.

As president, Dansby's focus is to conceive, coordinate and execute marketing plans and events to meet her clients' specific needs, as well as provide entertainment and celebrities to enhance corporate, fundraising, and private events. Major clients have included the NFL Cleveland Browns and the United Black Fund of Greater Cleveland.

In addition to event management, Dansby and her partner also consult with and provide public relations for former heavyweight champions Ken Norton, Sr. and Mike Weaver, songwriter Norman Whitfield, The Four Tops, Bobby Womack, and the legendary Jim Brown.

Prior to the formation of Imagine That…, Dansby worked in the marketing departments of FOX8 Cleveland and the NFL Cleveland Browns Trust.

Dansby has numerous professional honors and affiliations. These include being the 2003 Goodwill Ambassador for the Nelson Mandela Children's Fund, and president of the associate board of the United Black Fund of Greater Cleveland, Inc.

Dansby is single and resides in Euclid, Ohio.

Hezekiah M. Davidson
President & Chief Executive Officer
Right Hand Management & Productions, Inc.

Larry E. Fulton
Founder and President
LEFCO Industries

Hezekiah Davidson is president and CEO of Right Hand Management & Production, Inc., which he founded in 1998. Currently based in Akron, Right Hand Management & Production is a multifaceted client management and event production company. Hezekiah's client division specializes in managing the careers of a variety of high profile personalities, celebrities, established authors, and lecturers. His events division specializes in the production, marketing, and management of promotional events, workshops, expos, and seminars.

Prior to his own management and production company, Hezekiah spent ten years in the mortgage industry as a processor, loan originator, underwriter, and licensed broker. In addition, he spent more than 12 years working with several youth organizations serving as director, assistant director, group life supervisor, counselor, and sports instructor.

A native of Akron, Hezekiah still travels the country with his clients but never forgets his hometown. An avid believer in helping our youth succeed in life, he is a mentor and presently serves on the board of the National Youth Sports Program in Akron.

Larry E. Fulton is the founder and president of LEFCO Industries, a manufacturer of material handling products. LEFCO provides custom designed steel returnable racking systems, steel crates and pallets, wood crating products, and specialty wooden shipping platforms and containers. LEFCO serves customers in the defense, aerospace, transportation, and general industrial markets.

Previous to LEFCO, Larry was general manager of Alcoa Sub-Assembly & Logistics, a line of business of Alcoa, Inc. His earlier career included financial analysis and due diligence for merger and acquisitions, and business and strategic planning for small-sized companies.

Larry received his degree in business administration from the School of Business & Industry at Florida A&M University, and a master of business administration degree in management policy and entrepreneurialism from the Weatherhead School of Management at Case Western Reserve University.

Larry is a member of the 100 Black Men of Cleveland, Inc., a Prince Hall Mason, and is actively involved in the music ministry at New Community Bible Fellowship.

Larry is happily married to Arlishea, an attorney, and is the proud father of Larry, Jr. and Ashley Morgan.

James E. Greene, D.D.S.
Dentist
James G. Greene, D.D.S., Inc.

Teresa Hamilton
Owner & President
My Baby's Bubblegum

James E. Greene, D.D.S. joined his father in dental practice in the Mt. Pleasant area of Cleveland in 1978, after completing dental school at Howard University, and residency in general dentistry at D.C. General Hospital in Washington D.C. Practicing for 25 years with his father, now retired, Greene remains in Cleveland, located in the Shaker Square district. His practice is one of only four African-American dental practices located within city limits and treating people of all ages.

A past president of Forest City Dental Society and active as Junior Warden at St. Andrew's Episcopal Church, Greene obtained his bachelor of arts degree from Wesleyan University in Middleton, Connecticut. There, he was captain of the football team, named to first team, All-New England.

Greene is the long-running chair of the Kappa Alpha Psi Annual Golf Tournament and is vice-president of Kappa Management, overseeing operations at the Kappa Alpha Psi-owned HUD housing facility on Shaker Boulevard.

Married to Giesele Robinson Greene, M.D. for more than 28 years, Greene is the proud father of three children in addition to raising a niece and two nephews.

Teresa "Tesa" Hamilton is the owner and president of My Baby's Bubblegum, located in Cleveland since 1994. She sells thousands of promotional products including silkscreen and embroidered apparel. As the owner and president, she oversees the business and operates the equipment.

Tesa was featured in the National Register's *Who's Who in Executive Professionals* 2003-2005 editions and The American Biographical Institute, Inc.'s *Great Women of the 21st Century* 2004 edition.

A Cleveland native, Tesa uses Christian principles in the ownership and operation of her business. Her family, including husband Andrew Hamilton, works together in her business. The Hamiltons, with their children Tamika, Denzel, and MyTisha, enjoy playing basketball together.

Tesa and her family place Jesus Christ first in everything they do. They are members of Calvary Apostolic Assembly where Tesa has served on the usher board, the pastors aide committee, and the baptism committee.

Tesa's favorite quote is Acts 2:38: "Repent, and be baptized every one of you in the name of Jesus Christ for the remission of your sins, and ye shall receive the gift of the Holy Ghost."

Suzan E. Jackson
President & Founder
Creative Business Webs

Dr. Roselyn Brooks Kennedy
Pediatric Dentist
Kennedy Pediatric Dentistry, Inc.

Suzan E. Jackson has parlayed more than 30 years of experience in public relations and communications into providing marketing solutions for small, female, and minority businesses. The president and founder of Creative Business Webs, Suzan works with her clients to implement technology-driven, guerilla marketing strategies resulting in maximum bang for her client's buck. With a national client base that includes commercial, professional, and nonprofit, she provides personalized strategies to meet their individual needs. Services include Web site and graphic design, marketing, image development, public relations, event planning, production, systems installation and training.

Suzan has served on numerous boards and committees including the NAACP, the YWCA, the African American Family Day Picnic, and the Hispanic Community Convencíon. She was the first female and minority president of the Greater Cleveland Chapter of the American Multi-Image Association, and she is published through the U.S. Department of Education. She has written for several area weekly newspapers, including an entire business and technology section and a lifestyle column.

Suzan holds a bachelor of arts degree in communications from Notre Dame College of Ohio. Her philosophy is, "Conceive, believe, achieve…but first believe."

Dr. Roselyn Brooks Kennedy, pediatric dentist, is a native of Richmond, Virginia. Kennedy Pediatric Dentistry, Inc., in Cleveland Heights, was established in 1990.

Dr. Kennedy attended Franklin College in Indiana on a four-year scholarship, majoring in biology. She graduated from the University of Pittsburgh School of Dental Medicine with a doctor of dental medicine degree, and completed residency programs at Provident Hospital in Baltimore, Maryland.

A veteran of the United States Air Force Dental Corp, she served at the Strategic Air Command Barksdale Air Force Base in Louisiana and obtained the rank of major.

To her credit, Kennedy was the first African American accepted into a dental specialty residency program at University Hospitals and Case Western Reserve University. She has served as an adjunct professor and assistant clinical professor at Case in the area of dentistry for children.

A member of the Board of Pediatric Dentists and numerous other dental organizations, Kennedy has assumed several dental leadership roles on the local and national levels. Early, consistent, and routine dental care for children has been her philosophy in preventing and combating dental disease in children.

Cecil King
Founder
American Merchandising Systems

Franklin F. Martin
Owner
The F. Martin Printing Company

Cecil King, founder of American Merchandising Systems, has truly experienced the American dream. An active supporter of the civil rights movement and the late Dr. Martin Luther King, Jr.'s teachings of self-reliance, Cecil felt that blacks needed to become business owners—not just employees in other businesses.

In 1968, Cecil established American Dream Soap Company, selling soaps and related products. This company was the catalyst for his next entrepreneurial endeavor, American Merchandising Systems (AMS). Established in 1977, AMS sells laboratory, chemical, safety, maintenance, and office supplies.

Cecil King speaks at countless seminars and sits on the boards of directors for various local entities. AMS has received awards and recognitions from city, state, and federal agencies as well as corporate entities. Cecil takes the most pride and sense of achievement from the encouragement and motivation that he has instilled in other minorities to start their own businesses.

A veteran of the U.S. Air Force, Cecil holds a bachelor's degree in business administration from Fenn College. A Cleveland native, he has been married to his wife Norma for more than 35 years. They have seven children and numerous grandchildren.

Franklin F. Martin is owner of The F. Martin Printing Company and chief operations officer of the 100 Black Men of Greater Cleveland, Inc. A Cleveland native, Martin majored in instrumental music at Cleveland State University and served in the U.S. Air Force. He is a member of Affinity Missionary Baptist Church where he serves as chairman of the trustee board and sings with the sanctuary choir.

Since 1983, Martin has been a member of the Black Professionals Association, where he was chairman of the board from 1995 until 2000. He currently serves on the Workforce Development Board for the City of Cleveland, the African-American advisory board of the Cleveland Foundation, The Cleveland Museum of Art's African-American and Convening the Community boards, as well as the Old Stone Center for Education board of directors. Martin is also a charter member of the 100 Black Men of Greater Cleveland.

He has received numerous honors including recognition in *Black Enterprise* for business, Knights of St. Peter Claver through the Catholic Diocese, and the Cleveland Educators and Alumni Achievers Hall of Fame Award.

Martin has one adult daughter who is an architect.

Greg Mayo III
Founder & Principal Instructor
Northern Wind

Debra Milton, M.S.
Lifestyle Empowerment Consultant
Gemini Empowerment Group

Master Greg Mayo III is the founder and principal instructor of Northern Wind, a martial arts training center located in downtown Cleveland specializing in intensive self-defense training, personal safety and awareness, kickboxing, and mental/physical body conditioning. Known as the "G-Man," he has a heart of gold and is genuinely dedicated and committed to serving children and families in Northeast Ohio.

Since 1982, Master Mayo has personally trained, shaped, and counseled more than 500 men, women, and children. He has provided protection services for many notable entertainers, including Halle Berry, Jamie Foxx, Usher, and Sinbad. He also serves as director of security for Cleveland's CBS 19 and WUAB 43.

As a fourth degree master of Gung Fu, and a licensed martial arts instructor, Master Mayo is a well-known leader in the field of executive protection. He has received outstanding notoriety and demands for his service from many high profile celebrities, civic, business, and community leaders. Master Mayo is one of Cleveland's leading and most prominent executive protection professionals.

Debra Milton became an entrepreneur in 1982, after employment at Cleveland State University, Cuyahoga Community College, Western Illinois University, and Cathedral Christian Academy. She owns Gemini Empowerment Group.

A lifestyle empowerment consultant and motivational speaker, Milton provides consulting services for human resources training, development, and organizational growth. She provides financial literacy training for asset building. A network business developer, she advocates asset creation, wellness, and quality of life.

Milton's affiliations include Cathedral Church of God in Christ, the Christian Business League, the Consortium of African American Organizations, Faith Community United Credit Union, and the African American Women's Agenda Education Foundation. She is chair of the Cleveland Women's Health Care Commission, serves on the City of Cleveland Health Advisory Committee, and is a member of Cleveland Saves, Earn Income Tax Credit/VITA Sites Coalition, and Delta Sigma Theta Sorority, Inc.

A former Cleveland International Program board member and United We Can executive board member, Milton was a VISTA Volunteer, a founding member of Operation Greater Cleveland Big Vote, and worked with the Minority Regional Purchasing Council.

Milton graduated with a master of science degree from East Texas State University.

Donnie Minter
Co-Founder & Managing Partner
Professional Associates Accounting Inc.

Evan M. Morse, Jr., DVM
President
Warrensville Animal Hospital

Donnie Minter is co-founder and managing partner of Professional Associates Accounting Inc., located in Shaker Heights, Ohio. He is currently the account manager of the certified public accounting firm's business, individual, and nonprofit clientele.

Donnie is a member and co-chairman of membership in the National Association of Black Accountants, Cleveland chapter. He is also a member of the Ohio Society of Certified Public Accountants, and participates in the Adopt-A-Classroom mentoring program at his alma mater, Cleveland Glenville High School. In addition, Donnie participates in *The Cleveland Plain Dealer*'s "Ask the Tax Expert" call-in feature.

In 1983, Donnie received a bachelor of science degree in accounting from The University of Akron. In 1984, he received an honorable discharge from the United Stated Marine Corps after six years of reserve military duty.

Donnie is the proud father of two sons, Dontay and Najee. His hobbies include reading, weight lifting, exercise training, sports, and dancing.

Dr. Evan Morse, president of Warrensville Animal Hospital, has practiced veterinary medicine since 1968. The only African-American veterinarian in the state of Ohio for many years, Dr. Morse broke the color barrier when he served as president of the Cleveland Academy of Veterinary Medicine. Currently, he is chairman of the diversity task force for the Ohio Veterinary Medical Association, and he is a member of the American Veterinary Medical Association task force on diversity.

Northern Ohio Live recognized Morse for his leadership as president of the Northeast Ohio Jazz Society. He has served on numerous boards, including the Cleveland Museum of Natural History, Cleveland Institute of Music, and Cleveland Public Radio.

Morse has appeared as staff veterinarian on WEWS *Morning Exchange* and Fox 8 *News in the Morning*. Recently, he was featured in the national PBS broadcast of the *Nature* series entitled *Dogs: The Early Years*.

A Leadership Cleveland graduate, Morse holds bachelor of science and doctor of veterinary medicine degrees from Tuskegee University.

A native of Richmond, Virginia, Dr. Morse and his wife, Randi, have two daughters, Natalie and Halle.

Claudia Y. Owens
President & Chief Executive Officer
Evoice of Networking Solutions, LLC

Mark A. Parks, Jr., CPA
President & Chief Executive Officer
MarCon Consulting

Claudia Y. Owens, publicist, is president and CEO of Evoice of Networking Solutions, LLC (EVONS). EVONS specializes in all phases of entertainment publicity and sports promotions, including organizing special events and working with authors, actors, recording artists, corporate executives, and athletes. R & C Group, an EVONS company, specializes in sports publications.

Previously, Owens was the director of business attractions for the Rockford Area Council of 100. She received a mayoral proclamation for her work in promoting the City of Rockford.

A member of Mt. Zion of Oakwood Village Church, Owens is also a member of Alpha Kappa Alpha Sorority, Inc., the Entertainment Publicist Professional Society, and the Black Entertainment & Sports Lawyers Association. A Cleveland native, she is on the board of trustees of Educational Foundation, Inc.; Family Transitional Housing, Inc.; and the Northwestern University Diversity Council.

Owens has a bachelor of science degree in communication studies from Northwestern University, and a master of arts degree in applied communications theory and methodology from Cleveland State University. She has received a certificate of completion from the Economic Development Institute at the University of Oklahoma.

Mark Parks is the president and CEO of MarCon Consulting, a regional CPA firm with offices in five cities. In this position, he is responsible for operations of the firm. Mark is also a principal with the I3 Group (I-Cubed), a consortium of accountants. He is a 2005 graduate of the President's Council Emerging Entrepreneur Program.

Mark is a councilman in Orange Village. He is a trustee for Continue Life Inc., a homeless shelter and transitional housing for pregnant teens; CAUSE, an organization that educates at risk youth; and Women On Wheels (W.O.W.), a company utilizing technology for positive community outcomes. He serves on the ambassadors council and the community relations committee of The Club at Key Center, and he is the keeper of finance for Omega Psi Phi Fraternity, Inc.

Mark received a bachelor of arts degree from Baldwin-Wallace College, majoring in both business administration and political science. He will earn a master of business administration degree in e-business in May of 2006.

A native of East Cleveland, Ohio, Mark is the husband of Connie Parks, and father of Mark, III and Charles.

Simon C. Pittman, CPA
Managing Partner & Co-Founder
Professional Associates Accounting Inc.

Dr. Madge Potts-Williams
Dentist
Madge Potts-Williams, D.D.S.

Simon C. Pittman is a certified public accountant and managing partner and co-founder of Professional Associates Accounting Inc. in Shaker Heights, Ohio. In this position, he is in charge of managing corporate taxes and accounting for small businesses.

Simon works in conjunction with the Ohio Society of Certified Public Accountants and Cleveland Public Schools in their Adopt-a-Classroom mentoring program. He also serves as a panelist with *The Plain Dealer*'s annual tax clinic.

In 1996, Simon was awarded the United States Congress Achievement Award in recognition of being honored by the national sorority of Phi Delta Kappa, Inc.

In 1980, Simon received his bachelor's degree in science from Myers University (formerly Dyke College).

He is a member and co-membership chairman of the Cleveland chapter of the National Association of Black Accountants. In addition, he is a member of the Ohio Society of Public Accountants.

A native of Cleveland, Simon is the husband of Mardest Pittman. Simon is a member of Our Redeemer Lutheran Church in Solon, Ohio. He is a sports enthusiast with a great love for the outdoors.

Dr. Madge Potts-Williams practices restorative dentistry in Greater Cleveland, treating patients with TMJ disorder and occlusal traumatism. She is also a clinical instructor at Case Western Reserve University (CWRU) School of Dental Medicine.

Potts-Williams received the 2005 Phenomenal Woman Community Leadership Award from Colgate/Palmolive at the National Dental Association (NDA) Convention. Likewise, she received the Dr. Kenneth W. Clement Award for Community Service and Academic Excellence, and she is an inductee in JFK High School's "George E. Mills Gallery of Excellence."

Potts-Williams was recently elected national assistant secretary of the NDA, is the president of The Forest City Dental Society, and is active in Delta Sigma Theta Sorority, Inc. and Euclid Avenue Congregational Church. She serves on the Cuyahoga Community College School of Dental Hygiene advisory board.

A JFK High School graduate, Potts-Williams attended Kent State University, and received her doctorate of dental science degree from CWRU School of Dentistry. She also completed study at OBI, The Institute for Comprehensive Oral Diagnosis and Rehabilitation.

Dr. Potts-Williams, a native Clevelander, is married to Charles E. Williams, Sr. and has three stepchildren and three grandchildren.

Georgio Sabino III
Photographer
GS3

Jane B. Sheats
Realtor
Realty Corporation of America

Great art stimulates imagination, while diversity in fashion and design focuses the mind on artistic concepts. In the click of a plush black button, seasoned photographer Georgio Sabino III fuses these media to capture photographs that challenge the intellect and stimulate the imagination, while building a collecting public.

His love for the fine arts began at the early age of 12. A desire to combine fashion and design with photography intensified as he began to take on the local and national media scenes.

Through the fusion of art, fashion and design, Sabino continues to bring a flash of familiarity and a style to photography that promises to have critics and customers appreciating this innovative artist.

A licensed realtor since 1978, Jane B. Sheats has returned from retirement to the field full-time. She is a realtor with Realty Corporation of America, housed in the prestigious Cleveland Athletic Club downtown. Jane has been at the forefront of Cleveland's most noted political events. Her intensity, proclivity for perfection, and management style are respected and legendary.

Jane's career in government is marked by historic firsts. She was the first African American to chair a board of election; the first woman regional manager of a lottery office in Ohio; and the first woman to chair a board of managers for the YMCA.

Jane is a 2000 inductee into the Glenville Hall of Fame in the area of government. A devoted volunteer throughout Northeast Ohio, she continues to mentor Cleveland's emerging public servants. She is a corporate member and trustee of the Ohio Motorist Association and a member of the East Cleveland Library Board.

The widow of Marvin Sheats, Jane is the proud mother of Debra Woods, Marian Lindsley, and Lorna Sheats. She is also grandmother to Brandon, Shaina, Crystal, Tamara, Alexia, and Cordell Lindsley and Jamella Woods.

Glen Shumate
President
World Tourism Marketing

Dr. Maurice A.E. Soremekun
President & Chief Executive Officer
Women's Healthcare, Inc.

Glen Shumate is a marketing and communication executive with extensive experience in advertising, sales, public affairs, and communications. Currently, he is president of World Tourism Marketing, a tourism sales and marketing company representing clients in Florida and Ohio.

Shumate is the former vice president of tourism development for the Greater Cleveland Convention & Visitors Bureau (CVB). There, he oversaw the 750-member organization's nearly $3 million tourism marketing, sales, and services programs for leisure and group travel, as well as office services, community affairs, and the Spirit of Cleveland (foundation). These efforts included domestic and international tourism programs, visitor information and services, communications, international offices, community and philanthropic programs, mailroom hospitality training, and development of regional tourism initiatives.

Shumate's civic and professional involvement includes serving on the board of directors of Leadership Cleveland and Tri-C Jazzfest Cleveland, the Cleveland Advertising Association, and the National Association of Market Developers. He is the diversity committee chairman for the Student Youth Travel Association.

Prior to joining the CVB, Shumate served as director of community relations for the Cleveland Indians, and worked for the IRS, Hillcrest Hospital, and Cedar Point, Inc.

Dr. Maurice A.E. Soremekun is a distinguished physician who specializes in obstetrics and gynecology in the greater Cleveland area. He is also the president and chief executive officer of Women's Healthcare, Inc., through which he provides specialized health care services for women. He is the former chief of obstetrics and gynecology for Kaiser Permanente of Cleveland, and the former president of the Nigerian Community of Greater Cleveland Association.

Dr. Soremekun received his medical doctorate degree from the University of Michigan in Ann Arbor, and a master of science degree in biochemistry from the University of Western Ontario in Ontario, Canada. He has received numerous honors and awards through the years, including the Entrepreneurial Pioneer Award from the Center for the Study and Development of Minority Businesses at Kent State University. He also received the Merit Award of Achievement from the Methodist Boys High School Association, and an award for distinguished contributions from the Nigerian Community of Greater Cleveland Association.

Dr. Soremekun is married to Dr. Bessie House-Soremekun, a professor at Kent State University and entrepreneur, and together they have three children, Yomi, Jadesola, and Adrianna.

Tommye Stoudermire
Owner & Director
Tommye's New Attitude Modeling Studio

Lavonda Talbert
CEO & Principal Partner
jbmedia, inc.

Tommye Stoudermire is owner and director of Tommye's New Attitude Modeling Studio and The Miss Sweetheart Pageant Productions. Also a histology technician at University Hospital, she attended Alabama A&M University, Lakeland Community College, and the Institute of Pathology at Case Western Reserve University.

Tommye has modeled and taught modeling for the past 30 years, and her students have appeared on national television programs, commercials, in print work, and on runways. She is a past president of the Modeling Association of America International (MAAI).

An experienced pageant consultant and judge, Tommye has judged in many states. Since 1998 she has trained winners for the National American Miss and the Miss Sweetheart Pageant, on local, state and national levels. One of her former students currently holds the title of Miss University of Georgia.

Tommye is a member of Unity Baptist Church. She is married to Henry and has one son and one granddaughter. She enjoys traveling, sewing, dancing, and working with youth and senior citizens. Her motto is: "If I can help somebody as I travel this road, then my living will not be in vain."

Lavonda Talbert is CEO and principal partner of jbmedia, inc. In this position, Lavonda markets and designs collateral materials for nonprofit and profit businesses. She has also successfully managed public relations for WEA, Inc., a nonprofit organization.

Lavonda is a member of Phi Theta Kappa and is listed in *The National Dean's List®*, 2002-2003. She is vice president of the The Black Crayon, a publishing company that publishes books that help minority children to learn about their heritage and develop self-esteem. A recipient of the President's Award in 2005 from WEA, Inc., Lavonda is also founder of the nonprofit organization LaVenue Corporation.

Lavonda has served on the public relations committee for Lee Memorial A.M.E. located in Cleveland, Ohio. She has also volunteered for Ronald McDonald House, Habitat for Humanity, the Cleveland Clinic Hospital, and the American Cancer Society.

Lavonda received a bachelor of science degree from Bowling Green State University, and she holds certification in multimedia studies from Lakeland Community College.

A Cleveland native, Lavonda's key to success begins with her favorite saying, "Pray and move forward."

Eunice D. Ware-Spires
Producer & Founder
Spires Method

Timothy B. Williams
President & Chief Executive Officer
Nationwide Protective Service, Inc.

Eunice D. Ware-Spires is the producer and founder of the Spires Method, a six-week gospel music course she wrote and produced in order to teach individuals how to play their favorite gospel songs on the piano.

A graduate of Youngstown Public Schools, Spires attended Youngstown University. From 1980 through 1984, she attended Case Western University in Cleveland.

Spires has been recognized for outstanding accomplishments as a gospel singer and musician. In the early 80s, she was inducted to the Hall of Fame in her hometown of Youngstown, Ohio.

Spires has traveled extensively within the United States and abroad. She was the lead singer for the Ervin Singers of Youngstown, Ohio, and she recorded gospel records with the famous Raymond Raspberry Singers, a legendary gospel group from Cleveland. Spires also worked with other gospel artists including the Argo Singers of Chicago, and she is currently involved in many organizations.

Spires is the mother of three children and she has six grandchildren and one great-grandchild.

Timothy Williams is the president and CEO of Nationwide Protective Service, Inc. In this position, he manages the overall operation, marketing, and sales of the company. Timothy is also the licensed agent of the company in Ohio, Florida, Michigan, and Illinois. He provides off-duty police, security officers, bodyguards, and executive protection to government facilities, private sector organizations, and corporate businesses.

Timothy has more than 15 years of law enforcement and security experience. He has worked as a military policeman, security officer, correctional officer, and is now a full-time police officer. Timothy was featured in *The Plain Dealer* and the *New York Times* for articles on executive protection. He has provided executive protection for local political candidates, national political candidates, corporate executives, entertainers, and sports figures.

Timothy is a graduate of Shaker Heights High School. He received a law enforcement associate degree from Cuyahoga Community College and an urban studies bachelor's degree from Cleveland State University.

A resident of Cleveland, Ohio, Timothy is single and the proud father of Marie Williams.

Victoria R. Winbush
President
VRW Consulting, Inc.

Renea A. Woods
Chief Executive Officer
Overstreet Financial Group, LLC

Victoria (Vikki) Winbush is president of VRW Consulting, Inc., which provides coaching and counseling, facilitation and training, and organization development services.

Vikki is co-chair of the Gestalt Training Program at the Gestalt Institute of Cleveland, a personal and professional development program designed to inspire participants toward growth and transformation. She is also a member of the teaching faculty of the Diversity Management Program, a master's level program in Cleveland State University's psychology department. The major themes of Vikki's teaching and consulting practice are diversity and change.

Vikki received her bachelor of arts degree from Barnard College. She holds a master's in public health administration from the University of Michigan and a master's in social service administration from Case Western Reserve University's Mandel School of Applied Social Sciences. She is also a doctoral fellow in clinical social work at the Smith College School for Social Work.

A Cleveland native, Vikki is a member of the Western Reserve Chapter of The Links, Inc., and the Cleveland chapter of Jack and Jill, Inc. She is the proud mother of Nicole Winbush, M.D., and Nicolas Winbush, a talented high school basketball player.

Renea A. Woods has made a significant mark on the city of Akron and an impressive mark throughout the state of Ohio since starting in her home in 1999 to being featured in the *Akron Beacon Journal* in 2002. Overstreet Financial Group, LLC, a certified female minority-owned entity, is a full-service accounting firm that offers business coaching, taxes, payroll, and investment services.

Renea was featured in *Who's Who in Black Cleveland*®, 2004. She is highly sought after for speaking engagements, and is remembered long after her presentations. In 2004, Renea was chosen as keynote speaker for the City of Elyria's 18th Annual Martin Luther King, Jr. Celebration, and was the first female to speak at this yearly event. She has elevated herself to a significant stage, as a recognized and highly respected business executive, and she is known by her slogan, "Make it Happen–Today!"

Renea earned her certification in construction management at Auburn University, and attended The University of Akron for accounting.

Cleveland's
PROFESSIONALS

Celebrating African-American Achievements

Ferne A. Ziglar
President
The Ferneway Company

Ferne A. Ziglar is a communications and marketing practitioner with more than 25 years of experience in public relations, marketing, fund development, special events management, and organization administration.

Ziglar's firm, The Ferneway Company, is an Ohio-based public relations and marketing agency that provides counseling and project execution to mid-sized businesses and nonprofit organizations. Ziglar has won international, regional, and local awards for feature writing, video production, newsletter editing, design, and layout. She earned recognition for her achievements in the public relations profession as an Accredited Business Communicator (ABC) from the International Association of Business Communicators (IABC), a leading public relations trade association.

Active in the community, Ziglar is the former two-term president of the Cleveland Chapter of IABC and the president of the Ohio University Greater Cleveland Black Alumni Chapter. Other affiliations include the National Association of Black Journalists, Minority Women with Breast Cancer Uniting, Inc., and Abundant Grace Fellowship.

Ziglar received a bachelor of arts degree in Spanish from Ohio University and completed graduate courses in journalism at Kent State University. She is a graduate of the Presidents' Council Foundation's Emerging Entrepreneurs Program.

Cleveland's
PROFESSIONALS

"You can either try to get inside and have some influence, or you can stay outside and be pure and powerless."

JAMES BROWN, 1933-
Entertainer

Lynnette L. Al-Shidhani
Associate Attorney
Ulmer & Berne LLP

Lyn Al-Shidhani is an associate attorney at Ulmer & Berne LLP. There, she represents employers accused of discrimination or unfair labor practices, and defends workers' compensation claims before administrative bodies and in court. She also represents an international fast food franchise in cases of food-related claims and personal injury.

Prior to joining Ulmer & Berne, Lyn was a field attorney for the National Labor Relations Board. There, she investigated allegations of unfair labor practices and conducted union elections.

Lyn has also worked as a political consultant to the Cleveland City Council as a project manager for The Project Group. She proposed and drafted the first version of what has become the Fannie Lewis Law, which requires contractors to employ a certain percentage of City residents on City-funded construction projects. In this way, the number of minorities and females working on the projects has increased.

Lyn is Cleveland born, bred and educated. She received a bachelor of arts degree from Cleveland State University. She also earned a master's degree in public administration and a juris doctorate degree from Cleveland State University.

Dolores Del Anderson
Retired Educator
Cleveland Municipal School District

Dolores Del Anderson is a retired educator with the Cleveland Municipal School District. She established the Dolores Del Anderson Historically Black Colleges & Universities Annual Scholarship Award with her sorority, Delta Sigma Theta, Inc., and her church, Imani Temple Ministries.

Anderson was the president of the Cleveland chapter of the National Association of Negro Business and Professional Women's Clubs, Inc., Karamu Women's Committee, and the Kathryn R. Tyler Neighborhood Center. She has also served in leadership positions with AARP, Karamu House, the League of Women Voters, and the University Memory and Aging Center.

Anderson received the Sojourner Truth Award, and was recognized by Congressman Louis Stokes, former Mayor George Voinovich, and the Northeastern Neighborhood Development Corporation. She considers her greatest personal achievement to be the growth of the Ebony Fashion Fair between 1965 and 1973, while she was the chairperson. Dolores was inducted into the GradsNet Cleveland Educators and Alumni Achievers Hall of Fame in May of 2005.

A graduate of John Adams High School, Dolores holds a bachelor of science degree from Bowling Green State University and a master of education degree from John Carroll University.

Kim Banks currently serves as the Ohio Lottery's sponsorship manager, overseeing a $2.5 million sponsorship budget. She is responsible for reviewing sponsorship proposals and meeting with more than 160 marketing-sponsorship accounts a year. As part of her responsibilities, she develops, implements, and monitors promotions with sponsorship partners to ensure Lottery guidelines are met. She previously served as a sponsorship/advertising coordinator.

Prior to her work with sponsorships, Banks served as a research analyst in the Office of Marketing, tracking and placing media purchase authorizations for the division. She also provided research support to assist the division with special events and marketing promotions.

Banks held various positions in the office of sales and the office of information technology before joining marketing in 2001. She has been employed by the Ohio Lottery since 1981.

Kim Banks
Sponsorship Manager
Office of Marketing Services
Ohio Lottery

Dr. Emma Bowman Benning, a retired assistant superintendent of Cleveland Municipal School District, serves as civil service commissioner for the City of Shaker Heights, and is a supervisor of teachers-in-training at Cleveland State University. Her professional background includes curricula development in addition to teacher and parent workshop facilitation.

A member of Imani Temple Ministries, Dr. Benning is also a member of the Shaker Heights Public Library Board, the Cleveland Museum of Art Women's Council, the African American Community Task Force, The Links, Inc., and Delta Sigma Theta Sorority, Inc. She is a life member of the Jack and Jill of America Foundation and served as its national president.

Some of Benning's many honors include listings in *World's Who's Who, Who's Who of Women, Who's Who Among Black Women*, and *Who's Who in American Education.* She was a Community Hero Olympic Torch Bearer for the 1996 Olympics.

Dr. Benning is married to Calvin and is the mother of Dr. Sheryl Thomas, Nathaniel, and Dr. Eric. She has two grandchildren, Khalia and Shaura, one great-granddaughter, Annisia Alesandra, and one sponsored child, Odwuor Akach of Nairobi, Kenya.

Dr. Emma Bowman Benning
Supervisor of Teachers-in-Training
Cleveland State University

Gregory E. Bobbitt III
Community Outreach Specialist
SGT, Inc.
NASA Glenn Research Center

Gregory Bobbitt serves as a community outreach specialist for SGT, Inc. in the external programs directorate at the NASA Glenn Research Center in Cleveland. He is responsible for developing, organizing, coordinating, and expanding community outreach events in line with the agency's vision and mission.

Bobbitt has also served as an administrative coordinator for NASA's minority university research and educational program office. His commitment to minority issues, especially education and empowerment, is staggering in such a young man. He pours energy into projects designed to insure equality and justice for scholarships and other programs offered by the nation's academic institutions. His impact is measured one student at a time, when NASA receives thank you notes and letters of appreciation from young people who are affected by the benefits of improved educational standards due to agency initiatives.

Bobbitt currently studies political science at Cuyahoga Community College, and enjoys mentoring and tutoring. He never hesitates to be a positive influence on his younger family members or children in his neighborhood by lending a helping hand with homework, or serving as a strong role model.

Denise Booker-Wade,
R.N., CDE
Medical Surgical Case Manager
Visiting Nurse Association

Denise Booker-Wade, R.N., CDE, is a medical surgical care manager at the Visiting Nurse Association. Denise is responsible for providing skilled nursing care as well as coordinating care with outside agencies. As a certified diabetic educator, Denise provides diabetic education on preventing and controlling diabetes to her patients and their families.

Denise is the recipient of the 2005 Belle Sherwin Nurse Award. She is also a member of the Ohio Nurse Association, the American Nurse Association, the Greater Cleveland Nurse Association, and the American Association of Diabetic Educators. Denise also is a member of the Cleveland Church of Christ.

Denise volunteers on the nurses' guild, where she helps coordinate health check up days, and she provides a diabetic seminar for the community.

Denise received her associate of art degree and science degree in nursing from Cuyahoga Community College in June of 1983. She received her diabetic educator certification in May of 2003.

She is the wife of Donald Wade and has one son and two grandchildren.

At the time of her appointment in 1972, Conella Coulter Brown became the first and highest ranking African-American female administrator in a major Ohio school system. Her responsibilities included the development and implementation of human relations policies and practices throughout Ohio's largest school system. She accomplished much of her human relations pioneering during a period of heightened racial tension and a contentious school desegregation lawsuit.

Some of Brown's honors include being listed in *Who's Who Among Black Americans*, a Fulbright fellowship, and the President's Award from the Cleveland Urban League.

Brown is a member of Delta Sigma Theta Sorority, Inc., the National Sorority of Phi Delta Kappa, the NAACP, and St. James AME Church.

Brown earned her bachelor of arts degree from the University of Kansas City in 1953 and her master of arts degree from Case Western Reserve University in 1963.

Born and raised in Kansas City, Missouri, Conella is married to retired U.S. Army Major Arnold A. Brown, former principal of Franklin D. Roosevelt Junior High School. A music lover, Conella also enjoys reading and providing support to victims of chronic fatigue immune dysfunction syndrome.

Conella Coulter Brown
Assistant Superintendent, Retired
Cleveland Municipal School District

Diana Brown-Brumfield is the clinical nurse specialist for the department of surgery at Cleveland Clinic Foundation. In this position, she works collaboratively with the OR healthcare team members toward the best outcomes for the surgical patient. Diana serves as a leader in the appropriate use of research in evidence-based practice innovations that improve patient outcomes in the OR. She develops, plans, guides and directs programs for the department of surgery and provides direction to nursing personnel and others in these programs.

Diana received her bachelor's and master's degrees in nursing, and post-master's certificate as a family nurse practitioner, from Ursuline College. She is an active member of Chi Eta Phi Sorority, Inc. and Sigma Theta Tau International.

A native of Cleveland, Ohio, Diana is the wife of Willie Brumfield and the proud mother of three sons and one daughter, David, Jacquelyn, Jonathan, and Durell. She also has eight grandchildren.

Diana Brown-Brumfield
APRN, MSN, RN
CNS-Surgical Services
Cleveland Clinic Foundation

Eugene Cranford
Construction Administrator
Moody•Nolan, Inc.

Eugene Cranford provides construction administration, marketing/business development, and management services for Moody•Nolan's Cleveland office. Eugene assists clients and oversees projects in Northeast Ohio, including the new 630-student Cleveland Memorial Elementary School, one of the first new elementary schools in Cleveland in many years. He also works on the Mid-Town Development Design Review Board and the Northeast Shores Neighborhood Board.

A graduate of Cuyahoga Community College and the New York Institute of Technologies in Architecture, Eugene worked for more than 10 years in planning and zoning for the City of Cleveland, most recently serving as secretary of the Board of Zoning Appeals and the Board of Building Standards and Building Appeals. Prior to his opportunities with the City of Cleveland, he worked in architectural design and planning for several prominent Cleveland architectural and construction firms. He has experience in retail, corporate, education, and residential design projects.

Eugene and his wife reside in Cleveland and attend Zion Chapel Missionary Baptist Church, where he serves as the president of the mass choir and vice president of the usher board.

Lester Cumberlander, AIA
Project Manager
Moody•Nolan, Inc.

Lester Cumberlander, AIA, is a project manager for Moody•Nolan, Inc., the largest African-American architectural firm in the United States. In this position, he manages the planning design and construction of building projects. His most recent project is the newly completeled Cleveland Memorial Elementary School.

Over the years, his other significant projects while at area architectural firms include the Continental Airlines renovation, Cleveland Browns Municipal Stadium, Gund Arena, and the Cleveland Museum of Natural History.

A graduate of Kent State University architecture program, he is a member of the American Institute of Architects (AIA), the Society of American Registered Architects (SARA) and the Society of Marketing Professional Services (SMPS).

A resident of Cleveland Heights, Lester and his wife have three daughters. Lester, a deacon at Good Shepherd Baptist Church, also serves as vice president of the usher board of his church.

Cleveland's
PROFESSIONALS

Cheri Daniels is the business manager for the *Call & Post* newspapers. In this role, she oversees multiple departments: accounting, human resources, and circulation. Her main responsibility is to manage the financial operations of the company.

She has more than 25 years of financial experience and held various leadership positions with several major corporations such as IBM and National City Bank. Prior to joining the *Call & Post*, Cheri wanted to expand her horizons and gain international finance experience. She lived in Bermuda for 13 years, and worked for The Bank of Bermuda, Exxon Financial, and Esso Bermuda, both a division of ExxonMobil. These companies allowed her to travel and work in Europe and Asia.

In 1977, Cheri graduated from Central State University where she received a business administration degree in management with a minor in psychology.

Actively involved in the community, she is a member of Delta Sigma Theta Sorority, Inc., and she is the president of the Orange Alliance of Black Parents. She enjoys working with youth and reading.

A Cleveland native, Cheri is the proud mother of three children, Alexandria, Courtney, and Ronald, Jr.

Cheri Coleman Daniels
Business Manager
Call & Post

After 32 years with the Cleveland Municipal School District, Constance served as a staff attorney in the Court of Claims in Columbus, Ohio. A law clerk for Judges Eddie Corrigan and Robert Malaga, she was also a referee for the Shaker Heights Court. Currently, Constance is a court-appointed attorney in the Probate Court of Cuyahoga County.

Constance received a bachelor of science degree in education from The Ohio State University, a master of science degree in education from St. John's College, and a juris doctorate from Howard University. Further, she was selected by the Gund Foundation to study in Africa and Europe.

A member of the Ohio State and National Bar Associations, Constance is a charter member of Concerned Parents of Shaker Heights. Previously, she served as trustee of Alta House and East View United Church of Christ. She received Public Recognition Awards in 1974, 1977, and 1983 from Delta Sigma Theta Sorority, Inc.

Constance is the widow of Attorney Will H. Farmer; the mother of Gaynell Chapman Farmer and Joi Constance Rumph; and the grandmother of Mercedes, Eliza, Victoria, and Zachary.

Constance C. Farmer
Court-Appointed Attorney
Probate Court of Cuyahoga County

Mildred O. Foster
Retired Educator

Mildred Odelle Foster is a retired administrator of the Cleveland Municipal School District. She was the principal at Miles Park Elementary School until 1994, and assistant principal at Marion Sterling School. She became a student teaching supervisor for Kent State University in the School of Education, and has served as an educational consultant.

Mildred is a golden life member of Delta Sigma Theta Sorority, Inc., and she recently received the Soror of the Year Award from the Greater Cleveland Alumnae Chapter. A member of Advent Lutheran Church, she has served numerous civic and religious committees.

Mildred has received awards from several organizations. A member of Phi Delta Kappa International, she received a bachelor of science degree in education from Kent State University and a master of education degree in supervision and administration from John Carroll University. She s a graduate of John Adams High School.

A native of Alabama, Mildred is the wife of Rufus Foster and the proud mother of Shelley, Angela, Kathleen, and Louis C. She is the doting grandmother of 11, and her favorite saying is, "God is in control!"

Arlishea L. Fulton
Associate, Attorney at Law
Ulmer & Berne, LLP

Attorney at law Arlishea L. Fulton, Esq. focuses her legal practice on business law and real estate matters. She is a member of Ulmer & Berne, LLP's business law, real estate, nonprofit, and mergers and acquisitions groups. Her experience includes the representation of various business entities in formations, general business, commercial matters, and general legal counsel.

Arlishea is involved in the negotiation and documentation of a variety of business transactions including mergers, and the purchase and sale of businesses through both asset purchase and stock purchase agreements. She regularly represents buyers and sellers in the acquisition and sale of a variety of commercial real estate properties, and she represents landlords and tenants in the leasing of such properties.

A member of the American, Ohio State, and Cleveland Bar Associations, Arlishea is also a member of Commercial Real Estate Women of Cleveland, Inc. She earned her juris doctorate degree from Case Western Reserve University in 1999 and her bachelor's degree, magna cum laude, from Florida A&M University in 1994.

Arlishea is married to Larry E. Fulton. The couple has two children, Larry, Jr. and Ashley.

Greg Gaiter currently serves as a chain account representative in the Ohio Lottery's Office of Marketing Services, overseeing 12 chain accounts, including such well-known stores as Meijer Inc., Giant Eagle, CVS, and Certified Oil. One of his most recent accomplishments was to bring Ohio Lottery games to 20 Meijer gasoline convenience stores, in addition to selling lottery games in more than 50 Meijer discount department and grocery store outlets. Meijer's secured $26 million in lottery game sales in fiscal year 2005.

In 1993, Gaiter joined the Ohio Lottery Commission as a purchasing manager in the Division of Finance. He was promoted to assistant manager for the Cleveland regional sales office in 1996 before securing his current position as a chain accounts representative.

Prior to the Lottery, Gaiter served in the U.S. Air Force, working as a procurement specialist providing business supplies and other services for construction contracts in the Washington, D.C. area.

Greg Gaiter
Chain Account Representative
Office of Marketing Services
Ohio Lottery

J. Florence Goolsby is a retired educator. She retired from the Cleveland Municipal School District in 1995 after 30 years of service. She was principal of James Ford Rhodes High School at the time of her retirement. Presently, she works as an educational consultant with the Ohio State Department of Education in the Cleveland Scholarship and Tutoring Program.

Florence is a member of Antioch Baptist Church; a life member of the NAACP; a golden life member of Delta Sigma Theta Sorority, Inc.; and a life member of the Ohio Retired Teachers Association.

Florence received a bachelor of science degree from Bluefield State College and a master of education degree from Cleveland State University.

A native of Virginia, Florence enjoys arts and crafts as well as scrap booking.

J. Florence Goolsby
Educational Consultant
Ohio State Department of Education

Debra Green
Manager of Community Relations
Medical Mutual

Debra Green is manager of community relations for Medical Mutual. She oversees all company community relations activities and involvement. This includes coordinating volunteer efforts, managing company-sponsored events with charities and other organizations, and serving as spokesperson for company-sponsored programs.

Green is involved in a number of charitable and civic activities. She is on the board of the United Black Fund, Dress for Success, League of Women Voters Education Fund, and the Urban League of Greater Cleveland. In 1999, *Kaleidoscope Magazine* selected her as one of the area's leading women. In 2002, she was the recipient of the Woman of Professional Excellence Award, presented by the YWCA of Greater Cleveland. In 2004, *Kaleidoscope Magazine* recognized Green as a woman who makes a difference in the community.

A breast cancer survivor, Green is also active in a variety of efforts in the fight against the disease.

Green received her bachelor's degree in social work from Cleveland State University. She and her husband, Archie, live in Solon with their son and daughter.

Jeanette Haynes-Gordon
Fiscal Operations Manager
Community Action
Against Addiction, Inc.

Jeanette Haynes-Gordon is the fiscal operations manager for Community Action Against Addiction, Inc. She is responsible for the fiscal operations at the agency (i.e., budget, billing and financial reporting).

Jeanette is the vice president of operations for the National Black MBA Association, a professional membership organization comprised of African-American graduates with MBAs, advanced degrees, and entrepreneurs. She is also a trustee of Black Professionals Association Charitable Foundation, in which she holds the position of secretary. This organization raises thousands of dollars to give scholarships to African-American students pursuing undergraduate degrees. Jeanette also serves on the United Black Fund associate board, the Phyllis Wheatly Association board, and the David's Challenge board.

Jeanette earned her executive master of business administration degree in healthcare from Baldwin-Wallace College in 2000. She earned a bachelor of science degree from Myers University in 1983.

Born in Cleveland, Ohio, she has been married for 18 years to John J. Gordon.

Lynnette Jackson is currently a full-time graduate student at the Weatherhead School of Management at Case Western Reserve University. She is a candidate for a master of business administration degree in May of 2007.

Most recently, Jackson served as the school planning chief for the City of Cleveland and was responsible for engaging community leaders in the planning and design work for the Cleveland Municipal School District's $1.5 billion facilities plan for rebuilding Cleveland's schools.

Jackson serves on the board of directors for the Rock and Roll Hall of Fame and Museum (mayoral appointee), Salvation Army, and Cleveland Bridge Builders. She was featured in *Crain's Cleveland Business* "Forty under 40" in 2004 and in *Kaleidoscope Magazine's* "Forty under 40" in 2002. She is an American Marshall Memorial fellow, a group committed to fostering transatlantic relationships. A member of Alpha Kappa Alpha Sorority, Inc., she has received the Crescendo Award in Public Service from the Cleveland Boy's Choir and the Alumnae of the Year award from Cleveland Bridge Builders. She holds a bachelor of science degree from Hampton University.

Lynnette Jackson
Graduate Student
Weatherhead School of Management
Case Western Reserve University

Michele Jackson is a certified financial manager for Merrill Lynch Global Private Client Group. In this role, she helps clients develop and implement financial planning strategies to help build wealth and achieve personal goals. Michele is one of only a few women of color in the region providing financial advice with a major wire-house firm.

Michele has a commitment to providing financial education to people of color regardless of age or economic status. She is a member of the Urban League's Young Professionals and the Cleveland chapter of the National Association of Black MBA's. She is on the education committee for the Ohio Government Officers Association and is a member of the Ohio Municipal Officers Association. At Lee Road Baptist Church, she is the superintendent of Sunday schools.

Michele received her bachelor of arts degree from Cleveland State University, and she is currently attending Case Weatherhead School of Management to earn a master of business administration degree with an economics concentration.

Living in Aurora with her daughter Erika, Michele is member of Cooking In Cleveland.

Michele Jackson
Certified Financial Manager
Merrill Lynch Global
Private Client Group

Dr. Cheryl J. Johnson
Resident Physician
Summa Health System/
Akron City Hospital

D r. Cheryl Johnson is a second-year resident physician in obstetrics and gynecology at Summa Health System/Akron City Hospital. Her responsibilities include supervision of interns and medical students on labor and delivery, care of patients in the Women's Health Center, and performance of gynecologic surgeries under the direction of Summa's attending physicians. Johnson's formal rotations include maternal-fetal medicine, reproductive endocrinology and infertility, gynecologic oncology, urogynecology, and reconstructive pelvic surgery.

Johnson graduated from Laurel School (1995) and holds a bachelor's degree in biology from Hampton University. In 2004 she graduated from The Ohio State University College of Medicine and Public Health with the intentions of combining knowledge and empathy to alleviate human suffering.

Johnson is a member of the National Medical Association, the American College of Obstetricians and Gynecologists, Alpha Kappa Alpha Sorority, Inc., and Jack and Jill of America, Inc. She has also conducted research with several journal publications at the Cleveland Clinic Foundation.

Presently, Johnson and her husband, Ronald, reside in Aurora with their son, Carter. She believes: "Be not afraid of greatness; some are born great, some achieve greatness, and others have greatness thrust upon them."

Eric Lee
Call Center Manager
Progressive Insurance

E ric Lee is a call center manager for the Progressive Group of Insurance Companies, the third largest auto insurance group in the country. Eric brings tremendous enthusiasm and positive energy to his role as manager of a 20-member team of customer service representatives. He coordinates the activities of his team to meet business objectives and provides constructive feedback to team members on their performance. He also is involved in hiring decisions.

Eric worked his way up to his current position after joining Progressive in 1996 and holding a variety of responsible positions including manager of mail and delivery services. Previously, he worked as a counselor to physically and emotionally abused teenagers who had been removed from their homes.

Eric, married and the proud father of four, also finds time to pursue his passion of photography. His entrepreneurial spirit led him to form his own company, ELee's World of Photography, where he specializes in weddings with the goal of capturing once-in-a-lifetime moments between the bride and groom. Eric is in the process of developing a program to teach photography to inner city children.

Tia M. Melton, M.D., joined the faculty at Case Western Reserve University Medical School, Department of Obstetrics and Gynecology in July of 2005. As clinical instructor of reproductive biology at the MacDonald Women's Hospital, a division of University Hospitals of Cleveland, Melton supervises and lectures medical students, teaches clinical and surgical skills to residents, and attends patients in Richmond Heights and Landerbrook offices.

In 1989, she graduated from the University of Cincinnati, where she was named Outstanding Woman in Arts and Sciences and appeared in *Who's Who Among American Universities and Colleges.* She graduated from the University of Cincinnati's College of Medicine in 1993, served her residency, and began work with indigent populations as assistant professor of obstetrics and gynecology. Since 1998, she has been in private practice at University Hospitals Health System.

Melton has served villagers in South Africa, Honduras, the Dominican Republic, Nicaragua, and Egypt. She has attended medical and religious conferences in Arizona, California, and Florida, and in the nations of Chile, China, Greece, and Spain.

Melton is a member of Delta Sigma Theta Sorority, Inc., and she enjoys reading, music, and scuba diving.

Tia Meychelle Melton, M.D.
Clinical Instructor,
Reproductive Biology
Case Western Reserve University

Paula D. Morrison is an administrative manager for the City of Cleveland's Department of Public Utilities. In this position, she is responsible for producing informative, educational programming for TV23, the city's cable station.

Paula's career spans both the public and private sectors. Prior to joining the City of Cleveland, Paula was media coordinator for University Hospitals of Cleveland where she produced several network television specials.

Paula began her journalism career at WEWS-TV (ABC) in 1991, where she was an investigative-special assignment producer. She is a multi-Emmy Award and National Headliner Award winner.

Her experience ranges from media relations and crisis communications to strategic positioning. Paula recently founded Morrison Media Group, a full-service marketing and public relations agency. Morrison Media Group provides comprehensive marketing, media, creative, and communicative applications. The agency specializes in business-to-business development, public and media relations efforts, and special event management.

Paula attended Beaumont School For Girls in Cleveland Heights, Ohio and earned a bachelor of arts in journalism from Baldwin-Wallace College in Berea, Ohio.

She is a member of Mount Sinai Baptist Church.

Paula D. Morrison
Administrative Manager,
Department of Public Utilities
City of Cleveland

Tony Nicholas
Songwriter/Producer

Edwin "Tony" Nicholas is an accomplished songwriter/record producer whose credits include recordings by Joe, The Backstreet Boys, 3LW, Patti LaBelle, and many others.

Tony received his bachelor of arts degree in music from Denison University in Granville, Ohio in 1984. He relocated to Cleveland in 1988 to become keyboardist for the R&B trio Levert. Tony became the musical director for the band in 1990 and remained in that capacity for ten years.

When R&B legend Gerald Levert decided to embark on a solo project in that same year, he and Tony collaborated to produce *Private Line*, the platinum selling solo debut that successfully launched Gerald's solo career.

Gerald and Tony went on to write and produce a string of hits together, including songs for The O'Jays, L.S.G., Barry White, Keith Sweat, New Edition, Keith Washington, 702, and the Cleveland-based Rude Boys. They also worked on seven subsequent Gerald Levert solo records that include appearances by Mary J. Blige, Eddie Levert, Tamia, Faith Evans, and others.

Tony makes his home in Bratenahl and attends the New Jerusalem Baptist Church.

Olumuyiwa Omonogun
Advanced Management Trainee
Cintas Corporation

Olumuyiwa Omonogun is an advanced management trainee with Cintas Corporation in Strongsville. He is currently responsible for driving catalog sales for Cintas' rental division by training and developing service sales representatives, as well as by selling accounts.

Olumuyiwa received his bachelor of science degree in economics from the University of Ilorin, Nigeria. After receiving his bachelor's degree, he obtained his master of business administration degree from Cleveland State University in 2003, with a concentration in management and labor relations. While at Cleveland State University, Olumuyiwa served as a resident assistant, and in 2003 he was elected to *Who's Who Among Students in American Universities and Colleges*.

Olumuyiwa spends his free time volunteering at church and enjoys playing tennis, basketball, and billiards.

Tonya Perkins is president of the Cleveland Women's Council of the National Association of Real Estate Brokers (NAREB). She also holds the position of financial secretary of the national organization. The Women's Council is an affiliate of the NAREB, the oldest minority trade organization in the country. The Women's Council takes great pride in their service to the community. The organization creates such programs and opportunities in the community as down payment assistance, closing cost assistance, continuing education for its membership, the annual Minority Lupus Awareness Walk, and the annual Health and Safety Fair, which provides health screenings and book bags filled with supplies for children.

Tonya and her chapter received the 2005 Par Excellence Award, one of the highest honors awarded by the National Women's Council.

Tonya is also a member of the National Association of Negro Women, Rotary International (Cleveland East Club), co-chair of the housing committee of the NAACP, and serves on the board of Girls Club of America.

Tonya is the proud parent of two sons, Jeremiah and Joshua. Her passion is providing home ownership opportunities and education to low or moderate-income individuals.

Tonya Perkins
President
Cleveland Women's Council of NAREB

Jocelyn N. Prewitt-Stanley is an associate in the Cleveland office of Vorys, Sater, Seymour and Pease LLP, where she practices in the litigation group. She has represented banks and lending institutions, state universities, and insurance companies in complex litigation, adversary proceedings, and appeals at the state and federal levels. Jocelyn is admitted to practice in the State of Ohio, United States District Court for the Northern District of Ohio, and the United States Sixth Circuit Court of Appeals. She is also a member of the Ohio State Bar Association.

While attending law school at the University of Iowa College of Law, Jocelyn was a member of the *Journal of Gender, Race & Justice.* She received a bachelor of arts degree in political science from Grinnell College in Grinnell, Iowa.

A native of Warrensville Heights, Ohio, Jocelyn is married to Ted J. Stanley, head football coach at Kenyon College in Gambier, Ohio.

Jocelyn N. Prewitt-Stanley
Associate, Attorney at Law
Vorys, Sater, Seymour and Pease LLP

Delisa Y. Russell
Associate, Corporate
Transactions & Securities
Thompson Hine LLP

Delisa Russell is an associate in Thompson Hine LLP's corporate transactions and securities practice group. She focuses her practice on mergers and acquisitions; joint ventures; federal and state securities law filings and compliance, including public and private securities offerings; and corporate organization and governance matters. Delisa is admitted to practice in Ohio and Indiana.

Delisa received her juris doctorate degree from Indiana University School of Law, and her bachelor of science degree from Southern Illinois University at Edwardsville. In law school, she was the executive symposium editor for the *Indiana International & Comparative Law Review.*

A member of the American Bar Association, Ohio State Bar Association and Cleveland Bar Association, Delisa's awards and honors include *Who's Who Among American Law Students* (1999- 2001) and *Who's Who in Black Cleveland®* (2005). Her community activities include Junior League of Indianapolis (member 1998-2001) and the Bellflower Center for Prevention of Child Abuse (board of directors 2005).

Kimberly St.
John-Stevenson
Senior Consultant
BrownFlynn

Kim St. John-Stevenson is a senior consultant with the marketing communications firm BrownFlynn. In this position, Kim applies strategic solutions to community relations/marketing projects for a variety of clients. Before joining BrownFlynn, Kim was development director for Great Lakes Theater, where she raised $2 million annually for the theater's programming.

Kim holds a bachelor of arts degree in journalism/marketing from the University of Connecticut. Since moving to Cleveland in 1995, she has worked with numerous organizations, including ideastream's community advisory board, the Community Partnership for Arts and Culture, the Steamship W.G. Mather strategic planning committee, The Cleveland Foundation African-American outreach committee, the YWCA of Greater Cleveland, and the National Conference for Community and Justice (NCCJ). In 2003, she was appointed by the Cuyahoga County Commissioners to serve on a leadership task force on public funding for the arts.

Kim is a 1995 graduate of Leadership Greater Hartford, a 2003 graduate of NCCJ's LeadDIVERSITY program, and a 2000 inductee in *Kaleidoscope Magazine's* Forty Under 40 Club.

Kim resides in Cleveland Heights with her husband, Anthony Stevenson, and her daughters Jessica and Sydney.

S hirley Smith Seaton is liaison for community affairs/interim associate director of multicultural affairs at John Carroll University (JCU) in University Heights, Ohio. She has been a classroom and television teacher, principal, and administrator. In 2005, the Office of Multicultural Affairs at JCU renamed its cultural awareness series in her honor.

Shirley is a commissioner for Administrative Services in Cleveland Heights. She is coordinator of "We the People, the Citizen and the Constitution" for Ohio's 11th Congressional District and is regional chairperson for Fulbright Teacher Exchange.

Shirley received outstanding teacher awards from Cleveland City Council, the Ohio House, and Fulbright Awards to Italy and China.

She holds memberships in Phi Delta Kappa, Alpha Kappa Alpha, Coalition of 100 Black Women, American Association of University Women, National Alliance of Black School Educators, Phi Beta Delta, and Alpha Sigma Nu.

Shirley received bachelor's and master's degrees in history from Howard University, a master's degree in education from Case Western Reserve University, and a doctorate in education from the University of Akron.

She is married to Lawrence Seaton and is the mother of Eric Dean Seaton.

Dr. Shirley Smith Seaton
Liaison for Community Affairs
Interim Associate Director of
Multicultural Affairs
John Carroll University

M ichael G. Shinn writes the nationally syndicated financial planning column, "Your Money Really Matters." He is a certified financial planner and investment advisor representative for Financial Network Investment Corporation.

Mike retired from General Electric after a career as engineer, manager and corporate staff consultant. Each year the National Society of Black Engineers honors him by presenting the Mike Shinn Distinguished Fellow Award to the society's top scholar.

Currently, Mike is chairman of the board of trustees at Mt. Zion Congregational Church, UCC and chairman of the board of governance of the Shaker Lakes Nature Center.

At Kansas University (KU), Mike serves on the Endowment Association Board and the Engineering Advisory Board, and he recently received the KU Alumni Association's highest award, the Fred Ellsworth Medallion.

A native of Topeka, Kansas, Mike received a bachelor of science degree in aerospace engineering from Kansas University and a master of business administration degree from Case Western Reserve University.

Mike lives in Shaker Heights, Ohio with his wife, Joyce, and son, Stephen. He is a Leadership Cleveland alumnus and past Polemach of the Cleveland Alumni Chapter of Kappa Alpha Psi Fraternity.

Michael G. Shinn, CFP
Investment Advisor Representative
Financial Network Investment
Corporation

Jacques O. Smith, Sr.
Coordinator, Community Outreach
& Public Relations
Cuyahoga Community College

Jacques O. Smith, Sr. is the coordinator of community outreach and public relations for Cuyahoga Community College (Tri-C), and has served in this capacity for the last seven years. Before joining Tri-C, he worked as a case manager and employment specialist for the Urban League of Greater Cleveland.

A Cleveland native, Jacques attended school in the Cleveland Heights/University Heights Public School System. He earned an associate of arts degree from Cuyahoga Community College, Eastern Campus, and attended Cleveland State University, where he earned a bachelor of arts degree. Currently, Jacques attends the University of Phoenix, pursuing a master's degree in business administration.

A life member of Alpha Phi Alpha Fraternity, Inc., Delta Alpha Lambda Chapter, Jacques is a lifetime member of the NAACP. He holds several other memberships, including the United Way and 100 Black Men of Greater Cleveland. He also serves on numerous boards and as a motivational speaker.

Jacques is a proud father of two and lives in Cleveland. He gives all honor to God and his best friends, his parents, Rev. and Mrs. Hilton O. Smith.

Michael E. Taylor
Business Liaison
Congresswoman Stephanie
Tubbs Jones

Michael E. Taylor is the business liaison for Congresswoman Stephanie Tubbs Jones. He is responsible for representing the district office in numerous matters, including federal transportation, community development, and housing (specifically predatory lending, Fannie Mae, and HUD issues). He also represents the office in regard to Doanbrook, NASA, education, and youth issues.

A wrestling coach for Warrensville Heights Elementary Schools, Michael sits on the United Way of Greater Cleveland's health and caring investment committee. He also serves on the Cleveland State University Black Studies Department advisory board and the WECO board of directors.

He has received numerous awards for service to businesses (Cleveland Realtist Association) and youth organizations (Boys and Girls Club of Cleveland and the Girls Club of Ohio).

Michael is an alumnus of Ashland College with a bachelor of arts degree in criminal justice, a recipient of the National Urban/Rural Fellows Program at Bernard M. Baruch College in public administration, and a graduate of the Cleveland State Leadership Academy.

A native of the Warrensville Heights area, Michael is married to Chanté Thomas-Taylor, who is an educator in the public school system.

Cleveland's
PROFESSIONALS

Lisa Tomlin-Houston, M.Ed. is director of career services at Baldwin-Wallace College. She possesses 15 years of experience as a career services professional, human resources manager, and management consultant. She shares her knowledge and perspectives with corporate leaders, nonprofit managers, faculty and students, and organizational teams to help them achieve career and business success.

Lisa earned her master's degree from Rutgers University Graduate School of Education in counseling psychology, and she holds a bachelor's degree in psychology from Oberlin College. She served as a career counselor at the University of Pennsylvania and also was the director of career and student services at Carnegie Mellon University's H. John Heinz III Graduate School of Public Policy and Management.

In addition, Lisa served as a management consultant and thought partner to the Ford Foundation and Barclays Capital, a division of Barclays Bank.

Lisa's civic affiliations include the Cleveland Social Venture Partners, the YWCA of Greater Cleveland's Women's Leadership Initiative, and the Public Relations Society of America, Cleveland Chapter.

Lisa lives in Cleveland with her husband, Anthony D. Houston, who is a regent on the Ohio Board of Regents.

Lisa Tomlin-Houston
Director of Career Services
Baldwin-Wallace College

Carol A. Wagner is a personnel management specialist for the Department of Defense (DoD), Civilian Personnel Management Services. In this position, she serves as an advisor to DoD activities, civilian personnel offices, and the Office of Workers' Compensation's programs offices. Additionally, she helps manage the Federal Employees Compensation Act (FECA) program in six states.

Carol received the Phenomenal Women Award from the Phenomenal Woman's Foundation in 2001. She is currently president of the National Pan-Hellenic Council of Greater Cleveland. A golden life member of Delta Sigma Theta Sorority, Inc., Carol was president of the Greater Cleveland Alumnae chapter from 1999 to 2003. She is a board member of the Greater Cleveland Delta Foundation Life Development Center, and a member of Blacks in Government and Bethany Baptist Church.

Carol received an associate degree in applied business from Youngstown State University and a bachelor of arts degree in human resource management from Capital University.

A Youngstown, Ohio native, Carol is married to Larry Wagner and is the proud mother of Jason and Danielle. She is the proud mother-in-law of Keisha and the loving grandmother of Justin.

Carol A. Wagner
Personnel Management Specialist
Department of Defense

A native of Cincinnati, Booker Du'Bois Wright, Jr. now lives with his wife, Gina, and two daughters, Chantal and Nia, in Shaker Heights. Booker and his family moved to the Cleveland area in 1998 after he took a sales position with the pharmaceutical giant Pfizer Inc. Booker is currently a senior therapeutic specialty representative with Pfizer. He has won numerous awards and contests, including Pfizer's coveted Vice Presidents Cabinet Award. His plans are to move into management to help coach and develop sales people. One of Booker's philosophies is to "always do whatever you can to get better at what you do." This approach has helped him throughout life.

Booker is a proud financial member of Kappa Alpha Psi Fraternity, Inc. The fundamental purpose of his fraternity is achievement in all fields of human endeavors. He hopes to continue on the path of achievement. Booker has a true passion for his hobbies of playing golf and chess. However, his number one priority is nurturing his two beautiful daughters into productive contributors to our community and society.

Booker Du'Bois Wright, Jr.
Senior Therapeutic Specialty Rep.
Pfizer Inc.

BIOGRAPHICAL INDEX

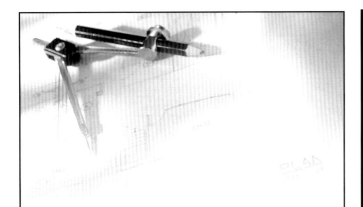

BIOGRAPHICAL INDEX

BIOGRAPHICAL INDEX

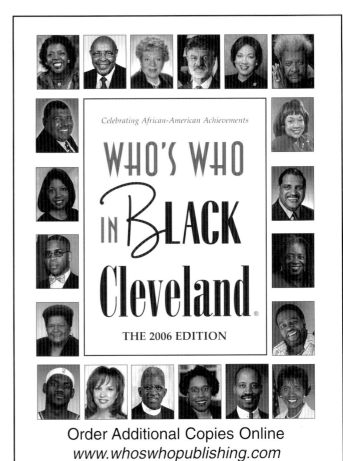

BIOGRAPHICAL INDEX

BIOGRAPHICAL INDEX

ADVERTISERS' INDEX

Reception Sponsors

Platinum Sponsors

Diamond Sponsors   *Emerald Sponsor*

Unveiling Reception Sponsors

Help us make a difference by exposing our children to positive role models!

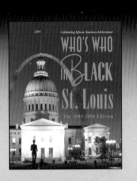
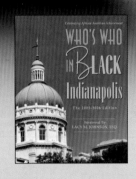
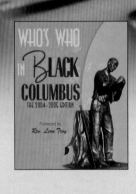
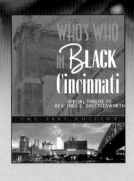
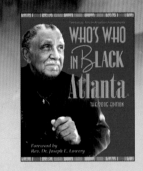

At Who's Who Publishing Co. LLC, we are dedicated to making an impact in our communities across the nation and in the lives of the next generation. Our coffee table-quality publications highlight the outstanding and significant achievements made by legendary and contemporary African Americans.

They are essential guides in acquainting our youth with people in their community who sacrificed, overcame and excelled. While the ancient African proverb wisely notes that "It takes a whole village to raise a child," we also realize that what our children see is what they become. Our books broaden the landscape of career opportunities for the next generation while inspiring them to reach for the top.

Who's Who publications are designed to encourage and inspire, to uplift and unite, and to forever memorialize the culture, contributions, and history that represents our rich heritage.

ORDER ONLINE OR CALL (614) 481-7300
www.whoswhopublishing.com